The
Truman Doctrine
of Aid to Greece:
A Fifty-Year Retrospective

Introduction by

Demetrios James Caraley

Edited by

Eugene T. Rossides

Published jointly by

The Academy of Political Science, New York

and the

American Hellenic Institute Foundation, Washington DC

Published jointly by
The Academy of Political Science
475 Riverside Drive, Suite 1274
New York, NY 10115
and the
American Hellenic Institute Foundation
1220 16th Street, N.W.
Washington, D.C. 20036

COVER CREDIT: WHITE HOUSE CURATOR'S OFFICE

Library of Congress Cataloging-in-Publication Data

The Truman doctrine of aid to Greece : a fifty-year retrospective /
    Introduction by Demetrios James Caraley : edited by Eugene T.
    Rossides.
        p.   cm.
    Includes index.
    ISBN 1-889247-02-2 (pbk. : alk. paper)
    1. United States—Foreign relations—Greece.   2. Greece—Foreign
relations—United States.   3. United States—Foreign
relations—1945-1953.   4. Truman, Harry S., 1884-1972.
I. Rossides, Eugene T.
E183.8.G8T78   1998
327.730495'09'044—dc21   98-19969
                                                              CIP

ISBN 1-889247-02-2

Printed in the United States of America

TABLE OF CONTENTS

PREFACE

March 12, 1997, marked the fiftieth anniversary of one of the most remarkable events in American history—the Truman Doctrine. The decision by President Harry S. Truman in 1947 to intervene in Greece to counter the threat of Soviet communism represented a turning point in world history: it committed the United States to the policy of containment of the Soviet Union. In terms of the preservation of human freedom and dignity, this policy represents perhaps the most successful foreign policy initiative undertaken by the United States in this century. Yet there is not a great awareness nor understanding of the Truman Doctrine among the general public, particularly in comparison to the Marshall Plan which followed it.

To commemorate this event and to mark its inception in Greece and Greece's central role, the American Hellenic Institute Foundation was pleased to initiate a two-day conference in Washington, D.C. on March 12-13, 1997. The conference was co-sponsored by the distinguished Academy of Political Science and held in cooperation with the Truman Library and the Marshall Foundation.

I was particularly pleased by the response of key individuals and organizations to our efforts. General Andrew J. Goodpaster, USA (Ret.), a fellow board member of the Eisenhower World Affairs Institute, was enthusiastic about the conference and readily agreed to be our luncheon speaker. During our initial discussion he coined the phrase "a turning point in world history."

Larry J. Hackman, Director of the Truman Library, graciously participated as chair of the panel The Truman Doctrine: From Inception to Implementation and also suggested speakers and arranged for a photographic exhibit for the conference.

The Marshall Foundation helped through the participation of Dr. Larry Bland, editor of the Marshall papers, and referred me to the biographer of General James A. Van Fleet.

A very special thanks to Professor Demetrios Caraley for the co-sponsorship of The Academy of Political Science and for his participation as chair of the panel on the military dimension.

Conference coordinators Dr. Van Coufoudakis, Dean, School of Arts and Sciences, Indiana University-Purdue University, and Dr. John O. Iatrides, Professor of Political Science at Southern Connecticut State University, are the ideal academic team with which to work. They were instrumental in developing the conference program and in recommending and obtaining outstanding speakers. Dr. Iatrides is recognized as a leading expert in the United States on this period in Greek history.

Many thanks to Lt. Gen. Pericles Papathanassiou (Ret.), who served on the Albanian front in World War II and in the Greek civil war, for chairing the panel The Greek Crisis and the Truman Doctrine.

The distinguished speakers, some of whom were active participants in the dramatic events of that era, deserve the most thanks for recreating the atmosphere of the time and discussing the background to President Truman's historic decision, its impact and legacy, the military dimension and the role of Greece. Their names and biographies are listed in the Appendix.

I acknowledge with gratitude the authorization from Dr. Joel Glassman, Director, Center for International Studies, University of Missouri-St. Louis and Dr. Christos P. Ioannides, chairman of factulty of The Speros Basil Vryonis Center for the Study of Hellenism, the co-sponsors of a conference on "The Truman Doctrine and its Impact on Greece" at Washington University, St. Louis, March 21-22, 1997, to include the addresses in this volume of Virginia Tsouderos, former Deputy Minister of Greece, and Professor Howard Jones of the University of Alabama.

Special thanks to the *Veterans of Foreign Wars* magazine for their permission to reprint the informative article by David Colley.

The conference was made possible through the generous contribution of the National Bank of Greece and several American Hellenic Institute Foundation members including John Charalambous, George C. Chryssis, Dr. Takey Crist, James H. Lagos, Esq., Dean C. Lomis, Ph.D., Ike Pappas, James Pedas, Theodore Pedas, Ted G. Spyropoulos, Savas Tsivicos, the American Hellenic Educational Progressive Association, the Hellenic American National Council, the Pan Cretan Association of America, and the United Hellenic American Action Societies of Delaware.

My thanks to Evanthia Allen who proofread the manuscript and Loren Morales, Business Manager of The Academy of Political Science, and Maria Hadjitheodosiou for their able assistance. A very special thanks to Yola Pakhchanian for her editorial and production assistance and for overseeing every step of this publication.

Eugene T. Rossides
President
American Hellenic Institute Foundation

INTRODUCTION

The Academy of Political Science is delighted to publish jointly with the American Hellenic Institute Foundation this set of excellent essays on the "Truman Doctrine of Aid to Greece: A Fifty Year Retrospective." They tell the story of a successful foreign and military policy intervention by the United States without loss in combat of any American lives. The essays provide a record of the numerous reasons for this success, reasons that have relevance today. Eugene T. Rossides, president of the American Hellenic Institute Foundation, deserves warm congratulations for the imagination and drive that brought together such a stellar cast of practitioners and scholars to write this retrospective analysis.

The hallmark of the Truman Doctrine was that it be "the policy of the United States to support free peoples who are resisting attempted subjugation by armed minorities or by outside pressures." On March 12, 1947, President Harry Truman went before a joint session of Congress and requested a program of economic aid, military equipment, and military advisers to help Greece defeat the heavily armed communist insurgents who were trying to topple the Greek government and turn Greece into a Soviet-dominated dictatorship. The insurgents were being helped by the three Soviet satellite states—Albania, Yugoslavia, and Bulgaria—on Greece's northern border. By May 9, 1947, both houses of the Republican-controlled 80th Congress passed the necessary legislation with bipartisan majorities: 287-108 in the House (Republicans 127-94; Democrats 160-13; Independent 0-1) and 67-23 in the Senate (Republicans 35-16; Democrats 32-7). By July 15, the American Mission for Assistance to Greece had arrived in Athens and by November 1, military equipment began to flow in. By August of 1949, after being increasingly depleted in numbers and confined to the northwest mountain areas of Greece, the insurgents were defeated in a major offensive and those who were not killed or captured fled over the border into Albania and Yugoslavia.

This brief summary may suggest that the launching and success of the Truman Doctrine had been in today's terms, a "no brainer." Would not any Amer-

DEMETRIOS CARALEY, Ph.D., is President of the Academy of Political Science, Editor of the journal *Political Science Quarterly*, Janet Robb Professor of the Social Sciences at Barnard College, and Professor of Political Science at the Graduate School of International and Public Affairs at Columbia University.

ican president recognize the critical location of Greece in the eastern Mediterranean for protecting American sea lanes to the Middle East and its oil, and seek to keep it from falling behind the Iron Curtain? And given these realities, would not any president be able to persuade Congress to back his initiative with bipartisan majorities? Also, wasn't it certain that the Greek government, the Greek army, and the Greek people would use the American support effectively and outfight the insurgents, in light of their ancient traditions and very recent World War II experience of resisting aggression and fighting for liberty? Finally wasn't it easy to adhere to the original strategy of not introducing American combat troops to prevent combat casualties even though on occasion it looked like the communists might score a major victory?

In fact, as the essays explain, none of what happened was inevitable, and the story might have ended very differently. Truman was a new president, having succeeded to the office after Franklin Roosevelt's death only two years before, and was largely untried in forging new foreign and military policy initiatives. He might not have been willing to break with all tradition and propose America's first peacetime foreign assistance program. The Republican-led Congress might have delayed or defeated the initiative of what they saw as a Democratic lame duck president in order to keep him from generating a successful record that he could use in his 1948 election campaign. True, the Greek government, army, and people had played a heroic role in World War II. They had rejected an October 1940 ultimatum to surrender and allow the Italian army that was invading from Albania to occupy Greece; instead they counterattacked, pushing the invading army back into Albania and almost destroying it by April 1941. Then, when Adolf Hitler dispatched large German forces to invade Greece through Yugoslavia in order to bail out his Italian ally, the Greeks offered fierce resistance on mainland Greece and then on the island of Crete. Because of the need for this German intervention and because of the unexpected ferocity of Greek resistance, the German attack on the Soviet Union was delayed from May to late June, undermining the German Army's ability to reach its major objectives in 1941 before the Russian winter set in.

Nevertheless, by 1947 the Greeks were war weary, for they had been fighting continuously since 1940, against the Italian and German armies, as part of the wartime resistance from the mountains, and finally against the communist insurgents. And while the Greek soldiers remained brave, the officer corps—largely tutored by British officers during the pre-World War II period and through the resistance—was imbued with cautious, unimaginative strategies and tactics that took the head of the American advisers, General James A. Van Fleet, considerable time to counteract. Finally it was not at all a given that the Soviet Army, which had crushed democratic forces in Poland and Czechoslovakia, would not come in force over Greece's northern borders through Yugoslavia or Bulgaria and overrun the Greek Army with its small cadre of American advisers. This would have posed to the United States the choice of accepting the loss of Greece to the Soviet Communist movement or taking on the risk of igniting a World War III by introducing major American combat units.

These essays, beyond fleshing out the historical record of how the Truman Doctrine was conceived and implemented in Washington and in Greece fifty years ago, also offer lessons for the present, especially now that the United States is the only remaining superpower. One reading of those lessons is that for an American military intervention in another country's civil war or counterinsurgency to succeed, (1) the president must educate the Congress and the public about the threat to American interests and the desirability but also the attainability of the objective, (2) the country receiving American aid must be willing to shoulder most of the burden of the fighting, (3) the objective of defeating the insurgents must be realistic given their resources and strategic positions versus those of the forces we wish to help, and (4) the nation and government we help should preferably be not just an enemy of our enemy but one that shares our own democratic and civil-libertarian values so that it can be counted upon to become a long-term friend, as Greece has been to the United States.

Finally, as some of the essays discuss in depth, the value of Greece's friendship with the United States did not end with the cold war. Greece's strategic location athwart sea lanes connecting the oil users of western Europe and the United States with the oil producers of the Middle East remains important to keep in the hands of a friendly government and a friendly people. As fewer and fewer governments in the Middle East are willing to give the United States bases for ground troops or warships, the superb harbors of mainland Greece and its islands are becoming more valuable for maintaining large American naval forces from which to project power in the eastern Mediterranean. And Greece's presence as a modern, economically-growing, stable democracy adjoining the war-torn states of the former Yugoslavia may yet prove valuable to bringing about a long-term reconciliation there through peaceful democratic processes.

Demetrios James Caraley
President, Academy of Political Science
Professor of Political Science,
Barnard College and Columbia University

THE ACADEMY OF POLITICAL SCIENCE

The Academy of Political Science is a nonpartisan, nonprofit organization founded in 1880 with a threefold mission: (1) to contribute to the scholarly examination of political institutions, processes, and public policies, (2) to enrich political discourse and channel the best social science research in an understandable way to political leaders for use in public policy making and the process of governing, and (3) to educate members of the general public so that they become informed voters in the democratic process. The major vehicles for accomplishing these goals are its journal, *Political Science Quarterly*, Academy conferences, and the publication of proceedings or symposia based on conference presentations. The prestige and authority of the Academy are such that statesman and scholars of all political persuasions have enrolled as members, participated in its conferences, and contributed to its publications. Former presidents Gerald Ford, Jimmy Carter, Ronald Reagan, and George Bush are honorary members of the Academy.

Published continuously since 1886, *Political Science Quarterly* (*PSQ*) is the most widely read and accessible scholarly journal on government, politics, and policy, both international and domestic. Dedicated to objective analysis based on evidence, *PSQ* has no ideological or methodological slant and is edited for both specialists and general readers who have a serious interest in public and foreign affairs. Each issue contains thirty to forty timely and thorough book reviews so that readers are kept up to date on new literature. *PSQ*'s editorial board is composed of outstanding scholars from the nation's leading universities and think tanks.

AMERICAN HELLENIC INSTITUTE FOUNDATION

The American Hellenic Institute Foundation, Inc., (AHIF), established in 1975, is a 501(c)(3) nonpartisan nonprofit tax-exempt educational and research organization. It is the first "think tank" devoted exclusively to the study of issues regarding the Greek American community and United States relations with Greece and Cyprus. AHIF conducts a program of research, publications, conferences, seminars and lectures, and maintains a library and an information center.

Current publications include: *Modern Greeks-Greece in World War II; The German Occupation and National Resistance; The Civil War* (1997) by Costas Stassinopoulos; *Doing Business in Greece* (1996) a two volume loose-leaf reference service; *Handbook on United States Relations with Greece and Cyprus* (1990) a loose-leaf reference service; and the *American Hellenic Who's Who, 1994-95* (5th ed.).

The Truman Doctrine:
From Inception to Implementation

Harry S. Truman and the Origins of the Truman Doctrine

ALONZO L. HAMBY

On March 12, 1947, President Harry S. Truman appeared before a joint session of Congress to request a major program of aid to Greece, struggling against a Communist-led insurgency, and Turkey, under direct pressure from the Soviet Union. The president called for $400 million, a sum that if adjusted for inflation would be equivalent to perhaps half of today's entire foreign aid budget. His speech, however, had more to it than this limited, if important purpose. It declared: "It must be the foreign policy of the United States to support free peoples who are resisting attempted subjugation by armed minorities or by outside pressure."

The March 12 speech was not the first U.S.-Soviet clash of the Cold War. A number of events in the previous year had presaged it: George F. Kennan's advocacy of a policy of "containment" of Soviet expansionism; the clash over Soviet reluctance to withdraw from Iran; belligerent statements by Soviet dictator Josef Stalin; Winston Churchill's "iron curtain" speech (delivered with Truman's apparent approval); the U.S.-Soviet deadlock over United Nations control of atomic energy; the dispatch of a U.S. naval fleet to the eastern Mediterranean; Secretary of State James Byrnes's pledge of support to anti-communist Germans at Stuttgart. Truman's dismissal of Secretary of Commerce Henry A. Wallace from the administration in September, 1946, had confirmed a hardening anti-Soviet line.

What Truman did on March 12, 1947, was to deliver an open confirmation of an American policy that already had taken shape in the previous year. Most importantly, he stated a broad and unequivocal rationale for it. The speech is justly remembered as a landmark event in the history of American foreign policy for two reasons: (1) It called for the first substantial commitment of funds to the containment of the Soviet Union; (2) It delivered in public for the first time the general statement of principle that I have just quoted—a "doctrine" that would drive U.S. foreign policy, the Truman Doctrine.

This essay attempts to explain how Truman came to the consciousness behind his speech of March 12. The declaration was important not simply as a

ALONZO L. HAMBY is Distinguished Professor of History at Ohio University. This essay is drawn from his book, *Man of the People: A Life of Harry S. Truman* (Oxford University Press, 1995).

U.S. commitment to Greece, nor even as a declaration of a vital U.S. interest in that area of the world we might call the Eastern Mediterranean/Middle East. It asserted an American mission in leading the world toward an international system built around liberal ideals. It was, of course, a group project, but one that required the assent and the voice of the president of the United States. Truman supplied both, readily and naturally. My question is how did he arrive at that disposition?

There is a well-developed cultural interpretation of Cold War foreign policymaking and of twentieth-century American international involvement. It holds that American foreign policy was the product of a White-Anglo-Saxon-Protestant patrician elite, mainly from the northeastern part of the United States, educated at exclusive private preparatory schools and universities, taught to envision the United States as an extension of what was beginning to be called "Western culture," dedicated to the defense of that culture, and Anglophilic to the core. There is much to be said for this argument; it is an especially good description of many of the men who made Truman's foreign policy: Dean Acheson, Robert Lovett, George Kennan, Paul Nitze, Averell Harriman, among others.

But it does not describe Truman—the offspring of a modest provincial family, educated in the Independence, Missouri, public schools, bereft of any kind of a liberal arts college experience, trained in the hard knocks of machine politics, possessing almost nothing in the way of a basis of common experience with the men I have just named. Yet nothing was foisted on him. His declaration was a heartfelt expression of deeply internalized values. What I want to do is follow the road that brought him to March 12, 1947.

EDUCATION AND CHILDHOOD IDENTITY

Let us begin by trying to visualize a fifteen- or sixteen-year old boy, a little pudgy, terribly nearsighted, altogether just a bit of a sissy, reading a history book through very thick and heavy eyeglasses in the local library or in a high school classroom around 1900 in Independence, Missouri. Young Harry Truman was a small-town boy, a rustic by the standards of the sophisticated Northeast, but none-the-less at the end of a cultural chain that stretched from Oxford and London through Boston and New York into the American heartland. Unknown to him another boy, somewhat less bookish but with at least as keen an intelligence, Franklin Roosevelt, was imbibing a similar education at one of America's elite preparatory schools, Groton.

Independence high school and Groton were worlds apart; yet they delivered to their students similar worldviews. Both Roosevelt and Truman received an education built around the classics, English literature, and history. Many educators today would disapprovingly call it Eurocentric. Young Harry seems to have learned little, if anything at all, about the Indians who less than a century earlier had been the inhabitants of what became Jackson county, Missouri.

He learned much about the Greeks of two thousand years ago, both as philosophers and warriors.

He developed a tempered admiration for Alexander the Great as a military leader of unparalleled courage and resourcefulness, who nevertheless exemplified the weakness of human nature by drinking himself into an early grave. He read Plato in translation and returned periodically to him later in life. He also took Latin, learned about Rome, and admired Hannibal and Caesar. More in Sunday school than in public school, he learned about the ancient Hebrews and the Biblical saga of Israel. He learned more ancient history in high school than most college graduates know today. The world of the eastern Mediterranean was alive and vivid for him as a child.

The same was true for the world of medieval and early modern Western Europe. Young Harry could discuss at length the lives and exploits of Charles Martel and Charlemagne, of Henri IV, Louis XIV, and Napoleon, of Henry VIII and Elizabeth I, of Gustavus Adolphus. Reared a Baptist and never questioning for a moment that Protestant Christianity was a progressive force of enormous importance, he adopted Martin Luther as a cultural hero. He sensed a direct connection between his own world and these worlds that had gone before. The idea of a "Western civilization" that began with the ancients and had developed up to his own time was fundamental to his consciousness.

It was equally fundamental that his education was infused with the optimistic outlook of Anglo-American liberalism that dominated the end of the Victorian age: history was the story of the expansion of liberty; moral and material progress was the overriding trend of human experience, whatever the bumps and interruptions along the way. He was taught to revere Lord Tennyson, who provided a glimpse of the end of history in his epic *Lockesley Hall*: an end to war, "the Parliament of Man, the Federation of the World," where "the common sense of most shall hold a fretful realm in awe/And the kindly earth shall slumber, lapt in universal law." By his own account, Truman carried those lines, copied and recopied, with him for a half-century.

For many twentieth-century intellectuals, World War I irrevocably destroyed the Victorian vision, and World War II obliterated the last vestiges of hope for its reestablishment. But, perhaps because he was not an intellectual, Harry Truman was an optimist to the last; he believed to his dying day that the best eras of human history were in the future, not in the past. And as the United States displaced England as the leader of the Anglo-American world, he came to believe that America had a special responsibility for moving the world in that direction, for promoting the spread of liberty and material progress.

WORLD WAR I

Far from dampening his hopes for progress, Truman's experience in World War I left them essentially untouched. First of all, the war drove home a lesson that already had been ingrained in him—power was the ultimate arbiter in relations among nations and indeed in most areas of life. From a very early age, he had known that his family was on the wrong side in the Civil War and that in some relatively benign ways, history had *happened* to them. To be a boy in Independence, Missouri in the 1890s was to understand that the very fact one was a citizen of the United States had been decided by a contest of arms in which the strongest prevailed. Moreover, Truman was to absorb this lesson at a time of national reconciliation that mixed nostalgia for the lost cause with a fervent sense of American patriotism and destiny.

Harry's mother and grandmother might grumble about Lincoln and the depredations of Kansas "redleg" guerrillas and think John Wilkes Booth a great man. Harry learned otherwise.

When the United States went to war with Spain in 1898, he and his teenage friends formed a pseudo-military company, marched, camped out, and shot a couple of stray chickens with their .22 rifles. Good fun, the experience was also a rudimentary display of patriotic pageantry.

Truman thus grew up with a strong sense of patriotism despite his parents' Confederate antecedents. He dreamed of going to West Point and becoming a professional solider. Instead, he became a bank clerk who found it a natural step to join the National Guard on his twenty-first birthday. He took pride in his affiliation even if his grandmother loathed his dress-blue uniform. As a young man in his twenties and thirties, he more consciously than ever fused American patriotism with American destiny. The agent who made that mix an enduring part of his outlook was Woodrow Wilson.

As Truman recalled it some years later, he rejoined the National Guard at the age of 33 in 1917 with the intention of going off to war primarily because he "was stirred in heart and soul by the war messages of Woodrow Wilson," secondarily because his reading of history told him "we owed France something for Lafayette." The two impulses were complementary. They joined a faith in liberal ideals with a conviction that liberal democracy had to be advanced by force of arms. Truman followed through on them with nearly two years of hard military duty, including three months of intermittent combat during the closing phase of the war in France. A courageous and resourceful junior officer, he survived brushes with death, found the realities of war hard and exasperating, but never lost his ideals.

It is correct that in early 1919, with World War I over, Captain Truman, trapped with his regiment in a mudhole of a makeshift camp in northern France, wanted only to go home and displayed a peevish impatience with his commander-in-chief's endeavors at Versailles. Complaining of "Woodie's" "pet peace plans," he wrote to his beloved Bess: "I don't give a whoop...whether there's a League of Nations or whether Russia has a Red government or a Purple one, and if the president of the Czecho-Slovaks wants to pry the throne from under the King of Bohemia, let him pry but send us home." (Dear Bess, 293) The quotation is a great one that reflected the real unhappiness of a homesick soldier, but let us not make too much of it. Woodrow Wilson was a great hero to Truman, and Wilson's foreign policy would establish the basis for his own thinking. Wilson's idea of an American mission to make the world safe for democracy would resonate powerfully with the mature politician as fully as with the younger captain. So would Wilson's determination to press for it with all of America's national power.

THE COMING OF WORLD WAR II, 1937-1941

Like many Americans, Truman appears to have paid little attention to foreign policy for the decade and a half or so after he returned from Europe. We do know enough, however, to realize that he never relinquished his belief in the Wilsonian vision of America's mission in the world. Nor did he compromise on his commitment to American power. His active membership in the Reserve Officers Corps, the 35th Division Association, and the American Legion all testified to a belief in military readiness as the ultimate protector of American interests and the instrument of the American mission. His disdain for Wilson's major critic within the Missouri Democratic party, former Senator James A. Reed, was ill-concealed.

It was as a U.S. senator that Truman again came face to face with foreign policy issues. He was elected in 1934 by an electorate fixated on the enormous problems of the Great Depression. There seems to have been no discussion whatsoever of foreign policy in either his primary or general election campaigns. He took his seat in January, 1935, one of thirteen freshman senators (all Democrats) who had been elected primarily by pledging unquestioning support for President Franklin Roosevelt and his New Deal. Caught up in the currents of the isolationist thirties, he pretty much followed a weaving administration foreign policy line. Roosevelt, an interventionist by every instinct, gave himself political cover by refusing to oppose the Neutrality Acts of 1935, 1936, and 1937; all of them embodied the premise that the United States could avoid involvement in a possible European war by avoiding the policies (or "mistakes") that had led to World War I. Truman voted for each of them. Roosevelt also pushed cautiously but persistently for increased military expenditures. Truman equally took up this theme, more forcefully than his chief.

On April 20, 1937, Truman delivered a speech at Larchmont, New York, that was the first shot in a sustained campaign for the revival of American power and the resumption of the American mission. It deserves close attention because it places him in the vanguard of elected officials who argued for increased international involvement. and because one can draw a straight line from it to the speech he would make about ten years later on March 12, 1947. By the spring of 1937, the post-World-War-I international system was in the intermediate stages of disintegration. Italy was consolidating its conquest of Ethiopia. Japan had long since swallowed up Manchuria, and most prescient observers knew that some incursion into the rest of China was likely. Spain was embroiled in a ghastly civil war that threatened to suck in every major European power. Germany, beginning its fifth year of Nazi rule, had occupied the Rhineland and undertaken a large rearmament program. No clear-eyed observer could look to the future with confidence. "Conditions in Europe," Truman declared, "have developed to a point likely to cause an explosion at any time." Or, to be only marginally more direct, war was likely and the United States probably would be drawn into it, just as had been the case a generation earlier.

He began with an interpretation of recent history: "We refused to sign the Treaty of Versailles, did not accept our responsibility as a world power, and tried, by tariff walls, to reap the benefits of world trade without giving anything in return. It did not work." Here was the Wilsonian arguing for an American mission of leadership in the world, positing liberal capitalism as the purpose of that mission. (Let us be clear, by the way, that in Truman's mind, liberalism [individual liberties and self-rule] and capitalism [individual economic enterprise] were two sides of the same coin. Both of them subject to regulation and interpretation, to be sure, but in tandem the highest development yet of human society.)

Truman virtually dismissed the very neutrality legislation for which he had just voted: "very laudable, and I hope it will help to keep us at peace. But, my friends, we are living in a world of realities....In the coming struggle between Democracy and Dictatorship, Democracy must be prepared to defend its principles and its wealth." From that point of departure, Senator Truman went on to call for a big navy, "an air force second to none," a well prepared army, and an industrial mobilization plan. "The world knows our honorable record in the World War," he concluded. "We fought for liberty and honor, just as we always have, and just as we always shall."

Consider all these words and the assumptions behind them. America should not have rejected world involvement and world leadership. American military power could serve a necessary and constructive purpose in improving the world. There were two kinds of nations, democracies and dictatorships. Not subtle. But not fundamentally wrong either, and stated with intense conviction more than six months before Roosevelt's much more tentative quarantine speech.

Truman repeated these arguments on numerous occasions, not just to distant audiences but to his Missouri constituency. Listen to this Armistice Day message, sent home to be read to his daughter's eighth grade class in Independence, Missouri, and published in the local paper: "We must take our place along with other peace-loving nations in world affairs and let the bandits and thugs among the world powers know that they will be punished for their thuggery." Or look at the way he wound up a speech to a group of Young Democrats in Bolivar, Missouri. This is on April 12, 1938, just weeks after the German

Anschluss with Austria. "We have more of the world's gold, the world's goods, and the world's productive land than any other nation has ever had. How long do you suppose we can keep those things for our own enjoyment if Hitler, Mussolini or the Emperor of Japan could walk in and take them?....That is why we need an adequate navy and a national defense policy."

Look at one more pronouncement, this one delivered to the Kiwanis Club of St. Joseph, Missouri, October 27, 1938, just a month after the Munich crisis. Here we have a policy undergirded by an interpretation of Western European history, built around two controlling themes: the tendency of warlike barbaric tribes from northern Europe to engage in wars of conquest and the periodic efforts of great national leaders to unify the continent, politically and economically. The last of those leaders, the natural successor to Julius Caesar, Henri IV, and Napoleon, had been Woodrow Wilson. "Wilson...clearly saw that Europe could never be at peace unless the economic barriers could be torn away and the races be made to understand each other and have a will to live in peace." Instead, he had been stymied by greedy and vengeful leaders among the victors. The peace of Versailles had collapsed. Japan had invaded China, Italy had subjugated Ethiopia, the German dictator was following their examples. One had to ask if the world had reached the end of another enlightened age, as had the Greeks when they experienced decline and defeat around 300 B.C. or the Romans centuries later. He concluded, "I still hope that some sort of a world arrangement along the lines laid out by King Henry IV or Woodrow Wilson may be worked out. Eventually it will have to be, or our civilization will end as all other great civilizations have, and we'll just start over from another Dark Age." As World War II approached, Senator Harry Truman more clearly than ever defined the American mission as the establishment of a universal world order.

With the outbreak of war in Europe, Truman emerged as a full-blown interventionist, supporting whatever aid Britain needed. In the fall of 1939, he backed modification of the Neutrality Acts to allow the sale of military equipment to the British on a cash-and-carry basis. In September 1940, as a candidate for relection to the Senate, he reversed an earlier position and voted in favor of a military draft. In the spring of 1941, he backed Lend-Lease. He asserted that all these stances were matters of self-interest for the United States. He also made no effort to conceal his sense that the United States was directly threatened by the Axis. In a stiff rejoinder to a constituent who was worried about the United States becoming embroiled in the war, he declared: "We are facing a bunch of thugs, and the only theory a thug understands is a gun and a bayonet."

In his private correspondence, Truman also began to use a new word—"totalitarian." It is an interesting addition to his vocabulary because it betrays an underlying conception of the stakes of international politics in the World War II era. The Senator's central concern was the threat presented by the Axis powers, but he also perceived a larger struggle going on the world. The war as he saw it was not simply a battle of the world's "progressive forces" against "fascism;" the United States represented ideals of liberalism and democracy that gave the armed struggle its ultimate meaning and, from the first, rendered the U.S. alliance with the Soviet Union problematic. Historians have often repeated his initial reaction to the surprise Nazi attack on Germany's former ally, the U.S.S.R: "If we see that Germany is winning, we should help Russia and if Russia is winning we ought to help Germany and that way let them kill as many as possible...." It is dangerous to invest too much significance into an offhand comment. The impulse was widespread—the great Nebraska progressive George Norris said much the same thing. And Truman said at the same time, "I don't want to see Hitler victorious under any circumstances." Still, he clearly perceived an underlying equation between Nazism and Soviet Communism. It troubled him throughout the war.

Truman's sense of the Soviet Union had numerous sources. Perhaps the most fundamental was his worldview that assumed liberal capitalism as a norm. It had room for class conflict between "the people" and "the interests" but not for the promotion of class warfare, the liquidation of the bourgeoisie, the abolition of private property, and the dictatorship of the proletariat. In his mind, dictatorship was dictatorship. Gangsters were gangsters. Writing to his wife at the end of 1941, he remarked that the Soviet leaders were "as untrustworthy as Hitler and Al Capone."

But he was also a practical man. A person who understands that power is the prime force in human affairs naturally enough realizes the limitations of ideals and knows that they often need to be compromised. Most of Truman's life pointed him in that direction—not just the experience of World War I but also the experience of being a machine politician. If the Soviet Union had once been an unfriendly state, it was on the side of the United States in the fight against Nazi Germany. "I am perfectly willing to help Russia as long as they are willing to fight Germany to a stand-still," he declared in 1943. He never was swept up in the wartime romanticism that hailed the valiant Soviet state as a new and perhaps higher type of democracy, but he did envision the Soviets as deserving allies and potential partners in the postwar world order.

The shape of that world order derived from the Wilsonian side of Truman's consciousness. He was a vocal campaigner, not just for American involvement in the postwar world, but for an international organization, driven by President Roosevelt's Four Freedoms, possessing "a powerful international police force," and "controlled by Britain, China, Russia and the United States in the name of all and for the welfare of all." The gesture toward a partnership of the Big Four was not devious, but assuredly Truman saw the new United Nations as an organization that would exist for the promotion of Anglo-American liberal values, the causes for which in the minds of most Americans the war was being fought. A Soviet Union that did not move in the direction of those values, or at least consent to their hegemony, would be an uneasy ally indeed. A Soviet Union that sought to impose its own values and ideology would no longer be an ally at all.

By mid-1944, Senator Harry S. Truman had established himself as a prominent Democratic foreign policy spokesman. He was an idealist in his liberal values and faith in progress, a realist in his understanding of human nature and appreciation of the role of power in politics. Both visions would continue to inform his presidency.

THE COMING OF THE COLD WAR

The first year of the Truman presidency was among the most momentous twelve-month spans in presidential history—the surrender of Germany, the establishment of the United Nations, the Potsdam conference, the atomic bomb and the capitulation of Japan, enormous economic stresses and strains in the domestic American transition from war to peace. Perhaps the most persistent of all the issues Truman faced was that of the U.S. relationship to the Soviet Union. To this problem, he brought all the impulses of his earlier years: a distaste for Soviet totalitarianism, a belief in the superiority (and indeed the inevitability) of liberal values, a determination to make America a world leader—and a desire to preserve the wartime alliance. To these impulses, he added another conviction—agreements had to be kept. The U.S.S.R., he believed, was failing to keep the agreements it had made at Yalta for "free elections" in Eastern Europe.

Yet his policy on Eastern Europe was ultimately more bark than bite. If he dressed down Soviet Foreign Minister Molotov, if he was understandably outraged by, among many issues, the subversion of Polish independence and the blatant repression of Bulgarian democrats, he realized that there was little the United States could do about it. He needed the Soviet Union on other matters: the United Nations, the war against Japan. Faced with Soviet intransigence in Poland, Bulgaria, and other Eastern European nations, he found himself with no other option than to search for a fig leaf that might hide at least the worst Soviet indecencies. Writing in his diary on May 23, he conceded that Eastern Europe made little difference to American interests, that Stalin could hold elections as free as those Boss Pendergast might have staged in Kansas City or Boss Hague in Jersey City. He left the Potsdam conference with considerable optimism that he could work with Stalin to achieve a decent, if imperfect, world order. Dismay over the naked extension of Soviet power into Eastern Europe and the occasionally harsh rhetoric accompanying it had a role in the beginning of the Cold War, but Truman realized that principle, however admirable, did not necessarily constitute a national interest. The clash of important interests that precipitated the Cold War would begin elsewhere.

That area was in the Eastern Mediterranean world that had existed so vividly for Truman since his childhood. Not Greece at first; that was still an area of British influence. Rather Iran and Turkey, the front and rear gateways to the Middle East. In early 1946, Truman authorized strong pressure on the Soviet Union to withdraw its troops from northwestern Iran. He exaggerated when he later claimed that he had sent an "ultimatum" to Stalin, but there can be no doubt of his emotional involvement and his determination to maintain Iranian independence. Later in the year, he used the U.S. navy to provide strong symbolic support to Turkey, which was under strong pressure to turn over control of the Black Sea straits to the Soviets. First, there was the return of the remains of the deceased Turkish ambassador aboard the U.S.S. *Missouri*, a floating hearse that just happened to have nine 16-inch guns. Then, late in the summer, the president approved a decision to station a U.S. naval task force in the region on a permanent basis. Truman had no sentimental attachment to Turkey nor much interest in its history, but he knew his geography. Turkey was a linchpin upon which the security of the Middle East and the eastern Mediterranean rested. He wanted American intentions to be clear and firm.

On August 15, meeting with national security officials, Truman approved a policy memorandum that declared a vital American interest in Turkish independence. He told Undersecretary of State Dean Acheson that he would stand by it "to the end." He remarked to Secretary of the Navy James Forrestal that we might as well find out now if the Russians were bent on world conquest. He also produced from his desk a map of the Middle East and lectured the group on its strategic importance. (Exactly how that map got there I have never learned. We know only that it does testify to Truman's sense of the region's importance.)

The commitments to Iran and Turkey led inexorably to the last piece of the puzzle—Greece.

THE DECISION TO AID GREECE AND TURKEY

Until late 1946, Greece had not loomed large in the consciousness of American policy makers. It long had been part of the British sphere of influence in that part of the world. But by late 1946, British power and capabilities were crumbling in Egypt, Palestine, and Greece. That fall, the Truman administration received advance notice that Britain could no longer support the Greek government against communist insurgents. What followed was a carefully orchestrated national security process—an American fact-finding mission, high-level discussions in Washington—that could lead to only one decision.

Most American policy makers, including Truman, found the right-wing government in Athens unpalatable. Undersecretary of State Dean Acheson described its premier, Constantine Tsaldaris, as "a weak, pleasant, but silly man" with little practical sense about the limits of American support. Before the war, the royal family, which was of German origin, had been altogether too cozy with the Nazis. Too many of the leading members of the government appeared authoritarian, perhaps protofascist. Truman, I have suggested, had a sense of Greek history and some pro-Greek sentiments. But he did not think he was moving to preserve Athenian democracy; nor would he have found any of the Greek leaders of 1947 worthy successors to Alexander the Great or Plato. He acted primarily out of a sense of strategic imperatives. He and his aides, moreover, readily accepted the need to couple aid to Greece with aid to Turkey, thereby making an implicit statement that the United States was confronting a regional crisis.

There remained the need to sell the program to an economy-minded Republican Congress. The president, Secretary of State Marshall, and Under-secretary Acheson met with congressional leaders on February 27, 1947. The story of that meeting is well known: Marshall's sober presentation of the need to fill the regional power vacuum or face the prospect of a series of crises "which might extend Soviet domination to Europe, the Middle East, and Asia;" congressional apprehension about "pulling British chestnuts out of the fire;" Dean Acheson's emotional invocation of the global struggle between totalitarianism and democracy; and Senator Vandenberg's assertion that the president needed to use the undersecretary's rhetoric to "scare the hell out of the American people" and thereby sell the program. I will leave it to others to decide whether Acheson's role was quite as pivotal as he later claimed. I have read Marshall's presentation; on paper, it looks both impressive and suffi-ciently scary to me.

What we can say with certainty is that Truman and his lieutenants had come to see the eastern Mediterranean crisis of 1946-47 as a situation with far larger implications. They understood that this was only one target of Soviet expansionism. They already sensed that the Greek-Turkish aid program was but the first step in a far larger design still to be worked out in the form of the Marshall Plan and the North Atlantic Treaty. The decision to justify it with a universal principle, the Truman Doctrine, was not just a tactical judge-ment; it reflected a realistic understanding of the Stalinist challenge to lib-eral democracy in the immediate postwar era. To fragment Cold War policy into a series of specific challenges and responses would have been to deprive it of intellectual coherence and to fail to inform the public of a genuine tran-scendent meaning.

But just what did the "Truman Doctrine" mean? Support free peoples, anywhere, anytime, with any amount of resources? One could find that impli-cation in it. By definition, broad general statements do not hedge. It is pretty clear, however, that the Truman administration had a sense of limits and a precision that is often ignored by the Truman Doctrine's critics. Those limits were derived from the Eurocentric outlook of the president and his national security officials and from their practical sense of the resources available to their foreign policy. For these reasons, the Truman Doctrine never applied to Chiang Kai-shek's China. General principles do not have to lead to an out-of-control crusade.

CONCLUSION

The American decision to aid Greece was part of a larger response to a regional crisis that the Truman administration had addressed for over a year. It was based on broad strategic considerations, not sentiment. But it was made all the easier by Truman's sense of history and by his apparent belief that it was natural and fitting for the United States to assume Britain's role as not simply a stabilizing influence but also a carrier of liberal values in the Eastern Mediterranean.

The president's education and experience, long before he reached the presidency, made the Truman Doctrine a natural stance for him. His sense of Western civilization, his mixed view of human nature, his understanding of the balance between power and ideals, and his belief in America's mission as the preeminent exemplar of liberal values all came together on March 12, 1947.

Critics of the Cold War have routinely deplored the Truman Doctrine, arguing that it unleashed a needless crusade against an exaggerated menace. We all can agree that it lacked subtlety. So did Franklin D. Roosevelt's Four Freedoms. Both were statements that needed to be made, and if they smacked more of Platonic ideal types than real world possibilities, they nevertheless expressed important principles that deserved to be stated without being hedged to death. The Truman Doctrine gave legitimate expression to the humane side of the great issue of the twentieth century—the struggle of liberal democracy against a totalitarian impulse that was as insidious in its so-called "left" version as in its right-wing variation. And it seems altogether fitting that, whatever the shortcomings of the Greek regime of 1947, it was stated in support of assistance to the nation that had given birth to the idea of democracy. ☐

A Reassessment of the Truman Doctrine and Its Impact on Greece and U.S. Foreign Policy

HOWARD JONES

The role of the Truman Doctrine in helping to prevent the fall of Greece to communism during the late 1940s provided a model for Washington's policymakers that they used throughout the Cold War. President Harry Truman's response to the Korean crisis in 1950 rested on his assertion that "this is the Greece of the Far East. If we are tough enough now," he declared, "there won't be another step." President Dwight D. Eisenhower viewed the threats to Indochina and the Middle East through the lessons learned in Greece, warning that if these areas fell to communism, Europe and other regions could likewise collapse. During the early 1960s both President John F. Kennedy and Democrat Adlai Stevenson argued that Greece provided an example for American action in Vietnam. Walt Rostow, chair of the State Department's policy planning council, assured Secretary of State Dean Rusk that "there is no reason we cannot win as clear a victory in South Vietnam as in Greece, Malaysia, and the Philippines." Henry Cabot Lodge, Jr., a Republican who had supported the Truman Doctrine in its formative years, declared in a 1964 speech that "We, of the Free World, won in Greece....And we can win in Vietnam." In 1965, shortly after the United States dispatched its first combat troops to Vietnam, President Lyndon B. Johnson referred to the Truman Doctrine in assuring Americans that they would win the war against communist aggression in Southeast Asia as they had won the war in Greece. The following year Rusk quoted from President Truman's 1947 address to Congress in justifying the U.S. involvement in Vietnam.[1]

HOWARD JONES is University Research Professor and Chair, Department of History, University of Alabama. A recipient of the John F. Burnum Distinguished Faculty Award for teaching and research, he teaches courses in American foreign relations and the U.S.-Vietnam War.

1. Bruce R. Kunihold, *The Origins of the Cold War in the Near East: Great Power Conflict and Diplomacy in Iran, Turkey, and Greece* (Princeton, New Jersey: Princeton University Press, 1980), 420; Ernest R. May, *"Lessons" of the Past: The Use and Misuse of History in American Foreign* Policy (New York: Oxford University Press, 1973), 108; Lyndon B. Johnson, *The Vantage Point: Perspectives of the Presidency, 1963-1969* (New York: Holt, Rinehart & Winston, 1971), 31, 422; Stephen G. Xydis, "The Truman Doctrine in Perspective," *Balkan* Studies 8 (1967), 256 n. 74; Rusk cited in Adam B. Ulam, *The Rivals: America and Russia Since World War II* (New York: Viking, 1971). 346-47; Theodore C. Sorensen, *Kennedy* (New York: Harper, 1965), 660-61; Lawrence S. Wittner, *American Intervention in Greece, 1943-1949* (New York: Columbia University Press, 1982), 307-09, 409 n.58; William J. Miller, *Henry Cabot Lodge: A Biography* (New York: Heineman, 1967), 373.

In the Truman administration's exuberance to sell a revolutionary foreign aid program to a reluctant Congress and American people, it launched a propaganda campaign that portrayed Soviet-American differences as an irreconcilable conflict between ideologies and thereby left little for compromise or accommodation. Indeed, it encouraged the development of a rigid mindset that automatically defined nearly every instance of unrest all over the globe as communist-imposed. According to Senator J. William Fulbright in the early 1970s, "More by far than any other factor the anti-communism of the Truman Doctrine has been the guiding spirit of American foreign policy since World War II."[2] "Like medieval theologians," the former chair of the Senate Foreign Relations Committee argued, "we have a philosophy that explained everything to us in advance, and everything that did not fit could be readily identified as a fraud or a lie or an illusion....The preciousness of the anti-Communist ideology of the Truman Doctrine arises not from any patent falsehood but from its distortion and simplification of reality, from its universalization and its elevation to the status of a revealed truth."[3]

At first glance, Fulbright's assessment seems accurate. Anti-communism certainly became the controlling force of the nation's containment policy. South Korea, like Greece, seemed to be under siege from communists acting in accordance with the Kremlin's orders and hence was a test of U.S. credibility as chief defender of the free world. In Vietnam, the situation appeared to be identical to that in Greece. Both crises had resulted from guerrilla wars fomented by internal problems, terrorist tactics, and outside assistance. And the government's enemies in both cases were led by communist guerrillas whose strings seemed attached to Moscow. Truly the future of freedom appeared to be at stake in these troubled areas.

But Fulbright's analysis was not entirely correct because those policymakers who sought to emulate the American experience in Greece had created a flawed analogy. The reality in Greece was far different from the appearance. Although the United States pronounced both Vietnam and Greece as centerpieces of world security during the time of trial, it nonetheless maintained a limited commitment in Greece. Most important, the Truman administration resisted tremendous pressure to send combat troops. American advisers in the period after the Greek crisis, however, did not discern these crucial differences in determining the course of involvement in other hot spots around the world. They failed to grasp the principles of flexibility and restraint underlying the Truman Doctrine and therefore extracted the wrong lessons from the

2. John L. Gaddis, *The United States and the Origins of the Cold War, 1941-1947* (New York University Press, 1972), 317-18; J. William Fulbright, *The Crippled Giant: American Foreign Policy and Its Domestic Consequences* (New York: Random House, 1972), 6-24.
3. J. William Fulbright, "Reflections In Thrall to Fear," *The New Yorker,* 47 (Jan. 8, 1972), 43.

experience in Greece.[4] Such realities necessitate a reassessment of the Truman Doctrine's impact on American foreign policy.

I

President Truman's famous congressional speech on March 12, 1947, shaped America's national security policy for four decades of Cold War and continues to provide a guideline for those foreign policy leaders who wish to help others help themselves in promoting their own security. The British government had recently declared an imminent end to its long-standing aid program in Greece and Turkey, and President Truman felt compelled to break a long-standing isolationist tradition in calling on Congress to approve a peacetime foreign assistance program that entangled the United States in European political and military affairs. Of the two troubled areas, Greece stood in greater danger of falling to communism. The government in Athens was engaged in a vicious guerrilla war with communist-led insurgents operating out of the northern mountainous regions of the country and receiving assistance from the neighboring communist regimes of Yugoslavia, Bulgaria, and Albania. The widespread perception, which had become for all intents and purposes the reality, was that the entire northern tier of Greece, Turkey, and Iran were at stake. Indeed, the area was crucial to control of the so-called world island or that veritable crossroads between East and West: the eastern Mediterranean, which offered access to the oil-rich Middle East and therefore presented the alluring possibility of America's enemies forcing the demise of its West European allies without firing a single shot. Although Truman's focus remained fixed on Greece and Turkey, he had actually thrust the United States once again into the ancient struggle between liberty and tyranny.[5]

Midway into his brief address, the president highlighted the essence of what became known as the Truman Doctrine: "I believe that it must be the policy of the United States to support free peoples who are resisting attempted subjugation by armed minorities or by outside pressures." The fall of Greece and Turkey, he warned, would signal other parts of the world that the United States's assurances of self-determination were mere rhetoric. The president soon got what he requested: a congressional appropriation of $400 million in military and economic aid for Greece and Turkey, along with civilian and military advisers. The bulk of the assistance was military aid for Greece.

The Truman Doctrine has been the subject of debate since its announcement. Critics have called it the "first shot of the Cold War;" a global license for American imperialism; an exaggerated response to an imagined communist

---

4. See Howard Jones, *"A New Kind of War:"* America's Global Strategy and the Truman Doctrine in Greece (New York: Oxford University Press, 1989); George F. Kennan, *Memoirs, 1925-1950* (Boston: Little, Brown, 1967), 314-17.
5. For text of speech, see U.S., President, *Public Papers of the Presidents: Harry S. Truman, 1947* (Washington, D.C.: U.S. Government Printing Office, 1963), 176-79.

menace that contributed to the nightmare of McCarthyism; a reactionary policy that placed the United States on the side opposite to freedom and reform; proof of an "arrogance of power" that repeatedly dragged Americans into other countries' domestic quarrels.[6] Defenders of the Truman Doctrine have praised the pronouncement as evidence of America's determination to contain Soviet communism; and assurance of its commitment to free world principles against totalitarianism—a magnanimous aid program designed to help first Greece and Turkey and then any nation that proved need.[7] Yet, in focusing on these issues, writers have failed to credit the Truman administration with devising a foreign policy designed to preserve freedom by helping the victimized country help itself. President Truman's declaration looked forward to the Nixon Doctrine of the 1970s, which called for partnerships based on the threatened nation sharing the burden of protecting itself by, among other considerations, furnishing the bulk of the manpower needed for its security.[8]

The Truman Doctrine marked the beginning of a global foreign policy that was flexible, restrained, and not necessarily military in thrust. More than a decade before President Kennedy introduced his program of "flexible response," Truman and his advisers (some later joining Kennedy) crafted a foreign policy intended to combat the constantly shifting challenges to democracy with an arsenal of responses equivalent to the danger then at hand. The Truman administration's approach to the Greek problem proved

6. J. William Fulbright, *The Arrogance of Power* (New York: Random House, 1966); Richard M. Freeland, *The Truman Doctrine and the Origins of McCarthyism* (New York: Schocken Books, 1970); Andreas Papandreou, *Democracy at Gunpoint: The Greek Front* (Garden City, N.Y.: Doubleday, 1970); Joyce Kolko and Gabriel Kolko, *The Limits of Power: The World and United States Foreign Policy, 1945-1954* (New York: Harper & Row, 1972); Thomas G. Paterson, *Soviet-American Confrontation: Postwar Reconstruction and the Origins of the Cold War* (Baltimore: The Johns Hopkins University Press, 1973); Thomas G. Paterson, *On Every Front: The Making of the Cold War* (New York: Norton, 1979); Daniel H. Yergin, *Shattered Peace: The Origins of the Cold War and the National Security State* (Boston: Houghton Mifflin, 1977; rev. ed., 1990); Wittner, *American Intervention in Greece*; Jon V. Kofas, *Intervention and Underdevelopment: Greece During the Cold War* (University Park: Pennsylvania State University Press, 1989).
7. Gabell Phillips, *The Truman Presidency; The History of a Triumphant Succession* (New York: MacMillan, 1966); Herbert Feis, *From Trust to Terror: The Onset of the Cold War, 1945-1950* (New York: Norton, 1970); Gaddis Smith, *Dean Acheson* (New York: Cooper Square Publishers, 1972); Gaddis, *U.S. and Origins of Cold War;* John L. Gaddis, *Strategies of Containment: A Critical Appraisal of Postwar American National Security Policy* (New York: Oxford University Press, 1982); John L. Gaddis, *The Long Peace: Inquiries into the History of the Cold War* (New York: Oxford University Press, 1987); Richard F. Haynes, *The Awesome Power: Harry S. Truman as Commander in Chief* (Baton Rouge: Louisiana State University Press, 1973); David S. McLellan, *Dean Acheson: The State Department Years* (New York: Dodd, Mead, 1976); Robert J. Donovan, *Conflict and Crisis: The Presidency of Harry S. Truman, 1945-1948* (New York: Norton, 1977); Kuniholm, *Origins of Cold War in the Near East;* Robert H. Ferrell, *Harry S. Truman and the Modern American Presidency* (Boston: Little, Brown, 1983); Donald R. McCoy, *The Presidency of Harry S. Truman* (Lawrence: University Press of Kansas, 1984); Walter Isaacson and Evan Thomas, *The Wise Men: Six Friends and the World They Made* (New York: Simon and Schuster, 1986); Randall B. Woods and Howard Jones, *Dawning of the Cold War; The United States' Quest for Order* (Athens: University of Georgia Press, 1991).
8. Gaddis, *Strategies of Containment*, 304-5.

idealistic in purpose but realistic in application. Its composite thrust was political, economic, and military, allowing for adjustments as the nature of the
threat changed.[9] The policy constituted a viable response to multifaceted
aggressions in which victory lay in convincing democracy's enemies that they
could not win.

In early 1949 the *New York Times's* veteran correspondent in Athens, Anne
O'Hare McCormick, put her finger on the problem when she reported that
the Truman Doctrine in Greece had involved the United States in "a new kind
of war." The conflict was dark and murky, a war in the shadows whose verdict
did not rest on territorial acquisition or human and material loss. The enemy
seldom wore uniforms, often fought with confiscated weapons and usually in
unconventional fashion, and was heavily dependent on outside assistance. Bat-
tlefronts rarely existed, for the vastly outnumbered guerrillas had little choice
but to pursue the terrorist tactics of raiding, pillaging, sniping, and abducting
villagers and townspeople into their small and highly mobile force. Indeed,
McCormick declared, Greece provided a "preview of the frontless, almost face-
less, war of tomorrow....The battle line is everywhere and nowhere."[10]

Americans at home did not discern the care with which the Truman administration intended to deal with the Greek crisis and expressed alarm that the
aid program might lead to full-scale U.S. military involvement and ultimate war
with the Soviet Union. During congressional hearings over the aid bill, Undersecretary of State Dean Acheson offered assurances that proved more unsettling than comforting. The proposals "do not include our sending troops to
Greece or Turkey. We have not been asked to do so. We have no understand-
ings with either Greece or Turkey, oral or otherwise, in regard to the sending of
troops to those countries." When Democratic Representative Mike Mansfield
asked whether the administration's policy could lead to war, the crowded room
hushed into silence as Acheson rubbed his chin, hesitated, and finally responded in a low voice: "I was going to say—no possibility it would lead to war." But
then he paused again before adding: "I don't think it could lead to war."[11]

---

9. Jones, *"New Kind of War,"* viii, 36. Even Kennan failed to grasp the administration's recognition of the essential issues in Greece and criticized its actions as too military in orientation.
   Memoirs, 319-22.
10. *New York Times,* Feb. 5, 1949, clipping in Francis F. Lincoln Papers, Truman Library, Inde-
    pendence, Missouri; *New York Times,* Dec. 29, 1948, p.20; *Time,* Jan, 10, 1949, p.45; Stephen
    G. Xydis, "America, Britain, and the USSR in the Greek Arena, 1944-47," *Political Science
    Quarterly* 78 (1963): 581-96.
11. Acheson's written replied to Senate questions, 26,51,77,92, enclosed in Acheson to Sen.
    Arthur Vandenberg, March 24, 1947, U.S. Dept., of State, General Records, Decimal File: U.S.-
    Greek Internal Political Affairs, 1945-49, Diplomatic Branch, National Archives, Washington,
    D.C. (hereafter cited as NA); "Source of Supply of Equipment for the Greek Armed Forces,"
    ca. Mid-March 1947, unlabeled, ibid.; Acheson's testimony before House Foreign Affairs
    Committee, March 20, 1947, summary in McNaughton Papers, Truman Lib.; *PM,* March 21,
    1947, Democrat Clipping File, Trum. Lib. U.S. Ambassador Lincoln MacVeagh's testimony,
    March 25, 1947, in U.S. House of Representatives, *Military Assistance Programs, part 2. Assistance
    to Greece and Turkey* 6 (Washington, D.C.; U.S. Government Printing Office, 1976): 334.

In truth, the White House had feared from the outset that stronger military measures would become necessary in Greece for at least three reasons: the impending British troop withdrawal, the desperate condition of Greek armed forces, and the strategic and symbolic importance of the region. Near East specialist Loy Henderson remarked that the president had purposely worded the Truman Doctrine loosely enough to be either military or economic in thrust. George McGhee, soon to become coordinator of the aid program, declared that the chief attribute of the Truman Doctrine was its flexibility: Administrators could shift the emphasis to either military or economic aid. And State Department adviser Charles Bohlen solidified that implication when he insisted that the Truman Doctrine did not *assure* the use of armed force. But all agreed that the United States must maintain the military option.[12]

Many congressmen remained worried about the open-ended nature of the commitment, Republican Francis Case of South Dakota, who chaired the House Committee considering the bill, concluded that most of his peers supported the measure only because they saw no choice. But, he warned in a statement that deserved wide attention, "no country, ours or any other, is wise enough, or just plain big enough to run the rest of the world."[13]

Even as the aid bill went into effect in May 1947, the Truman administration recognized the impossibility of guaranteeing self-determination around the globe. "Our resources are not unlimited," the president declared. "We must apply them where they can serve the most effectively to bring production, freedom, and confidence back to the world." Undersecretary of State Robert Lovett later proclaimed that "the line must be drawn somewhere or the United States would find itself in the position of underwriting the security of the whole world....We must be careful not to over-extend ourselves." Some areas were crucial for strategic reasons; others furnished a showcase of America's capacity to help targeted peoples resist aggression; still others were untouchable because they lay within Soviet spheres of influence. In theory

12. Henderson interview with author, May 24, 1979; McGhee interview with author, May 24, 1979; Charles E. Bohlen, *Witness to History, 1929-1969* (New York: Norton, 1973), 310; Rusk interview with author, Nov. 3. 1978. See also John O. Iatrides, ed., Ambassador MacVeagh reports: Greece, 1933-1947 (Princeton, New Jersey: Princeton University Press, 1980), 709; MacVeagh to Sec. of State, March 4, 1947, in U.S. Dept. of State, *Foreign Relations of the United States V: Near East and Africa* (Washington, D.C.: U.S. Government Printing Office, 1971): 89-90 (hereafter cited as *FRUS*); Sec. of War Robert Paterson to Sec. of State, ca. March 11, 1947, ibid.: 105-6; Memo for record: conferences concerning Greek situations, March 5, 6, 1947, U.S. War Dept., Records, ABC (American-British Correspondence) 400.336 Greece, Sect. I-A, pp.2-3, MA; Acheson's written replies to Senate questions, 73, U.S. Dept. of State, General Records, Decimal File, NA; Sec. of War to sec. of State, March 11, 1947, U.S. Army, Staff Records, 092, sect. VI-A, case 95, p.2, Plans & Operations, Modern Military Division, NA; all testimonies on March 13, 1947, in U.S. Senate, *Legislative Origins of the Truman Doctrine: Hearings Held in Executive Session Before the Committee on Foreign Relations, 80th Cong., 1 sess., on 5,938: A Bill to Provide for Assistance to Greece and Turkey* (Washington, D.C.: U.S. Government Printing Office, 1973), 5-6, 10-11.
13. Case to Truman, May 10, 1947, Truman Papers, Official File, Trum. Lib.

and in ideal, the commitment to Greece and Turkey was part of a global strategy designed to protect freedom wherever challenged. In practice and in reality, that strategy was limited by circumstances—whether the troubled area could and should be saved. As long as ideal and reality remained distinguishable, congressional fears were groundless.[14]

II

Only on paper is it arguable that the Greek army should have put down the rebels with ease. It was five times larger than the guerrilla forces, but it was poorly led, ill-trained, undisciplined, inadequately provisioned, low in morale, and, not surprisingly, stubbornly reluctant to take the offensive. The Communists meanwhile infiltrated the cities, towns, and large villages, building an intricate intelligence and supply network that aided in recruiting soldiers, raising money, gathering information about government troop movements, and terrorizing the population. When the army launched a daylight offensive, the guerrillas dispersed, only to regroup at night after the regulars had returned to their posts.[15] Greek military strategy seemed sound: Soldiers were to advance toward the northern frontier, crushing the guerrillas or driving them out of the country and sealing the border. But the largely unmarked border sprawled over 600 miles of territory, and passageways northward were seldom paved and difficult to use. Mountains covered more than 60 percent of the country's surface and afforded the guerrillas further protection.[16]

From the first arrival of U.S. materiel in August 1947, the Truman administration pushed for a major offensive by the Greek military forces. But this central objective became blurred in the popular excitement and overblown expectations of the Truman Doctrine. British news correspondent Kenneth Matthews capsulized the misguided optimism in Greece. The United States brought the "prestige of limitless resources and an air of knowing how to put things straight in no time—in no time at all." Every problem would disappear. "Corruption in the administration?" The Americans "would plant their men

---

14. Truman's speech to Inter-American Conference at Rio de Janeiro, Sept. 2, 1947, *Public Papers of the Presidents: Harry S. Truman, 1947*, 430; Lovett memo of conversation with Turkish ambassador, July 21, 1948, *FRUS 1948 III: Western Europe* (Washington, D.C.: U.S. Government Printing Office, 1974), 197. See also Jones, "*New Kind of War*," 62; Kennan, *Memoirs, 1967*: 320, 373-75; Gaddis, *Strategies of Containment*, 59, 64-65; Gaddis, *U.S. and Origins of Cold War*, 351-52.

15. Gen. Stuart Rawlins (British) to Gen. Wiliam Morgan (British), Sept. 18, 1947, U.S. Army, Staff records, 091 Greece, sect. II, cases 8-17: 1-2, NA; U.S. Army, History of JUSMAGG [Joint U.S. Military Assistance Greep, Greece]: 64-65, NA; Edgar O' Ballance, *The Greek Civil War, 1944-49* (New York; Praeger, 1966), 140, 142,147-48.

16. Testimony on April 1, 1947 of Paul A. Porter, head of the 1946 U.S. economic mission to Greece, in U.S. Senate, *Legislative Origins of Truman Doctrine*, 26; Edwin P. Curtin, "American Advisory Group Aids Greece in War on Guerrillas," *Armed Cavalry Journal* 58 (Jan. -Feb, 1949): 10-11; D.M. Condit, *Case Study in Guerrilla War: Greece During World War II* (Washington, D.C.: Dept. of Army, 1961), 141-42, 188-89; Kenneth Matthews, *Memories of a Mountain War: Greece, 1944-1949* (London: Longman, 1972), 28.

inside the Greek ministries. Morale in the army? They would stiffen it with American officers, not sitting on their rumps at a headquarters desk, but slogging it right up there with the front-line fighters." By the time the Greek army launched its first great northern offensive in the summer of 1948, the Americans had provided nearly 3,000 motor vehicles, 7,000 tons of ammunition, and 75,000 weapons, including machine guns, mortars, and rifles. Soon to arrive was a large number of howitzers. Victory seemed certain.[17]

In the meantime, however, the Greek war effort continued to flounder and soon sparked a major debate within the Truman administration over whether to send American combat troops to Greece. The catalyst for this discussion actually began in the summer of 1947, when the British notified Washington that they intended to pull their last 5,000 troops. Unless the United States persuaded the British to reverse their policy, American involvement would become unilateral and much more volatile. U.S. advisers meanwhile determined the availability of their own military personnel; they scrutinized both the domestic and foreign impact of direct military involvement, and pondered the repercussions of either success or failure. Most important, they examined the steps toward termination of involvement if events did not follow the desired course.[18] Should the United States provide operational advice to Greek soldiers in the field? Or should it send Americans to fight the war?[19]

The Truman administration was in a quandary. It regarded the British troops as a symbol of Western opposition to communism. Their withdrawal would be emblematic of a Western concession to Soviet encroachments that could spread to other parts of the world. The "hot question" of the period, asserted *Time* magazine, was whether the United States would send troops to Greece and thus meet the "test" of fulfilling America's obligations in Europe. But the Truman administration had cut the nation's armed forces so drastically after World War II that it lacked sufficient numbers to prevent an inva-

---

17. Matthews, *Memories of a Mountain War*, 160-61; "Interim Historical Report," USAGG [U.S. Army Group Greece], enclosed in Gen. William L. Livesay to director, Aug. 8, 1947, U.S. Army, Staff Records, 091, Greece, sect. V, cases 74-86, p.10, NA; "President's Third Quarterly Report on Greek-Turkish Aid," May 12, 1948, Truman Papers, Official File 426, Trum. Lib.
18. Jones, "*New Kind of War*," 85 ff.; Gen. Cortland T. Van R. Schuyler to commanding general, USFMTO, Leghorn, Italy, Aug. 11, 1947, U.S. Army, Staff Records, 092, sect. VI-A, case 95, NA; Schuyler to Admiral C.D. Glover at al., Aug. 12, 1947, "The Greek Situation," U.S. War Dept. Records, ABC 370.5 Greece-Italy, sect. I-A, NA; Lt. Col. [?] Osmanksi, Strategic Plans, "Planning Bases for Dispatch of Task Force to Greece," Aug. 20, 1947, U.S. Army, Staff records, 320.2, sect. V. cases 74-86, p. 1, NA; Brig. Gen. A.W. Kissner to Commanding General, Army Air Forces, "Availability of Forces for Movement to Greece," Sept. 5, 1947, ibid.
19. Jones, "*New Kind of War*," 79. 85.

sion of Greece. The only recourse was nationwide mobilization—which was politically impossible.[20]

The Joint Chiefs of Staff at first pushed for the injection of U.S. troops. The British withdrawal, Washington's military leaders argued, necessitated American replacements as "a show of strength in the Eastern Mediterranean and...tangible evidence of U.S. determination to uphold its policy by military action if necessary." They insisted that the absence of a military force might encourage a full-scale insurrection as well as an invasion from the north. Either British or American troops must be in Greece.[21]

Practical considerations by the joint chiefs, however, soon won over their initial reaction and eased the pressure for combat troops. Army intelligence warned that northern Greece was indefensible. Moreover, the arrival of soldiers could escalate the fighting into an all-out war that was unwinnable in view of Soviet military superiority in the Balkans. In a telling admission, the joint chiefs dourly concluded that the United States was "not now capable of deploying sufficient armed forces in Greece to defeat an attack...by the combined forces of Albania, Yugoslavia and Bulgaria; most emphatically not if these countries receive either covert or active Soviet support."[22]

The argument for American combat involvement lost even more support when the joint chiefs tied the matter to global strategy. The use of combat forces in Greece rendered them unavailable for "more critical emergency use" elsewhere. The major considerations were "our own strength, together with our prospective or actual commitments elsewhere, and the latest and best estimate as to whether such overt action by us will precipitate overt action by Soviet satellite or U.S.S.R. forces." The joint chiefs brought focus to the

20. Ibid., 79-80; *Time*, Sept. 8, 1947, pg. 20; Terry H. Anderson, *The United States, Great Britain, and the Cold War, 1944-1947* (Columbia: University of Missouri Press, 1981), 151; Melvyn P. Leveler, *The Specter of Communism: The United States and the Origins of the Cold War, 1917-1953* (New York: Hill and Wang, 1994), 70. U.S. armed forces had been cut from their high in June 1945 of 12 million to one and a half million in June 1947. The Soviets' Red Army (including the Air Force) had been reduced from more than 11 million in May 1945 to fewer than 3 million by early 1948. See Yergin, *Shattered Peace*, 270-71, and Paterson, *On Every Front*, 155-56.

21. JCS to Brit. Chiefs of Staff, after Aug. 29, 1947, pp. 1-2, encl., in Sec. of Navy James V. Forrestal to sec. of state, Sept. 1, 1947, U.S. Army, Staff Records, 091 Greece, NA; Report by Joint Strategic Survey Committee to JCS—"Military Implications of Withdrawal of British Troops from Greece and Italy," Aug. 30, 1947, pp. 7-10, 16, U.S. War Dept. Records, ABC 370.5 Greece-Italy, sect. I-A, JCS 1801/1, NA; Memo for Joint Staff Planners for JCS from F.H. Schneider, secretary of ad hoc committee to consider plan of action regarding British withdrawal of troops from Greece, Sept. 2, 1947, pp. 1-3. ibid.; Sec. of War Kenneth Royall and Forrestal to sec. of state, Sept. 5, 1947, *FRUS V: Near East and Africa*, 127-29.

22. U.S. Assistance to Greece, " Sept. 16, 1947, pp. 8-9, 56-57, 59-60, U.S. War Dept. Records, ABC 370.5 Greece-Italy, JIC [Joint Intelligence Committee] 401.1, NA; JCS 1798/1-"U.S. Assistance to Greece," Oct. 15, 1947, pp. 57-58, ibid.; Intelligence Report #3899, "U.S. Assistance to Greece," Sept. 12, 1947, U.S. Army, Staff Records, 091 Greece, sect. II-A, case 13, pp. 13-14, NA; Jones, *"New Kind of War,"* 94.

central corollary of America's new global strategy: it could not overextend itself in one country at the risk of damaging American interests elsewhere.[23]

Several features of this administrative decision-making process are worthy of note. America's military analysts did not count on ingenuity or luck. They did not argue that the mere threat of direct military intervention would frighten the guerrillas into submission. They did not blindly advocate a military response that lacked a strategic balance between means and ends. They examined all aspects of the Greek crisis and realistically concluded that American combat forces could not guarantee victory.

The troop question finally dropped from debate in late 1947, when the British relented to Washington's pressure and announced that they would retain their force in Greece for an indefinite period. In a face-saving effort, British Foreign Secretary Ernest Bevin explained that the presence of his nation's soldiers lifted Greek morale and demonstrated Britain's desire to cooperate with the United States in establishing Greek stability. A high-ranking British diplomatic official emphasized the need to work with America in developing "parallel policies in the Middle East." Whatever the motivation, British troop retention bought time for American advisers to improve the Greek army to the point that it could fight the war.[24]

The Truman administration had meanwhile opted for a measure aimed at facilitating this cardinal objective but carrying its own dangerous ramifications: the dispatch in November 1947 of ninety military advisers authorized to provide operational advice to Greek soldiers in the field. The policy was fraught with danger. Besides putting Americans into the heat of battle and subjecting them to injury and death, the new policy provided them with a place of leadership in a war that automatically made the United States more responsible for the outcome. Yet the continued inept performance of the Greek army left the Truman administration with little choice. The American ambassador in Athens, Henry Grady, complained that the Greeks had adopted a simple formula for winning the war: "always more: more men, more money and more equipment." During a recent army offensive, "I watched

23. Jones, "*New Kind of War*," 123; Report to JCS on "Outline Plans for the Dispatch on Short Notice of U.S. Forces to Greece and for Their Deployment in That Country," pp. 33-35 (approved by JCS on Feb. 24, 1948), U.S. War Dept. Records, ABC 370.5 Greece-Italy, sect. I-B, JCS 1826/2, Jan. 29, 1948, NA; "Comments on Certain Courses of Action Proposed with Respect to Greece and Answers to Specific Questions Contained in the Memorandum by the Secretary of the National Security Council dated February 24, 1948," pp. 7-8 (encl. in memo for JCS from Sidney W. Souers, exec. sec. of NSC, Feb, 24, 1948; 1-2, in U.S Sec. of Defense, 1947-48, CD 6-1-21, Modern Military Division, NA; Leffler, *Specter of Communism*, 70.
24. Jones, "*New Kind of War*," 154-54; Note by sect. to JCS on reports by commanding gen., HQs, USAGG, AMAG, March 24, 1948, U.S. Army, Staff Records, 091 Greece, sect. III-A, case 21, JCS 1841/4, NA; Minutes of Chiefs of Staff Committee Meeting, Nov. 21, 1947, Great Britain, Foreign Office, FO 371, vol. 6114, AN 400, Public Record Office, Kew, England, Minutes of Orme Sargent, Dec. 3, 1947, GB, FO 371, vol. 68041, AN 45/45, ibid.

Greek artillery men using expensive ammunition irresponsibly, sending repeated volleys against rocky slopes of mountain ridges, …much in [the] manner of American children setting off firecrackers on July 4."[25]

The implementation of operational advice again demonstrated the perils of this new kind of war. *New York Times* correspondent Cyrus Sulzberger confided to his diary that the Americans "appear to be in charge of operations and there is not much disguising this fact, although everyone pretends it isn't so." British observer Christopher Woodhouse later wrote: "Both on ground and in the air, American support was becoming increasingly active, and the theoretical line between advice, intelligence and combat was a narrow one." Washington nonetheless attempted to distinguish between an American officer serving as "combatant" and as "adviser." In reality, however, the distinction did not exist. An American officer standing beside Greek soldiers firing at the guerrillas became part of the fighting force, even if he did not pull a trigger. Moreover, advising and carrying out advice were inseparable parts of combat. An American shot on the battlefield counted as a casualty, even if he was technically an observer. Indeed, as the opposing sides exchanged firepower the Americans on the scene doubtless recalled their commanding general's assurance of safety as they prepared to join the Greek army in the field: "Neither your actions *nor your talk* should leave the impression that you are a 'combatant.'" If you "get caught in an operation, …take cover" and "don't get involved in the combat." But "don't give the Greeks the idea you are afraid when you take cover.…You are not armed and that is your protection." A captured guerrilla underlined the futility of these directives. He was under orders to shoot *any* Americans "interfering with operations."[26]

III

The war's growing savagery became evident as the tone of fighting took on that of a vendetta. Families closed ranks, seeking vengeance against anyone who wronged one of their own. In many cases these feuds developed into small wars—especially when blood members became divided in loyalties. Stories abounded of atrocities by both sides. Supporters of the Greek govern-

25. Gen. Stephen J. Chamberlin report to Chief of Staff, "The Greek Situation," Oct. 20, 1947, p. 55, U.S. Sec. Of Defense, 1947-48, CD 2-1-6, NA; Cyrus L. Sulzberger, *A Long Row of Candles: Memoirs and Diaries [1934-1954]* (New York: Macmillan, 1969), 394; Grady to sec. of state, Nov. 22, 1948, *FRUS IV: Eastern Europe: The Soviet Union* (Washington, D.C.: U.S. Government Printing Office, 1974), 187-89; JCS to Forrestal (SANACC) [State-War-Navy-Air Force Coordinating Committee] 358/8. Nov, 24, 1948, ibid., 191-92; Grady to sec. of state, Dec. 7, 1948, ibid., 210-22; Leffler, *Specter of Communism*, 70.

26. Sulzberger, *Long Row of Candles*, 394; Christopher M. Woodhouse, *The Struggle for Greece, 1941-1949* (Brooklyn Heights, N.Y.; Beekman-Esanu, 260-61; Gen. Livesay's address to American advisers to Greek army, Jan. 16, 1948: 1-2, 6-7, William L. Livesay Papers, U.S. Army Military History Institute, Carlisle Military Barracks, Pennsylvania; *The New York Times*, Feb. 13, 1948, p. 11; Jones, *"New Kind of War,"* 128-30.

ment bitterly complained of village raids, forced recruiting by the guerrillas, and terrorist executions by guns, knives and axes—including the gangland-style assassination of CBS newsman George Polk and the strangling (by wire), scalping, and mutilation of an American military adviser downed in a Greek plane. Critics of the government denounced its brutal efforts to restore domestic order—particularly the mass executions of Communist prisoners—and excoriated those Greek army commanders who used political prisoners as "mine detectors" in having them precede truck convoys. A London newspaper shocked the world by carrying a photo of Greek soldiers on horseback swinging the heads of female guerrillas by the hair, en route to collect government bounties.[27]

The driving force behind America's intervention in Greece was the belief in Soviet involvement. Without Soviet and Eastern European documentation, Americans acted out of perceptions based on circumstantial evidence, first- and second-hand observations, an intelligence network that was not always accurate, and, most important, a deep suspicion of Soviet trouble-making all over the world. Although critics later established the Kremlin's inability to engage in such far-ranging activity, America's leaders at that time could not have been sure. Admittedly, more than a few contemporary observers questioned whether Moscow had a blueprint for conquest; but hardly anyone was willing to take the chance.[28]

The Truman administration correctly charged various East European communist states with aiding the Greek guerrillas; but its strong suspicion of Soviet assistance does not seem warranted. Recent documentation shows that Yugoslavia sent rifles, machine guns, anti-tank weapons, land mines, clothing, and food. In addition, the guerrillas received weapons from Albania and Bulgaria, along with assorted non-military items from Hungary, Rumania, and Czechoslovakia. The lack of Soviet support suggests that Soviet Premier Joseph Stalin placed primary emphasis on ridding the eastern Mediterranean and Near East of Western influence, and that he knew his involvement in Greece would attract a greater U.S. presence highly dangerous to his interests. But to American leaders already inclined to believe the worst of the Kremlin, the perception of Soviet complicity in the Greek civil war remained a critical determinant of their policy. The White House became convinced that Greece con-

27. Edmund Keeley, *The Salonika Bay Murder: Cold War Politics and the Polk Affair* (Princeton, New Jersey: Princeton University Press, 1989); Condit, *Case Study in Guerrilla War*, 143; Constantine Poulos, "Fruits of the Truman Doctrine," *The Nation* (New York), Dec. 6, 1947: 614; *Time*, Aug. 25, 1947, p. 27; Wittner, *American Intervention in Greece*, 137; Dominique Eudes, *The Kapetanios: Partisans and Civil War in Greece, 1943-1949* (New York: Monthly Review Press, 1972), 305; Jones, "*New Kind of War*" 162-67.
28. Jones, "*New Kind of War*," 5; CIA Report 2, "Review of the World Situation as It Relates to the Security of the United States," Nov, 14. 1947, pp. 1, 5, Truman Papers, President's Secretary's Files, Trum. Lib.; Leffler, *Preponderance of Power*, 146.

stituted the chief obstacle to Soviet penetration of the eastern Mediterranean, making Soviet involvement in Greece almost axiomatic. The guerrillas received enough outside assistance from their communist neighbors to make Greece an international issue and hence a battleground of the Cold War.[29]

Although the White House could not have known, Stalin angrily told Bulgarian and Yugoslav representatives summoned to Moscow in February 1948 that the conflict in Greece must end. Stalin had changed his initial inaction toward the civil war to outright opposition—probably because the Truman Doctrine had injected the United States into the mix and thereby threatened the Soviet alliance system in Eastern Europe and surrounding areas. The conflict had originally been between the guerrillas and the Greek army supported by the British, thereby permitting the Soviets and their counterparts to launch a propaganda campaign against the "monarcho-fascist" Greek and British governments. But in the summer and fall of 1947, the deepening involvement of the United States posed a threat to Stalin's interests in the region and forced him to demand an end to the fighting in Greece.[30]

When his visitors objected to the order to stop the war, Stalin could not contain his wrath: "We do not agree with the Yugoslav comrades that they should help further the Greek partisans; in this matter, we think that we are right and not the Yugoslavs." Thus "the uprising in Greece has to fold up." But the Yugoslav vice-premier, Edvard Kardelj, persisted in believing a Greek guerrilla victory possible "if foreign intervention does not grow and if serious political and military errors are not made." Stalin stormed back: "If, if! No, they have no prospect of success at all. What do you think, that Great Britain and the United States—the United States, the most powerful state in the world—will permit you to break their line of communication in the Mediterranean Sea! Nonsense....The uprising in Greece must be stopped, and as quickly as possible."[31]

29. Vladimir Dedijer, *Novi Prilozi za Josipa Tita, Treci Tom* (Belgrade, 1984), 266-67; Elisabeth Barker, The Yugoslavs and the Greek Civil War, 1945-1949," in *Studies in the History of the Greek Civil War, 1945-1949*, Lars Baerentzen, John O. Iatrides, and Ole L. Smith (Copenhagen; Museum Tusculanum Press, 1987), 303; Leffler, *Preponderance of Power*, 126, 143; CIG [Central Intelligence Group], ORE 6/1, pp. 11, 12, "The Greek Situation," Feb. 7, 1947, Truman Papers, President's Secretary's Files, Trum. Lib. For a penetrating analysis of Stalin's policy of "inaction," see Peter J. Stavrakis, "Soviet Policy in Areas of Limited Control: The Case of Greece, 1944-1949," in John O. Iatrides and Linda Wringley, eds., *Greece at the Crossroads: The Civil War and Its Legacy* (University Park: Pennsylvania State University Press, 1995), 227-57.
30. Jones, *"New Kind of War,"* 133-34; Dimitrios G. Kousoulas, *Revolution and Defeat: The Story of the Greek Communist Party* (London: Oxford University Press, 1965), 250; Eudes, *Kapetanios*, 310; Vladimir Dedijer, *The Battle Stalin Lost: Memoirs of Yugoslavia, 1948-1953* (New York: Viking, 1971), 269-270; Svetozar Vukmanovic-Tempo, *How and Why the People's Liberation Struggle of Greece Met with Defeat* (London: Merrit & Hatcher, 1950), 3; Milovan Djilas, *Conversations with Stalin* (New York: Harcourt, Brace, 1962), 131-32, 181-82.
31. Vladimir Dedijer, *Tito* (New York: Simon and Schuster, 1953), 316-22; Dedijer, *The Battle Stalin Lost*, 68-69; Dimitrios G. Kousoulas, "The Truman Doctrine and the Stalin-Tito Rift; A Reappraisal," *South Atlantic Quarterly* 72 (1973): 430-32; Djilas, *Conversations with Stalin*, 181-82.

In retrospect, Stalin's directives in Moscow revealed that the Truman Doctrine had in unexpected ways encouraged a Western victory in Greece. Although American advisers knew nothing of the Soviet premier's new policy, they had learned of growing troubles between the Cominform and Yugoslavia's communist leader, Josip Broz Tito, and hoped to exploit a potential crack in the Soviet alliance. The payoff proved larger than ever envisioned. Tito's rift with Stalin led Yugoslavia to close its borders to the Greek guerrillas, denying them refuge and forcing them to meet a steadily improving Greek army on its own terms. U.S. military assistance had meanwhile grown to include napalm and Navy Helldivers. After a massive government artillery and infantry sweep of the north had either scattered or killed the guerrillas or driven them into Albania and Bulgaria, the war came to an end in October 1949, when rebel leaders announced a cease-fire.[32]

IV

Although historians have long debated the reasons for the Greek government's victory, one observation is certain: American military aid alone had not been solely responsible. The communists could have gone on indefinitely if they had not switched from guerrilla tactics to conventional warfare and if they had continued to receive refuge and outside assistance. The conclusion is tempting: that Tito's defection from the Soviet bloc broke the guerrillas' resistance and allowed American firepower to finish the task. Although these ingredients surely proved vital to the outcome, the full explanation does not lie in either the events in the Balkans or in American military assistance.[33]

The Truman administration achieved its objectives in Greece because of a flexible foreign policy that was global in theory but restrained by reality. White House advisers had defined the nation's interests in Greece in relation to the rest of the world, developed a strategy that had manageable goals, and worked within the limitations of America's capacity to influence events and people. Most important, they cultivated a Greek populace rich in democratic tradition and staunchly nationalistic, and who opposed communism and wel-

32. Jones, *New Kind of War*, 135, 222; Dedijer, *The Battle Stalin Lost*, 270; Woodhouse, *Struggle for Greece*, 285; O'Ballance, *Greek Civil War*, 195, 201; William H. McNeill, *Greece: American Aid in Action, 1947-1956* (New York: Twentieth Century Fund, 1957) 42; Cavendish Cannon (U.S. Ambassador in Yugoslavia) to sec. of state, July 13, 1949, *FRUS VI: The Near East, South Asia and Africa* (Washington, D.C.: U.S. Government Printing Office, 1977), 368; Grady to acting sec. of state, Oct. 3, 1949, ibid., 431-33; U.S. Army, History of JUSMAGG [Joint U.S. Military Assistance Group, Greece] History, 71, 73-74, Jont U.S. Military Assistance Group Air Adjutant Section 314.7 Military Histories [U.S. Air Force Section], JUSMAGG, Modern Military Division, NA; J.C. Murray, "The Anti-Bandit War," Part 5, *Marine Corps Gazette* 38 (May 1954): 52; *Times* (London), Aug. 26, 1949, p.3; ibid., Sept. 5, 1949, p. 25; Evangelos Averoff-Tossaizza, *By Fire and Axe: The Communist Party and the Civil War in Greece, 1944-1949* (New Rochelle, N.Y.: Caratzas Brothers, 1978), 345-46.
33. Jones, *New Kind of War*, 223.

comed U.S. help. All the while, America's policymakers kept the struggle within the technical confines of a civil war, repeatedly refusing to allow the conflict to grow into a larger war. After winning the aid bill, the administration toned down its rhetoric to avoid confrontation with the communists, quietly persuaded its British ally to remain in Greece as part of a bilateral effort and thus gained time for the strategy to work.[34]

The Truman Doctrine provided the basis for a global strategy that rested on equivalent and limited responses to carefully defined and continually changing levels of danger. In 1947 the emergency in Greece necessitated military aid and operational advice; once that threat had subsided in late 1949, the United States shifted its focus to concentrate on long-range economic rehabilitation. During the Greek involvement, the Truman administration considered every option ranging from outright withdrawal to direct combat intervention. Decisions resulted from proposals thrashed out not only by specialists in Greek and Turkish affairs but also by those who brought both European and Asian perspectives to the problem. Information came from British and Greek observers, the State and Defense departments, National Security Council, Joint Chiefs of Staff, CIA, and other intelligence groups. The new policy derived from hard considerations: its impact on Greece and neighboring states, on America's allies and the nonaligned countries, and on Americans at home; the necessity of averting a unilateral and more dangerous involvement; the possibility of graceful de-escalation or even withdrawal; the effect of events in Greece on global strategy. The White House, meanwhile, maintained an ongoing reassessment of the Greek problem to keep the commitment flexible and under control.[35]

Not all the American advisers in the period following the Greek civil war misread the nation's limited involvement as a prototype for broader interventionist activities. The Truman administration itself fought off heavy pressure to aid the Chinese Nationalists in their losing battle against communist guerrillas. President Eisenhower rejected the advice of those in his administration who sought direct military intervention in Indochina on behalf of the French. The Korean experience weighed heavily on his decision, of course, but perhaps so too did the lessons of restraint exercised in Greece. President Kennedy recognized the danger of unlimited commitments and resisted inordinate pressure from numerous advisers who urged him to send American combat troops to Vietnam. Kennedy's caution was not surprising: Acheson and other former Truman advisers had convinced him of the wisdom of meeting the challenges of limited warfare with a flexible and restrained policy that relied on short-of-war tactics based on a series of controlled and variable responses.

---

34. Ibid., 225; Woods and Jones, *Dawning of Cold War*, 243-46.
35. Jones, *New Kind of War*, 225.

The Johnson administration, however, failed to discern the subtleties of this foreign policy strategy and mistakenly cited the Greek war as justification for using the military option in Vietnam. *The parallel was flawed.* In seeking a military solution as the overarching objective rather than as only one of several means to the broader end of peace and stability, the Johnson White House acted rashly and thus demonstrated its failure to understand the reasons for success in Greece: limitations on America's involvement in the war, and an effective strategy that kept means and ends in balance. The Truman administration avoided an over-commitment by formulating Greek policy within the perspective of global realities. Johnson's decision to intervene in Vietnam did not rest on these restraints, and the result was a near disaster.[36]

Now, over fifty years since the declaration of the Truman Doctrine, the time has come to reassess its overall impact on the Cold War. In the 1940s well-known columnist Walter Lippmann called the containment policy a "strategic monstrosity" and denounced America's intervention in Greece as an unwarranted involvement in a purely domestic matter. Soviet specialist George F. Kennan criticized the messianic tone of the president's message. Almost thirty years later, during the peak period of American torment over Vietnam, Senator Fulbright attributed nearly every U.S. mistake in foreign policy to the Truman Doctrine.[37] No question exists that numerous Cold Warriors relied on the president's 1947 proclamation in molding a nationwide anti-communist mentality. But in assessing blame for this inflated fear of global communism, one should look more at the abusers than the creators of the Truman Doctrine. This is not to say that the president was blameless. He and his advisers aimed the aid program specifically at Greece and Turkey, though admittedly leaving room for applying its principles elsewhere as specific circumstances warranted. But in no instance did they advocate a blanket program that defined every problem in the world as Soviet-inspired and in need of an instant American military response.

The inherent danger in the Truman Doctrine lay in the exaggeration and distortion that resulted from its open-ended ideological language. To win support for an aid program defying the nearly mystical American belief in European noninvolvement, the president followed the advice of Republican Senator Arthur Vandenberg, chair of the Foreign Relations committee, in seeking to "scare the hell out of the country." Truman succeeded—and in magnificent fashion. He averted a direct challenge to the Kremlin by refusing to mention either the Soviet Union or communism in his address; instead, he placed the Greek and Turkish problems within the broad historical struggle between lib-

---

36. Donovan, *Conflict and Crisis,* 285; Gaddis, *U.S. and Origins of Cold War,* 351-52; Richard J. Powers, "Containment: From Greece to Vietnam and Back?", *Western Political Quarterly* 22 (1969): 846-61; McGhee interview with author.
37. Lippman quoted in Isaacson and Thomas, *Wise Men,* 422; Kennan, *Memoirs,* 319-20.

erty and tyranny and darkly proclaimed that the "fateful hour" had come when peoples all over the world "must choose between alternative ways of life." Acheson just as dramatically made the case when he repeatedly defined the conflict as "democracy" v. "totalitarianism."[38]

Such broad and emotion-laden terms inescapably give a global cast to the Truman Doctrine. Kennan had correctly cautioned against meshing America's "vital" and "peripheral" interests into a global involvement. But Acheson and others in the administration also recognized the crucial distinction and staunchly opposed a sweeping commitment. The problem was that less perceptive advisers in the post-Greek civil war period failed to discern this distinction. They defined the enemy as totally hostile, rejected all compromise as a pact with evil, and consequently over-extended the nation's foreign commitments. The most glaring sign of a growing inclination to universalism came with NSC-68, which in April 1950 attempted to reduce the world's complexities to a Manichean struggle between "free" and "slave" nations.[39] Seeing the danger in such a declaration, President Truman squelched this National Security Council report, and it remained buried in the archives until its accidental discovery in the early 1970s.

Along with the external danger of over-commitment came an internal threat to America's own constitutional system of checks and balances. Those who misused the Truman Doctrine fostered a tense international atmosphere based on ideological differences with the Soviet Union that encouraged flagrant encroachments on Congress's war-making power. Cold War presidents felt justified in taking such extraordinary action during a postwar era that became so explosive that many Americans regarded it as a continuation of the challenges to freedom posed by the dictators who brought on World War II. President Franklin D. Roosevelt had elevated his office into an "imperial" position during the war. Afterward, in the face of new foreign crises during the Cold War, succeeding presidents continued to concentrate more power in the Oval Office. The Truman Doctrine facilitated this process as Congress in 1947 deferred to the president in foreign affairs and continued to do so in the period afterward.

Constitutional checks and balances—in short, the entire doctrine of separation of powers-suffered one severe blow after another as strong-willed presidents virtually ignored Congress in waging undeclared war in Korea, Vietnam, and Central America. Military solutions to internal political and economic problems became the standard response, even though the results most

38. Vandenberg and Acheson quoted in Isaacson and Thomas, *Wise Men*, 395; Gaddis, *Strategies of Containment*, 23-24, 58-59, 108; *Public Papers of Presidents: Truman*, 1947, 178-79.
39. Leffter, *Specter of Communism*, 56-58. Malvyn P. Leffter, *A Preponderance of Power: National Security, the Truman Administration, and the Cold War* (Stanford, Calif.: Stanford University Press, 1992), 146; Gaddis, *Strategies of Containment*, 108-9.

often were increased hatred between opposing groups that only prolonged civil strife, and a general failure to make those domestic social, political, and economic reforms so vital to lasting peace. Congress succeeded in restraining President Woodrow Wilson after World War I, but it proved unable to harness the executive office after World War II. Not until the early 1970s did Congress reassert itself with the repeal of the Tonkin Gulf Resolution and passage of the War Powers Act. Even then, however, both actions failed to restore a balance between the two branches of government and the president continues to be the dominant force in making foreign policy.

Let me conclude by returning to where I began, with the lessons of history. We historians like to quote George Santayana's famous remark that people who don't know the past are doomed to repeat it, for that provides a powerful justification for our existence. But there is a corollary proposition, quite as important: that learning the *wrong* lessons from history dooms us just as surely as does ignorance. ☐

The Truman Doctrine:
A Turning Point in World History

GENERAL ANDREW J. GOODPASTER, USA (RET.)

The fifty-year retrospective of the Truman Doctrine enables us to recall the danger to Greece in 1947 and the beginnings of the Marshall Plan. I think it is important to keep memories of those events alive. This was a turning point in history, not just the history of the twentieth century, but a turning point in American history and particularly in the history of America's relationship with Europe. I am going to comment from the standpoint of the organizations which I was serving regarding the threat, at that time, to Greek independence and democracy and the response that was made to that threat. This was an issue that broadens into the response to the challenge of all of post-war Europe.

The organization in which I was working at that time was the Plans and Operations Division of the War Department, which was General George Marshall's command post in World War II. The particular units in which I served were the Strategy Section at the close of World War II, the Joint War Plans Committee, and the International Survey Section. During the war, their responsibilities had to do with a strategy for winning the war. When you served under General Marshall, it was very clear that that was the goal. It was not a strategy for carrying on the war, although that proved to be a part of it. But General Marshall insisted on having a clear goal and that goal was winning the war in the shortest possible time and with the least possible cost to our people and particularly to our armed forces.

Following the war, the same units were charged with dealing with post-war issues. It was, first of all, the question of the occupation of Germany and Austria. What should be the policy and how should that policy be carried forward? And that became one of the central disputes with the Soviet Union at that time.

It did not take long after the close of the war to discover that we had some real problems on our hands. There had been an agreement at the level of

GENERAL ANDREW J. GOODPASTER, USA (RET.), former Supreme Commander of NATO, is Chairman of the Atlantic Council of the United States, the George C. Marshall Foundation and former Chairman of the American Battle Monuments Commission, and the Eisenhower World Affairs Institute.

heads of government to establish Allied Control Commissions in the countries that had been overrun during the war. They included, in Central and Eastern Europe: Romania, Bulgaria, Hungary and Czechoslovakia. It became clear very soon that the Soviets had no desire to share the governance of these countries, but were instead intent on imposing their own control over each one. They had installed a puppet government in Poland by force even before the end of the war. The clouds of these problems were looming and the result was a growing confrontation. The Soviets were strongly opposed to any policy other than the continued suppression of Germany.

We had wise leaders at that time who were convinced that if that was our policy, we would simply be laying the ground work for another major war. The aim of our country should instead be to bring Germany into the circle of nations of the international community on the basis of the accepted international norms of the Western nations. There were threats beyond the nations I already mentioned. There where serious threats in Italy and in France and there was a feeling that the Soviets were on the march. They had by far the greatest military force in the world and that was combined with a policy that was then seen as a policy of ideologically based expansionism. This was a mortal threat to the freedom of the countries of Central, Eastern, and Western Europe.

Much of this was spelled out in the long telegram that George Kennan sent from Moscow in 1946. As I recall, when we received it, we studied it with very great care. We found it very penetrating and very persuasive and we began to realize the nature of the new situation with which we were confronted. There were two very important meetings of the Council of Foreign Ministers. The first, was attended on our part by then Secretary of State and former Governor James Byrnes, and the second by General Marshall after he was appointed Secretary of State to succeed Byrnes. It was apparent that we were at an impasse with the Soviet Union over the issue of the future of Germany and going quite far beyond that. For example, the Soviet Union was demanding a position in Libya; that was turned away by Foreign Minister Earnest Bevin of Britain. They were pressing for a position to control access to the Dardanelles. They were pressing for concessions from Greece that would endanger the whole future of that country. And then, in February 1947, Great Britain notified the United States that it would no longer be able to support Greece and Turkey against Soviet pressures and demands. President Truman, decisive as always, made the quick decision to provide support. President Truman stated in his address to the Congress:

> "It must be the policy of the United States to support free peoples who are resisting attempted subjugation by armed minorities or by outside pressures. We must assist free peoples to work their own destinies in their own way."

I have to say that there is a certain clarity that contrasts well with some of the mush we so often hear today.

I received a book just a few days ago from George McGhee, called *On the Front Lines of the Cold War*. In that book he made the point that I am making here. He said: "U.S. foreign policy had reached a turning point. Wherever aggression, direct or indirect, threatened the peace, American security was involved." That was the determination made by President Truman and he moved to propose to Congress the authorization of appropriate funds to provide aid. Now that was something new for our country. We did not have legislation that committed funds. The first time we saw the lack of legislation had to do with Austria. We came within one day of losing the authority we had to continue to support the recovery of that country. Urgent action was taken with the Congress to obtain legislation to prevent this.

Now it was necessary to go to the Congress again to obtain legislation for the aid program that President Truman wanted to carry out. My knowledge of this came from a report of the testimony of Dean Acheson, then undersecretary of state under General Marshall, in which there was an exchange between Secretary Acheson and Senator Vanderberg. Senator Vanderberg asked whether there was to be a succession of these individual requests for urgent and emergency action, or whether there could be a consolidated forward looking approach.

Dean Acheson reported that we were talking about that and thinking about it and were about to begin. To summarize Vanderberg's response, it was "well, get on with it." And within the government at that time, mid-March 1947, there was a tasking for the development of a consolidated and forward-looking proposal. General Marshall put a number of groups to work. Within the State Department he had George Kennan and Paul Nitze working on this. Others were involved within the War and Navy Departments.

We, in the War Department, were brought in through our membership in the State War Navy Coordination Committee (SWNCC). The task came to the Strategy and Policy Group of the Plans and Operations Division, a group which was headed by Brigadier General George A. Lincoln, one of the great figures in American military policy and planning. He had tasked our particular team, telling us that we must become more forehanded and forearmed. He served as the Army representative on this SWNCC committee and like other good executives he turned to the working-level staff, and that turned out to be me, participating in this work from early in the month of April into June of 1947. The object was to study the needs of foreign countries for aid and support within the framework of the Truman Doctrine.

As I mentioned, there were other concurrent efforts going on. One interesting issue that arose was whether the effort should be worldwide or focused on Europe. Three of the State-War-Navy participants thought it should be world-wide, whereas Kennan and Nitze thought it should be concentrated on Europe, largely because in Europe there was a foundation to build upon. There had been successful economic activity in Europe before the war and although this was to be extended, we would be restoring something that had existed there previously.

In providing the support with which the shattered economies could carry out their recovery, General Marshall very wisely went with the thinking of the Kennan-Nitze group to concentrate on Europe. The second thing he did, and this was part of his genius, was to call on the European governments to come together and to present a consolidated proposal for U.S. consideration. Rather than having us attempt to solve their problems, they would do it and we would respond to it.

Think for a moment of all that was avoided under the pressure of the necessity to come up with a single proposal. The European countries worked out their differences, their priorities and so on. Had we in the United States attempted to do that, we would have been subject to uncoordinated pressures from this country or that country, this group of their supporters or that group and so on. General Marshall's proposal, which was grasped by Britain's Foreign Minister Ernest Bevin, brought the governments of Europe together. First, his proposal gave the United States a sounder base to work from; it had been produced by people who knew something of what they were doing. Second, it saved us the type of interaction that I mentioned. Third, it caused the governments of Europe to work together to come up with a constructive proposal rather than looking for individual advantage. Instead of reverting to a competitive process, they were now beginning the process of coming together, which proved to be so important.

The Marshall Plan was aimed against hunger and disorder and it moved rapidly. It obtained support in the United States. It was looked after by a group of extremely capable leaders, Paul Hoffman being at the top. When George McGhee, who was serving under Under Secretary Will Clayton, was charged with the supervision at this end of the extension of aid to Greece and Turkey, within a very short period of time, there was a viable and strong aid program going forward. Its passage, in part I think it fair to say, was due largely to the behavior of the Soviet Union at that time. Not only did the Soviet Union not join in the Marshall Plan effort, but also forced the withdrawal of Poland and Czechoslovakia, which had initially indicated their desire to participate.

When the Marshall Plan was going forward, as you know, the struggle in Greece was also going forward. There was also the development and beginning of collective security institutions in Europe. Initially there was the Western European Union, in which Britain, France and the Low Countries came together in the interest of their common security. Then came the coup in Czechoslovakia by the Soviets in 1948, next the blockade of Berlin and the airlift organized and conducted brilliantly by General Curtis Lemay. Following the Czechoslovakia coup and the Berlin blockade came the agreement on the North Atlantic Treaty Organization, finally signed into agreement on April 4, 1949. And at that point came the beginnings of the collective military structure.

The next great event was the invasion of South Korea by North Korea. At the time we all attributed that to the expansionist policy of the Soviet Union. In later years, it was not so clear that the Soviet Union was in fact the instigator of it, but they were undeniably associated with it. In any case, great alarm spread through Europe at that time. The European countries came to the U.S. with the proposal to bring into being a collective military force in Western Europe as a means of further deterring any Soviet attempt at expansion. That was in the fall of 1950. As a result, in December of that year, there was an invitation to the U.S. to provide a Supreme Commander who would organize a collective military force. That turned out to be General Eisenhower. When the U.S. sent General Eisenhower with Mrs. Eisenhower to Europe it gave a message, not only to the countries of Western Europe, but also to the Soviet Union.

General Eisenhower was held in tremendously high regard in the Soviet Union. He was respected. He had been invited to stand on Lenin's tomb in Red Square to participate in the review of the victory of the Soviet Union in World War II, the only foreigner ever given that particular honor. I think the Soviets, as well as the Western Europeans, understood that the U.S. meant business when it sent Eisenhower to take the command.

Eisenhower worked diligently for a little over a year to bring that command into being. It was his persuasion, with the support of President Truman, that made possible the return of four American Army divisions to Europe. In the words of one European statesman "that put the glue into NATO." Why? Because that put a force on the ground that the Soviets would have to run over if they were to seize Western Europe. That said they would be engaged in large-scale conflict with the U.S. from the outset.

In February 1952, at the Lisbon meeting of the North Atlantic Council, the accession of Greece and Turkey was agreed upon. It was five years after 1947, and there was still much to be done. But we were no longer just reacting to Soviet moves. We had taken the initiative on the Western side with a positive program to insure security through a cooperative effort. In the process, many ancient quarrels had been overcome or confined. Some of their differences of course remained and remain to this day, but they do not override or endanger the collective security which has so clearly proved its worth. It has been responsible, in my view, not just for security but for the peace we have all been able to enjoy in Europe in this half-century.

Let me conclude with a statement made by General Eisenhower in 1952, when he prepared and submitted his first annual report as the Supreme Allied Commander. He spoke of the situation that had come to exist in Europe throughout the whole NATO community as an expanding spiral of strength and confidence. That is what got us successfully through the Cold War. It was no small achievement, and it retains its importance to this day. ☐

George C. Marshall: The Truman Doctrine and the Marshall Plan

LARRY I. BLAND

George C. Marshall's World War II boss, Secretary of War Henry L. Stimson, once said that people in public life tend to fall into two groups: those who thought primarily of what they could do for the job that they held, and those who thought of what the job could do for them. He put George C. Marshall, the first American military leader to be a truly global commander, at the top of the first category. "You are," Stimson said in 1942, "one of the most selfless public officials that I have ever known."[1]

George Marshall was an austere, demanding, efficient leader, whose cool blue eyes seemed to penetrate to the core of those with whom he talked; yet he had a saving sense of humor and a passion for simple justice. Marshall was also a master administrator; he ran an efficient organization and he had the knack of selecting good subordinates.[2]

Furthermore, as historians Richard Neustadt and Ernest May have observed in their book *Thinking in Time,* Marshall had developed the habit of "seeing time as a stream:" that is, of applying a consciousness of past problems, ideas, and solutions to the present rather than seeing every current problem in isolation and thus as new and unique.[3]

He was not a scholar of military or political history, but he read widely and was excellent at extracting accurate lessons from his reading and from his own experience. In many respects, Marshall sought during World War II to avoid the mistakes he had witnessed in World War I and its immediate aftermath.

LARRY I. BLAND, Ph.D., is the editor of *The Papers of George Catlett Marshall,* a multivolume documentary edition of General Marshall's papers published by The Johns Hopkins University Press.

1. Larry I. Bland and Sharon Ritenour Stevens, eds., *The Papers of George Catlett Marshall* (Baltimore: Johns Hopkins University Press, 1981-), 3: 499, 501.
2. The definitive and authorized biography of General Marshall is Forrest C. Pogue's *George C. Marshall,* 4 vols. (New York: Viking Press, 1963-87). Two valuable single-volume biographies are Mark A. Stoler, *George C. Marshall: Soldier-Statesman of the American Century* (Boston: Twayne Publishers, 1989), and Ed Cray, *General of the Army: George C. Marshall, Soldier and Statesman* (New York: W. W. Norton and Co., 1990).
3. Richard E. Neustadt and Ernest R. May, *Thinking in Time: The Uses of History for Decision-Makers* (New York: Free Press, 1986), pp. 247-48.

Consequently, Marshall was increasingly disturbed after the autumn of 1945 at what he considered the *disintegration* of American military power rather than the careful demobilization and reorganization for which he had planned since 1943. As he said publicly several times in the latter half of 1945, the United States courted disaster for itself and the world if it again fell "into a state of disinterested weakness" and failed to fulfill its international responsibilities for aid and assistance in postwar economic and political reconstruction.[4]

These could have remained the departing sentiments of a fading-away old soldier. Indeed, in late November 1945, Marshall longed to retire after forty-four years of active duty, but President Truman needed Marshall's prestige and skills to attempt to mediate the Chinese civil war and (as Marshall knew by early 1946) thereafter to take over from James Byrnes as secretary of state.[5]

One sometimes reads that Marshall was isolated in China, and thus when he became secretary of state in January 1947, he had been out of contact for thirteen months with the increasingly frigid Cold War. This is a great exaggeration. Marshall was always well briefed, and during World War II he often impressed reporters with his minute grasp of the status of the conflict in every theater. In China, he received a constant stream of detailed reports on political and international affairs from his personal staff in Washington, and he even had an Ultra clerk assigned to him so that he could receive Ultra-secret messages based on U.S. decryption of allies' and friends' transmissions.[6] Granted, the information Marshall had available to him in Chungking was inferior to that readily available to high-level representatives today, but Marshall was probably better informed on the world situation and the Washington scene than any of his contemporaries outside the capital.

Marshall's failure in China was not a result of his lack of negotiating skills but of the determination of both sides to seek a military solution to China's problems. Marshall considered the Chinese Communist Party ruthless dedicated Marxists who seemed to count on and encourage China's economic collapse as a way of furthering their objectives. What particularly pained him, however, was that Chiang Kai-shek's government was such a poor ally for the United States. Reactionaries within the Nationalist party presumed that America *had* to support the Nationalists, and they thus rejected the domestic re-

4. Speech to the Salvation Army National Convention, November 17, 1945, Speeches, Pentagon Office File, George C. Marshall Papers, George C. Marshall Library, Lexington, Virginia. See also, Speech to the *New York Herald Tribune* Forum, October 29, 1945, ibid.
5. In early February 1946, Marshall had suggested to Albert Wedemeyer, Commanding General of United States Forces, China Theater, that when Marshall became secretary of state, Wedemeyer might become ambassador to China. See Wedemeyer to Marshall, telegram, February 17, 1946, China Mission File, Marshall Papers.
6. On the Ultra clerk (officially "Special Security Officer"), see A. Fairfield Dana to Larry I. Bland, June 1, 1983, and Dana oral history interview, September 19, 1983, p. 12, Dana papers, Marshall Library.

forms that Marshall and other Truman administration leaders considered essential to undermining Communist growth.[7]

Thus, when Marshall came to Washington in January 1947, he had a good bit of experience in dealing with communists. Yet he was no hard-liner. Indeed, in many ways, he was one of the last high officials to give up on cooperating with the Soviets. Marshall tended to assume that all effective leaders were rational, practical, and understandable by outsiders. Thus he tended to think in terms of negotiations, deals, and compromise and not of crusades, holy wars, or righteous ideologies. He knew from experience that Stalin was a tough and "very astute negotiator," but in early 1947 Marshall did not believe that negotiations with Stalin were either dangerous or futile.[8]

One important reason that President Truman wanted Marshall as secretary of state was the general's tradition of good relations with Congress and his lack of partisanship. When Marshall stepped off the train at Union Station on January 21, 1947, his first statement to the press was designed to quash any suspicions that he might have political ambitions. He would never seek and could never be drafted to run for office, he asserted, thereby reassuring Senate Foreign Relations Committee Chairman Arthur Vandenberg and other GOP leaders and laying the foundation for a bipartisan foreign policy.[9]

Marshall professed himself "horrified" when he took over at State at how poorly organized the department was; he said that it had the most "nonsensical organization I have ever heard of."[10] Each department behaved as if it was autonomous. Decision-making was drastically decentralized; new ideas generally came from outside and implementation was dominated by other institutions. State's previous fifteen years of near-irrelevance on important aspects of foreign policy had not encouraged organizational efficiency and modernization. In early 1942 Marshall had reorganized the War Department, ultimately creating a reasonably efficient command post. In the first half of 1947 he did the same thing for State.

He induced Dean Acheson to stay on as under secretary and Marshall's chief of staff to run the department. Everything for the secretary had to go through Acheson, thus creating for the first time in history a chain of command and reducing the number of people who could run to the secretary on

7. On Marshall's publicly stated conclusions about his China mediation mission, see his January 7, 1947, statement in Department of State, United States Relations with China with Special Reference to the Period 1944-1949 (Washington: GPO, 1949), pp. 686-89, particularly p. 687. The most recent studies of Marshall's China Mission are in Larry L. Bland, ed., George C. Marshall's China Mediation Mission, December 1945-January 1947 (Lexington, Va: George C. Marshall Foundation, 1998).
8. Larry I. Bland, ed., George C. Marshall Interviews and Reminiscences for Forrest C. Pogue, 3d ed. (Lexington, Va.: George C. Marshall Foundation, 1996), p. 341.
9. Pogue, Marshall, 4:145.
10. Bland, ed., Marshall Interviews, p. 561.

minor matters or intramural disputes. There were numerous other reforms, but the most important one for our purposes here is Marshall's determination to separate long-range planning from immediate operations. This led to the creation of the Policy Planning Staff that was Marshall's think tank.[11] Marshall was military in organization and administration but not in ideas; there he had a most un-military and flexible cast of mind. Charles Bohlen, who was close to Marshall at state, later wrote that Marshall's "personality infected the entire State Department. It gave it a sense of direction and purpose....We realized we were working for a great man." Moreover, Marshall treated Truman with great deference, never forgetting, as Byrnes did, that Truman was president.[12]

American leaders were aware of Britain's growing economic weakness, the likely effects that would have on the Eastern Mediterranean, and the possibility that the Soviet Union or its surrogates would fill the power vacuum there. Even before the disastrous blizzard of December 1946 to January 1947 had pushed London to the edge, the U.S. was moving toward helping the Greek government against the communists. The suddenness of the British notification that it had to relinquish its traditional role in Greece put Washington under the gun to act quickly.[13] When the advance version of the British notes were presented on February 21, Marshall was out of town, on his way to Columbia University to receive an honorary degree and then to Princeton on the 22nd for his first speech as secretary of state. At Princeton, in the face of the recent elections, returning GOP majorities in both houses, that were infused with the rhetoric of tax-cutting, economic nationalism, and government down-sizing, Marshall reiterated his 1945 calls for Americans to learn from the lessons of past and assume their responsibilities as citizens of a great power.[14]

On Monday, February 24 Marshall returned to his office and Acheson presented the British memos, reports from Athens, and the staff's recommendations. The situation probably reminded Marshall of the situation in China fifteen months earlier. The staff recommended the unification of all Greek parties (this time excluding the Communists and the extreme right), domestic reforms in government and tax programs, and economic and military aid from the U.S.[15]

By February 27, Marshall's advisers had written a plan of action, which Marshall read to a White House meeting of congressional leaders and the

11. Pogue, *Marshall,* 4:146-50.
12. Charles E. Bohlen, *Witness to History, 1929-1969* (New York: W. W. Norton and Co., 1973), pp. 268-69.
13. Howard Jones, *"A New Kind of War": America's Global Strategy and the Truman Doctrine in Greece* (New York: Oxford University Press, 1989), 27-35.
14. Dean Acheson, *Present at the Creation: My Years in the State Department* (New York: W. W. Norton and Co., 1969), 217-18; Marshall's Washington Birthday Remarks at Princeton University, February 22, 1947, Marshall Papers, Secretary of State, Speeches file.
15. Acheson, *Present at the Creation,* 218; Jones, *"A New Kind of War,"* 37-41; Pogue, *Marshall,* 4:163.

president. Marshall was well acquainted with all the senators and congress-men and adopted his usual low-key but earnest approach to defending the policy of aid to Greece and Turkey. Using a version of what would later be called the domino thesis, Marshall asserted that a communist victory in Greece would be a disaster. "It is not alarmist," he said, "to say that we are faced with the first crisis of a series which might extend Soviet domination to Europe, the Middle East and Asia." Marshall made no call for the defense of democracy everywhere or for an anti-communist crusade, but for contain-ment of Soviet opportunism in the face of British weakness. American assis-tance would be aimed at boosting Greek public morale through financial and military equipment aid.[16]

Acheson thought that Marshall had failed to put the administration's case across and repainted the picture for the politicians in more vigorous strokes and in starker contrasts. Acheson asserts in his memoir, *Present at the Creation,* that only in this way were the congressmen sufficiently impressed to take action.[17] This approach cleared the way for more vigorous public rhetoric by the Truman administration.

Marshall was reluctant to put too militant a public face on the U.S. response to the Greek situation lest all hope of agreement on the treatment of Germany and Austria at the up-coming Moscow Foreign Ministers' Conference be lost. Moreover, should the Soviet Union be provoked into aggressive action, the United States was not prepared to offer effective resistance in Europe. Tru-man and certain of his advisers, however, believed that strong anticommunist rhetoric was essential to the aid bill's passage, and despite a March 7 note from Marshall in Paris urging some cooling of the rhetoric, Marshal had almost no influence on the final form of the March 12 Truman Doctrine speech.[18] His real influence to this point had been on the State Department itself.

Historian John Lewis Gaddis, a critic of the idea that the Truman Doctrine marked a turning point in American foreign policy, observed twenty-five years ago that "while it is clear from both contemporary and retrospective sources that the men who participated in this decision felt they were living through a revolution, one gets the impression that this sense of exhilaration stemmed from the *way* in which policy was formulated—not from the actual decisions that were made. For the first time in recent memory the State Department had actually done something, quickly, efficiently and decisively. This was the real revolution of 1947—and the only one."[19]

16. Statement by the Secretary of State, [February 27, 1947], Department of State, *Foreign Rela-tions of the United States, 1947,* 8 vols. (Washington: GPO, 1971-73), 5:160-62.
17. Acheson, *Present at the Creation,* 219.
18. Pogue, *Marshall,* 4: 166-67; Bohlen, *Witness to History,* 261; *Foreign Relations, 1947,* 5:100-101.
19. John Lewis Gaddis, "Was the Truman Doctrine a Real Turning Point?" *Foreign Affairs* 52 (Jan-uary 1974): 386-402; quote on 389-90.

Moreover, as it turned out, the president's pronouncement appeared to have no impact on the Soviet attitude at the Moscow Foreign Ministers' Conference. The conferees met forty-three times between March 10 and April 24 but found few areas of agreement. More important were Marshall's frequent discussions with the British and French, smoothing out disagreements and displaying American concern; Marshall also received a dire picture of Anglo-French economic and political problems.[20] As for the Soviets, Marshall concluded that they had decided to stall in the expectation that the spreading social disintegration would work to their benefit. Their attitude reminded Marshall of the 1944 Morgenthau plan's ideas of breaking up and pastoralizing Germany, and when he returned to Washington he re-read Henry Stimson's vehement critique of the plan.[21]

Marshall's second public address as secretary of state came in an April 28 national radio speech on the Moscow conference. Marshall still desired to avoid a rupture with the Soviet Union, but his optimism was rapidly waning. Europe, he asserted, needed American reconstruction help and relief, and there must not be further delay on a German settlement. "Disintegrating forces are becoming evident. The patient is sinking while the doctors deliberate." He called for bipartisan unity on the reconstruction of Europe.[22]

By this time, dozens of public figures and commentators in addition to Marshall were calling for aid to Europe. Studies were already underway in the State Department that would help to lay the groundwork for a new American initiative to restore the balance of power in Europe. But Marshall and his advisers faced countervailing pressures. On the one hand, increasing misery and communist voting strength in Western Europe demanded speed and decisiveness from the Truman administration. On the other hand, domestic politics encouraged the administration to caution. While the reaction to the Truman Doctrine had generally been positive, there was a worrisome undercurrent of opposition, and not just from GOP isolationists. Many Democratic congressmen warned that they would not stand for the presentation of another administration policy *fait accompli* regarding Europe. State Department officials went out of their way to avoid any further hints that the United States would seek everywhere to resist communism or the Soviet menace. Marshall himself went to considerable lengths to stroke Senator Arthur Vandenberg's ego and to reassure him that no budget-busting programs were under consideration.[23]

20. On the Moscow Conference, see Pogue, *Marshall*, 4:168-96, and Melvyn P. Leffler, *A Preponderance of Power: National Security, the Truman Administration, and the Cold War* (Stanford, Calif.: Stanford University Press, 1992), 151-56.
21. Bohlen, Witness to History, 263; Marshall to Stimson, April 28, 1947, Marshall Papers, Secretary of State.
22. Pogue, *Marshall*, 4:200.
23. Acheson, *Present at the Creation*, 232, 230.

By early May 1947, Marshall had decided upon a low-key approach to proposing American political-economic efforts in Europe. He proposed announcing a new initiative at a graduation ceremony. Acheson assured him that nobody paid any attention to what was said at those events, but Marshall knew that European leaders could be tipped off in advance. He first thought of announcing something at the University of Wisconsin on May 24; that venue had the advantage of bearding the very conservative and hostile Bert McCormick/*Chicago Tribune* tiger in its den; but key economic adviser Will Clayton was out of the country, the Policy Planning Staff was just getting started, and Marshall's advisers could not be ready in time. The next important venue considered was Amherst College on June 15, but it was quickly evident that the United States could not wait that long. Consequently, Marshall decided upon Harvard University on June 5 as the best time, and hurriedly arranged to receive a long-delayed honorary degree from that school.[24]

By the end of May, the planning was beginning to jell; all Marshall's advisers were by now agreed that the United States had to launch a massive aid program. On May 30, Marshall directed his staff to prepare a draft for a ten-minute talk. To avoid comparisons of the new approach with the controversial Truman Doctrine, Marshall agreed with Acheson's suggestion that he present the aid as a material or technological rather than an ideological problem, and to propose no American-inspired solution. Marshall's advisers were generally agreed on two other points: first, that European nations had to take the initiative and to coordinate policies; second, that the offer be made to all European states in order to avoid the implication that the United States sought to divide Europe into American and Soviet blocs, although it was assumed that the Soviets would never accept economic conditions such as openness, free trade, and American supervision.[25]

The Marshall Plan speech was deliberately low-key and no master plan was enunciated; the speech had just the right degree of vagueness to require European action, yet just the right degree of specificity to excite it. In time, the Marshall Plan program that evolved from the planning of the first half of 1947 would be adjudged one of the greatest of America's foreign policy successes. Harry Truman considered the Truman Doctrine and the Marshall Plan "two halves of the same walnut."[26]

---

24. Ibid., p. 232; Bland, ed., *Marshall Interviews,* pp. 336, 558; Pogue, *Marshall,* 4:208-9.
25. Acheson to Marshall, Memorandum, May 28, 1947, *Foreign Relations, 1947,* 3:232-33; Bohlen, *Witness to History,* 264-65.
26. Marshall's Harvard speech announcing what would be called the Marshall Plan is printed in *Foreign Relations, 1947,* 3:237-39. Gregory A. Fossedal, *Our Finest Hour: Will Clayton, the Marshall Plan, and the Triumph of Democracy* (Stanford, Calif.: Hoover Institution Press, 1993), 212, 234.

Let me conclude by summarizing what I consider George Marshall's most important contributions to American foreign policy in the first half of 1947. These were two: his personal status and his administrative philosophy.

By personal status I mean that public image, based upon his role as army chief of staff between 1939 and 1945, as the disinterested, non-partisan servant of the people; the trusted warrior, whose policies could be debated but whose integrity and well-meaningness could not; the organizer of victory revered by Harry Truman and most members of Congress and the media. His stature thus helped to pave the way for new initiatives.

By administrative philosophy I mean his application of those hard-learned lessons of how best to run an organization. Marshall resuscitated and reinvigorated the State Department, molding it into a reasonably efficient foreign policy tool. He chose good subordinates, gave them room to operate, and listened to their advice. All in all, I think, it was another masterful performance by General Marshall and one for which we can be thankful. □

Impressions of a Speechwriter

GEORGE ELSEY

I must comment first on the identification of me in the program as "President Truman's Speechwriter." I disclaim those words.

I was not the president's speechwriter nor was anyone else.

In contrast to the bloated—and at times out of control—White House staffs of recent administrations, Harry Truman's staff was astoundingly small. Scarcely a baker's dozen drew up chairs in a semi-circle around the President's desk at 9:00 o'clock each morning to discuss the day's business. Every man, if not a Jack-of-all-trades was certainly a Jack-of-many-trades. Each from time to time had a hand in the preparation or review of speeches and messages to Congress.

On matters of foreign affairs, the president expected the Department of State to submit a draft, just as he expected other departments to do the spadework on matters within their bailiwicks. The White House staff was too small to have the time or the necessary knowledge to write a speech from scratch.

In due course I became an administrative assistant to the president and participated in the morning meetings around his desk. However, at the time we are discussing—March 1947—I was a commander in the United States Naval Reserve serving as the only assistant to the special counsel to the president, Clark M. Clifford. I had moved with him a few months earlier when he was promoted from his former post as naval aide to the president.

Clifford had taken over as special counsel at a time of great turbulence. Strikes in major industries were causing massive economic and political problems. Clifford had no time for foreign affairs. He did not focus on them until the late summer of 1946 when I began feeding him—chapter by chapter as I wrote it—the document that has come to be known as the Clifford-Elsey Report. Entitled *American Relations with the Soviet Union,* it presented a grim picture of the international situation.

The top secret, 26,000-word-analysis was based on information I had requested, over Clifford's signature, from State, War, Navy, Justice and other knowledgeable sources about Soviet actions and intentions and their effect on

GEORGE ELSEY was a commander in the U.S. Naval Reserve serving as the only assistant to the special counsel to the president.

our national security. the report was intended for the president. Shaken by the information in it, Clifford realized that foreign affairs also demanded his attention. From then on he increasingly noted international developments and began discussing them with the President.

With respect to Greece and Turkey, I wrote (September 1946) "The Soviet Union is interested in obtaining the withdrawal of British troops from Greece and the establishment of a 'friendly' government there. It hopes to make Turkey a puppet state which could serve as a springboard for the domination of the eastern Mediterranean...." In its concluding chapter, the report recommended: "The United States should support and assist all democratic countries which are in any way menaced or endangered by the U.S.S.R....Providing military support in case of attack is a last resort: a more effective barrier to communism is strong economic support."

As the autumn of 1946 turned into the harshest winter in Europe in decades, cables from our embassies portrayed increasingly bleak military, economic and political situations in Greece and Turkey. Problems in those countries were thus well known at the White House when the British government dropped its bombshell on February 21, 1947, that it could not provide support for Greece and Turkey after March 31. The only surprise was the imminence of the British withdrawal and the sudden realization on our part that if those countries were not to fall into Soviet hands, it was up to us.

Secretary of State Marshall and Under Secretary Acheson discussed the crisis with President Truman before Marshall flew off to Moscow for a frustrating meeting of foreign ministers and Truman left for a long-scheduled visit to Mexico. Acheson was ordered to carry the ball in their absence. This meant he had to gear up much of the Executive Branch for action as well as prepare a presidential message to Congress. Drawing on memoranda from several officers of the State Department, Acheson directed draft after draft of a paper, uncertain as to whether he would go in person. That was settled at a Cabinet meeting on Friday, March 7, the day after Truman returned from Mexico. He would address a joint session of Congress.

It had not occurred to Acheson to share with the White House staff any of the several drafts of the message as it evolved, although he did discuss it with the president before the Friday Cabinet meeting. Clifford had to ask for a copy. Acheson, never lacking in self-confidence, seemed to think that anything he had a hand in needed no input from anyone else.

When a fifteen-page paper entitled "*The President's Message to Congress on the Greek Situation*" arrived late that Friday, Clifford passed it on to me with the comment: "We've got to get this thing into shape for the Boss. Read it tonight and tell me in the morning what you think."

I recognized at once that the title was misleading. This was much more than a message on the Greek situation. Buried in the verbiage were the seeds of a foreign policy that could shake the nation—and the world. I did not like the timing. Expressing my doubts in a long memorandum to Clifford written while he was in the Saturday morning staff meeting, I wrote: "I do not believe that this is the occasion for the 'all-out' speech. [There is] insufficient time to prepare what would be the most significant speech in the President's Administration. Much more time is necessary to develop the philosophy and ideas and do justice to the subject. I think the President should have two weeks to prepare such a speech…" And all we had were three days!

Unknown to me at the time, George Kennan was also expressing doubts. He thought the proposed message too sweeping and too soon. Acheson simply ignored Kennan. Clifford, in contrast, quickly filled me in on the crisis. He told me to drop what I was working on (a bill to unify the armed services) and to concentrate with him on the speech.

As a starter, Clifford asked Acheson to send over the writer of State's latest draft. Joseph M. Jones arrived Saturday morning, accompanied by Carl Humelsine, director of State's Executive Secretariat. Jones's presence at the White House was ironic. He had been arguing at State that the speech should be given by General Marshall because, said Jones, Marshall was the only man in government with the prestige to make a deep impression.

Clifford and I were critical of the State draft. In our view, the broad policy implications were not well spelled out. It was not clear enough that we were dealing with much more than Greece and Turkey, important though they were. And the draft placed too much emphasis on Britain's economic plight.

Jones returned to State with our comments. A swift and skillful writer, he turned out a new draft which was hand-carried to Clifford's office where Clifford and I were awaiting it at 9:30 Sunday morning. We rolled up our sleeves and plunged in, Clifford saying as we started that this was—I noted his remark on a slip of paper—"the opening gun in a campaign to bring people up to realization that the war isn't over by any means."

He and I shuffled paragraphs around and wrote new ones. We were striving to organize the flow of ideas so as to build the strongest possible case that action was vital to *our* national security. We certainly were not just pulling British chestnuts out of the fire because Britain was broke.

We also did our best to simplify. As always seemed to be the case with something from State, it might *read* well enough but it was not a speech. Least of all was it a *speech* that sounded like Harry Truman. Sentence structure and vocabulary were "Trumanized."

We went home Sunday afternoon having scratched up nearly every paragraph and written in the new ones. We left a mess for the typing pool.

I worked alone Monday morning on a clean version of our Sunday efforts while Clifford was at the morning staff meeting. I went through the text again line-by-line, catching points that had slipped by us the day before. I worried about the absence of a suitable reference to the United Nations, sensing that our failure to tip a hat in that direction would bring strong protests. I phoned Humelsine. He sent over innocuous but adequate language. In it went.

I was worried by the absence of what today would be called "a sound bite." Where were two or three sentences that would convey the essence of the President's policy? Where were the highly quotable words that the press and the public could grasp at once and know that this was a policy that went far beyond $400,000,000 of assistance for Greece and Turkey? Had we overlooked something? I went back to State's final draft and focused on one unwieldy paragraph. The key thoughts were there but they were buried in long sentences that would be hard for Truman to read and for listeners to grasp.

I stripped out needless words. I broke the paragraph into three sentences and re-phrased them. Each sentence was then set as a separate paragraph for emphasis. And each sentence then began with "I believe...."

You know the result:

> I believe that it must be the policy of the United States to support free peoples who are resisting attempted subjugation by armed minorities or by outside forces.

> I believe that we must assist free peoples to work out their own destinies in their own way.

> I believe that our help should be primarily through economic and financial aid which is essential to economic stabilization and orderly political process.

As Clifford wrote in his memoirs many years later, "I liked this idea enormously and immediately made it a part of the draft we were preparing for the president. These sentences, which George and I called 'the credo' finally seemed to leap at the listener."

As soon as a clean text came downstairs from the typing pool, Clifford carried the ribbon copy to the President. This was the time for final polishing. That afternoon Clifford and I sat at the Cabinet Room table with the President. Also there were Charles Ross (the press secretary) and William Hassett, a long-time White House staff member whose facility with the English language had led Franklin Roosevelt some years earlier to call him "My Bartlett, Roget and Buckle." We wrote in their suggestions, few in number but all to the point.

Clifford then crossed the street to Acheson's office in what today is known as the Old Executive Office Building to show him our version. Acheson proposed several changes. Clifford accepted some, rejected others. He did accede to Acheson's request that the word "forces" in the first sentence of " the credo" be changed to "pressures."

That was the only change offered by anyone in the three key sentences.

The president gave the text his last review at the Tuesday morning staff meeting. I then gave it a last-touch-up and passed it to Ross to be duplicated for distribution to the press Wednesday morning, sent a copy to State at 1:00 P.M. for translation into many languages for broadcast after delivery, and, most important of all, sent it to Miss Rose Conway to prepare the president's reading copy.

Beginning at 1:02 P.M. Wednesday, March 12, 1947, Harry Truman in his flat 120 words per minute speaking style called for aid to Greece and Turkey in the context of a dramatic new foreign policy. He proclaimed what will forever be known as "The Truman Doctrine," a policy succinctly summarized in the three "I believe" sentences. When he finished eighteen minutes later, he received a standing ovation from both sides of the aisle. As Dean Acheson reflected, "This was a tribute to a brave man rather than a unanimous acceptance of his policy."

To conclude, what did members of the White House staff contribute to the Truman Doctrine?

As to the policy, nothing. The policy was determined by Truman in consultation with Marshall before the latter left for Moscow and Truman took off for Mexico City.

The policy was hammered out on paper by State Department writers struggling with a speech draft under the whiplash of Dean Acheson.

So what *did* we at the White House do?

Were we policy makers? No.

Were we speechwriters? No.

But were we speech *editors*?

Yes, that we certainly were! ☐

Implementation of the Aid Program

GEORGE CREWS MCGHEE

The British had valiantly bore the burden of assistance to Greece and Turkey after the defeat and withdrawal of the German forces from Greece, which resulted in mass destruction of the means of transportation, industry and edifices in the major cities. The Greek economy had been brought to a standstill, the government was helpless in assuring food, housing, and fuel for the Greek people, despite efforts by the United Nations under UNRRA (United Nations Relief and Rehabilitation Administration). The British had been unable to support the Greek economy and army in coping with the communist-led guerrilla forces, which controlled most of the countryside outside of Athens and Salonica.

The fateful transfer of responsibility which resulted in the Truman Doctrine was initiated officially at 9:00 A.M. on Monday, 24 February 1947, when British Ambassador Lord Inverchapel handed to Secretary of State George Marshall two aide-memoirs—one on Greece, the other on Turkey. In essence, the British acknowledged the importance of protecting Greece and Turkey against Soviet influence, predicted the imminent fall of the Greek government in two weeks in the absence of rapid economic and military aid, and requested the United States to assume the major responsibility for providing the assistance that the British economy could no longer support.

Truman consulted with the new secretary of state, General George Marshall, and read the report prepared over the weekend by the State/War/Navy Co-ordination Committee created for this purpose. Based on the co-ordinating committee's report and after discussion with Secretary of War Robert Patterson and Secretary of the Navy James Forrestal, Marshall wrote to the president on 26 February that he believed the British were sincere about their financial constraints; the situation, particularly in Greece, was desperate; the collapse of the Greek government would put U.S. interests in peril; and we should, therefore, immediately extend all aid possible to Greece and, on a smaller scale, to Turkey.

Truman's conclusion, in light of all the advice given him, was the one he had already reached. Greece was in certain danger of being drawn behind the

GEORGE C. MCGHEE, a Petroleum producer and former U.S. government official, was coordinator of the Truman Doctrine Aid Program.

Iron Curtain, and if Greece were lost, Turkey's position would become untenable in a sea of communism. Conversely, Turkish acquiescence to Soviet demands would put the survival of the Greek government further at risk. Failure to meet this, the JCS advised that if Turkey succumbed in peacetime, all Middle East countries would rapidly fall to Soviet domination. "If Russia can absorb Turkey in peace, our ability to defend the Middle East in war will be virtually destroyed".[1]

Truman, without delay, launched into intensive consultations with government and congressional leaders. Sensitive to the reactions of Congress, particularly the Senate leadership of the opposition majority party, he carefully encouraged the support of Foreign Relations Committee Chairman Arthur Vandenberg, whose backing would prove essential to overwhelming congressional support. President Truman decided to request $400 million—$250 for Greece and $150 for Turkey, and preparations commenced on a presentation to a joint session of Congress that would explain the sense of Truman's position on aid and smooth the way for the requisite legislation. Marshall delegated Acheson to organize the effort, which culminated in President Truman's speech to Congress on the 12th of March and introduced to history the Truman Doctrine. In his meeting with Vandenberg Truman presented his case, which Acheson supported strongly. A long silence followed. Then Arthur Vandenberg said solemnly, "Mr. President, if you say that to the Congress and to the country, I will support you and I believe that most of the members will do the same."

U.S. foreign policy had reached a turning point. The Truman Doctrine made that departure by declaring that whatever aggression—direct or indirect—threatened the peace, U.S. security was involved. Truman's message to Congress and the nation rang with the conviction of American ideals and drew deeply on the American tradition of democracy. It could not fail to inspire:

> I believe…that it must be the policy of the United States to support free peoples who are resisting attempted subjugation by armed minorities or by outside pressures.

> I believe that we must assist free people to work out their own destinies in their own way.

> I believe that our help should be primarily through economic and financial aid which is essential to economic stability and orderly political processes.

Contrasting government that is empowered by the will of the majority with a government forcibly imposed by a few, Truman pleaded the urgency of maintaining the democratic spirit of peoples grown weary in their struggles for freedom and a better life. The forceful simplicity of his words left no mistake about the new role he envisioned for America:

---

1. U.S. Department of State, *Foreign Relations of the United States*, 1946, vol. 7, 857-8.

> The seeds of totalitarian regimes…are nurtured by misery and want. They spread and grow in the evil soil of poverty and strife. They reach their full growth when the hope of the people for a better life has died.
>
> We must keep that hope alive.
>
> The free peoples of the world look to us for support in maintaining their freedoms.
>
> If we falter in our leadership, we may endanger the peace of the world—and we shall surely endanger the welfare of our own nation.

When he had finished, every member of Congress, with one exception, rose and applauded. Free nations of the world joined in the acclaim, while the communist world lashed out savagely.

Truman's decision came just short of two years after he became president. It would, however, be a mistake to underestimate the importance of President Truman's own Cold War attitudes at that time in his decision to come to the aid of Greece and Turkey. Truman had served in "Wilson's War," which he believed had saved Europe from barbarism. He denounced Germany, Italy, and Russia as early as 1939 as having a "code little short of cave-man savagery." He opposed isolationism, supported the U.S. war effort once the decision was taken and announced early support for a postwar League of Nations. By early 1946 Truman said he was "tired of babying the Soviets" and by 1948 considered them worse than Hitler.

Truman came to see himself as the protector of liberty and freedom. As his Cold War attitudes evolved, enhanced by the similar opinions of his most trusted advisers (George Marshall, Dean Acheson, W. Averell Harriman, James Forrestal, George Kennan, and Will Clayton), Truman led an administration that characterized Russia as a "monstrous tyranny whose command of a massive military machine menaced Western civilization" and was bent on world domination. Soviet leaders were seen as secretive, sinister figures who relied on terror, propaganda, and subversion.

It was first necessary, of course, to determine how the new aid package would be administered. At the request of the president, the State Department took the lead among the executive agencies in coordinating the implementation of the policy, in drafting the necessary legislation, and in preparing its presentation to Congress. The Department of State was formally delegated responsibility for the administration of the act by executive order. The testimony of the executive agencies before the Congress and the reports of the House Foreign Affairs and Senate Foreign Relations committee envisaged small but competent advisory missions in both Greece and Turkey. Each would have a chief of mission, who would exercise a large part of the responsibility for the execution of the program. It was also made clear that the State Department would utilize fully in the execution of the program the agency or agencies of the government best qualified.

Foreign operations were only beginning to emerge from the remnants left from the war. The Greek-Turkish aid program was the first of the postwar aid programs, succeeding the war-end United Nations Relief and Works Agency (UNRWA). It was later to be absorbed by the much larger Marshall Plan and Mutual Security Agency.

Little thought had been given during the effort to get approval of the aid program as to how it would be administered. When this was finally decided there was no precedent to go by. There was, however, a plethora of former participants in the war effort who were eager and ready to take part in the new crusade unleashed by the Truman Doctrine. They called me and wrote me by the hundreds. I knew many of them from war days and was able to recruit excellent candidates for the Greek and Turkish aid missions. Although the State Department had never administered an aid program it was naively expected to do this through its normal administrative structure, which had been largely involved in leisurely policy-making and in administering only itself. It was decided, therefore, that a small central administrative staff was required; it was placed inconspicuously in a wing of the department basement.

As special assistant to Under Secretary for Economic Affairs William Clayton, I had been advising him on the Greek-Turkish aid issue and had become deeply involved, particularly in the government-wide effort to prepare for the presentation to the Appropriations Committee that would follow passage of the enabling legislation. As a result, I was named as coordinator for aid to Greece and Turkey, a statutory position created with the enabling legislation, Public Law 75 enacted on May the 22nd.

The rationale for creating such a position resulted from the personal experience of Secretary Marshall during his China Mission days. He had been in charge in the field but had requested a trusted Washington aide to serve as his channel of communications with the president, government agencies, and the Congress. The head of the mission in Turkey for the two years was Ambassador Wilson, and in Greece, former Nebraska Governor Dwight Griswold. He was chosen by President Truman, who was in the same unit with him in World War I.

As coordinator, I was their representative in Washington. I was to fight many battles on their behalf—in large part because the lines of authority between Griswold and the able Ambassador MacVeagh tended to overlap—until we realized that the two jobs had to be combined. A new ambassador, Henry Grady, was chosen for the task, reporting as ambassador through the regional assistant secretary. During the initial phases of broad planning and co-ordination of the program and its shepherding through the congressional process, I also had to focus on details such as which agencies of government would be involved with each aspect, and how suitable personnel would be selected and trained. All of these problems fell into my lap at once, before I had been able to select my own staff. On my first day as coordinator I received 137 telephone calls, of which I could return only a few. As quickly as I could, I filled my own staff of about twenty, bringing on Walter Wilds, an experienced administrator as deputy and William Rountree, a very capable and experienced foreign service officer who went on to assume important ambassadorships.

My single purchasing officer and I, with the assistance of the Army Corps of Engineers, opened negotiations with a consortium of American engineering firms the Corps had selected to rebuild the docks of Piraeus, the harbor for Athens, which had been destroyed by the retiring Nazis. Contracts on the usual Corps cost plus fee basis aggregating several tens of millions of dollars were ready for signature. When I presented the contracts for approval by Under Secretary Robert Lovett, a leading Wall Street financier who had been a senior partner in Brown Brothers Harriman, he hit the ceiling. "You mean you want to sign contracts for these amounts in the name of the State Department? The Department has never done anything like this before. We'll be crucified by criticism. No way."

Feeling that I had committed myself and the department, I spent a sleepless night. Early the next morning I called the chief of the Corps of the Engineers, who had been helping me, and explained my problem. Would he take over the problems and administer them if we would provide the funds? He would. I was off the hook. This increased the cost of the projects and imposed a delay while the Corps formed an Athens District, but the docks were built without scandal.

This being the first of the postwar aid programs, Congress, after putting up token resistance to appropriating the funds, took little interest in how they would be spent. I kept the appropriate committees informed but found no tendency on their part to interfere with administration. They had not yet discovered, much to the increasing distress of government administrators to this day, how interesting and politically profitable it was to second-guess the government's decisions. I well recall the day, after the Greek guerrillas had blown up several of the bridges we had just built, that I quietly, without getting anyone's approval outside of the department, sent the Treasury Department a check transferring $50,000,000 from the Greek economic program to the Defense Department to apply against defeating the guerrillas. No one ever complained or questioned. I concluded that the best way to survive in the Washington bureaucracy was when you had the authority, to "lie low."

Pursuant to this policy the army, navy, and air force departments assumed responsibility for the execution of the military aspects of both programs. The numerous other responsibilities were divided along the following lines: Department of Agriculture, the agricultural rehabilitation program envisaged as part of Greek recovery; Department of Commerce, the development of trade and procurement policies; U.S. Public Health Service, execution of the Greek public health program; Bureau of the Budget, the development of plans for the reorganization of the Greek government calculated to increase its effectiveness; Department of Treasury (although primarily in the development of financial and monetary policy), through the Federal Bureau of Supply, the procurement of all non-military supplies not purchased through private channels; Department of Labor, all matters affecting Greek labor; Federal Security Agency, Greek social insurance; and the Public Roads Administration, road building under the Turkish program.

When the missions began their work in Greece and Turkey, each of the substantive divisions developed direct lines of communication with their corresponding agencies in Washington. Although policy matters came from the chiefs of missions through embassy and Department of State channels, there was direct interchange, at the working level, of substantive information, ideas, and instructions. Many of the departments had furnished some of their key personnel for the aid missions and maintained a keen interest in their segments of the program. It was believed that one of the most important elements in the success of these missions was the bringing into play of all the potential contributions of the other executive agencies.

Both the Greek and Turkish aid programs involved close co-ordination with the three service departments and with the national military establishment. Recommendations on important policy decisions were obtained from the secretary of defense, who, when appropriate was to refer them to the JICs (Joint Intelligence Committee). However, day-to-day operational matters were handled directly by liaison with the minimum of formality. Excellent co-ordination between and with the services was achieved both in Washington and in the field. The size of the military missions, 450 in Greece and 363 in Turkey, at the end of 1948, gives some indication of the complexity of the problem. (Although original estimates had assumed only a small military mission in Turkey, the total number of U.S. personnel, including civilians, was to reach almost 25,000 at its peak. The large increase included many maintenance specialists but principally consisted of personnel engaged in radio intelligence, for which Turkey was ideally located.)

Important as co-ordination in Washington is in the execution of a foreign program, co-ordination in the field is more important. This I believe was successfully achieved in carrying out the program, and any lapses that occurred served only to highlight the importance of a united effort. Co-ordination between the economic and military aspects of the Greek aid program, which was vital to the success of the effort since each impinged on the other, was originally assured by the fact that the chief of the American Mission for Aid to Greece was responsible for both segments of the program.

During the two-year duration of Public Law 75 I made regular visits to Greece and Turkey to meet with the heads of mission, staff, and high officials of the host governments. In Athens I always visited King Paul and Queen Frederika as well as Prime Minister Tsaldaris. I once accompanied General Van

Fleet, our able chief of military mission, to view, at a respectful distance, the battle between Greek army and guerrilla forces for the Grammos Mountains.

The Greek army won, but our elation was destined to be short. The defeated guerrillas, having a sanctuary available in nearby Yugoslavia, wheeled along the border and entered Greece again unexpectedly, inflicting a crushing defeat, which represented a major setback to our aid program.

I will end with a brief summary of what I consider the most significant results of the Truman Doctrine.

1) President Truman pledged to "support free people who are resisting attempted subjugation by armed minorities (in Greece) or by outside pressure (against Turkey)," representing a significant change in American attitudes and in U.S. policy. The USSR could no longer be perceived as an ally in terms of our wartime alliance, but a real or possible enemy.

2) For the first time Americans authorized expenditure of major resources and the sending abroad of large numbers of civilian and military personnel to make good such a pledge. There had been created the necessary mission organization, lines of authority, and able staff for this purpose.

3) In missions to Greece and Turkey it was U.S. policy that our support precluded exposure to or participation in combat of our personnel. Over the two-year period of Greek-Turkish aid we suffered no loss in combat. Fortunately, we avoided direct combat in the Cold War with the USSR. Although other aid situations may involve combat, our assistance to South Vietnam in combat was, I believe, a mistake in which we intruded unwittingly into a civil war. Once we start shooting it is our war.

4) In two years, including $275 million allocated the second year for military assistance only, the $670 million of the Greek-Turkish Aid Act achieved victory in both countries, saving them from being drawn behind the Iron Curtain. By 1949 fewer than 2,000 guerrillas were fighting in Greece, compared with 28,000 two years earlier. Greece was enabled to rearm, restore its economy, and regain its confidence and stability. Both countries, with our assistance, gained entry into NATO, thereby preventing a USSR end-run around the NATO line and the conquest of the Middle East, access to which would otherwise have been wide open.

5) The Truman Doctrine is rightly credited with leading directly to the promulgation of the Marshall Plan four months later, which cost the United States only a bargain $14 billion; to the Berlin airlift, which broke the Soviet blockade of West Berlin; and to the success in July 1949 of the U.S. initiative in creating NATO. Ultimately, the impetus of the Truman Doctrine engendered programs of military and economic aid to most of the non-communist world. The United States currently supplies such aid at an annual rate of approximately $14 billion and continues to provide substantial military aid to Greece and Turkey. □

From Doubt to Decision: Celebrating the Fiftieth Anniversary of the Truman Doctrine

JOHN O. IATRIDES

This is indeed an appropriate moment to commemorate the Truman Doctrine, and not merely because March 1997 is the fiftieth anniversary of that historic policy pronouncement. With the collapse of the Soviet Union and the discrediting of communism as a state dogma it can be argued that the mission upon which President Harry S. Truman and his advisers launched this country in March 1947 has been crowned with success.

As with all great human undertakings, the Truman Doctrine was not without its ambiguities, its pitfalls and its critics. Nevertheless, its impact on American foreign policy in the aftermath of the Second World War—indeed, its impact upon the international system from the 1940s to the end of the 1980s—is clearly beyond question.

Historians of the American presidency rank Truman with the near greats, with Thomas Jefferson, Theodore Roosevelt and Woodrow Wilson. And while ranking presidents is inexact, highly subjective and changes over time, Truman's showing is almost always quite high and has been improving. Since there was little that was extraordinary about Truman the man, historians are obviously impressed by his performance on key national issues and by his impact on the presidency as an institution. Moreover, while domestic problems were important—for example, his showdown with the formidable John L. Lewis, head of the powerful United Mine Workers Union—it was primarily on issues of foreign and security policy that Truman earned his high marks. His decisions were tough and path-setting. In retrospect, one may question the wisdom of his policies, but one cannot doubt their historical importance.

In the realm of foreign and security affairs the cornerstone of United States policy under Truman was the containment of Soviet communism. This policy was to remain the fundamental rationale of America's global efforts until the final collapse of the U.S.S.R. a mere six or seven years ago. As with all grand strategies, containment had many components and phases. They

JOHN O. IATRIDES, Ph.D., is Professor of International Politics at Southern Connecticut State University. He received his education in Greece, the Netherlands and the United States.

included the Marshall Plan, the Berlin airlift, the North Atlantic Treaty, the Korean war, the adoption of NSC 68, which globalized U.S. defense strategies, and a host of official pronouncements, actions and international agreements. But the fundamental justification and blueprint for all components of containment—and the ultimate rationale of American foreign and security policies all through the Cold War—was the simple but compelling logic of the Truman Doctrine.

Considering the highly charged and exaggerated rhetoric which characterized the East-West dialogue during the Cold War, the message of Truman's speech of 12 March 1947 was rather unexceptional. In the view of the president and his advisers, less than two years after the defeat of the Nazi and Japanese aggressors and after all the sacrifices which that effort had entailed, the United States faced new and grave dangers which required new and bold initiatives. The world was being forcibly divided into two distinct "ways of life." The one, familiar to the president's audience, was "based upon the will of the majority, and is distinguished by free institutions, representative government, free elections, guarantees of individual liberty, freedom of speech and religion, and freedom from political oppression." In short, the president was describing the democratic way of life. Opposing and threatening it was another way, "based upon the will of a minority forcibly imposed upon the majority. It relies upon terror and oppression, a controlled press and radio, fixed elections, and the suppression of personal freedoms."

Without identifying it by name the president was clearly referring to Stalin's Soviet Union and the communist regimes which Moscow was imposing across East-Central Europe. Having portrayed the world as dangerously split into two irreconcilable camps Truman declared the purpose of his pronouncement: "I believe that it must be the policy of the United States to support free peoples who are resisting attempted subjugation by armed minorities or by outside pressures. I believe that we must assist free peoples to work out their own destinies in their own way."

The president struck a note of urgency: "We must take immediate and resolute action." Nor was this a question of appealing to compassion and humanitarian generosity. The president had opened his speech with ominous-sounding words: "The gravity of the situation which confronts the world today necessitates my appearance before a joint session of the Congress. The foreign policy and the national security of this country are involved."

In its particulars Truman's speech was devoted to an explanation of why it was necessary for the United States to go to the assistance of Greece and Turkey, the first facing an internal communist insurrection while the latter was under Soviet pressure to relinquish control over the Turkish Straits and of certain areas along the Black Sea. In his justification for assisting those two far-away countries, the president, focusing his attention on Greece, presented what would later be called the theory of the falling dominoes: "It is necessary only to glance at a map to realize that the survival and integrity of the Greek nation are of grave importance in a much wider situation. If Greece should fall under the control of an armed minority the effect upon its neighbor, Turkey, would be immediate and serious. Confusion and disorder might well spread throughout the entire Middle East. Moreover, the disappearance of Greece as an independent state would have a profound effect upon those countries in Europe whose peoples are struggling against great difficulties to maintain their freedoms and their independence while they repair the damages of war.... Collapse of free institutions and loss of independence would be disastrous not only for them but for the world.... Should we fail to aid Greece and Turkey in this fateful hour, the effect will be far reaching to the West as well as to the East."

Finally, the president brought his argument back to the central issue of enlightened self-interest: "The free peoples of the world look to us for support in maintaining their freedoms. If we falter in our leadership, we may endanger the peace of the world—and we shall surely endanger the welfare of our own nation."

During the long life of the Cold War, foreign aid—especially to countries believed to be facing communist threats—became a staple of American foreign policy. However, this was not the case before 1947, when the modest amounts of relief assistance to other nations were justified largely on humanitarian grounds. To appreciate the importance of the Truman Doctrine as a radical departure from traditional U.S. policy we need to see it not in the light of what followed but what had been the norm before it.

Reflecting the thinking of President Franklin Roosevelt as well as the presumed wishes of the American public, the new and inexperienced president had no conscious desire to pursue activist policies in Europe once the war was over. He was certainly not looking to assume new obligations and burdens beyond those created by the defeat of the Axis powers. Indeed, Roosevelt's intention to withdraw U.S. forces from Europe as soon as practicable, and to curtail American commitments in that continent, had been the principal reason the United States had been quite content to have the Soviets occupy and administer a large portion of defeated Germany.

For all the difficulties of the wartime alliance in dealing with Stalin—and despite remarks unsympathetic toward the Soviet Union, Truman had made while vice president—the fact remained that the Soviets had been an indispensable partner whose valiant war effort and terrible sacrifices had insured victory in Europe. To publicly declare the Soviet Union a threat to America's vital interests—even if this were done indirectly—was a sharp and difficult change of course. There is no evidence that Truman was looking for a show-down with Stalin. The sharp change in policy was necessary because of Moscow's hostile attitude and expansionist behavior all across East-Central Europe and down to Iran. In his own words, Truman was tired of "babying" the Russians.

Moreover, the new policy was not simply a verbal denunciation and a condemnation of the Soviets for establishing puppet regimes from Poland to Bulgaria and East Germany. The Truman Doctrine implied the promise that the United States would provide the assistance needed to help free peoples everywhere remain free. This pledge was likely to be a very costly and risky undertaking. At the very moment that the country was demobilizing and returning to peacetime norms could it afford to extend to others the assistance promised?

To be sure, in subsequent Congressional hearings the Truman administration was careful to explain that it had no intention of applying the new policy to China, where a civil war not very different from that in Greece was raging. And there was no indication that the president's advisers had any plans to assist those countries which had already fallen under communist domination. Nevertheless, Truman's speech gave the impression that the United States was committing itself to rescue victims of totalitarianism, whether homegrown or fostered from the outside, wherever they might be. Would a Republican-controlled Congress which had not taken the new president all that seriously, approve the funds needed for the new policy? Would the Republican leadership, which had coined the expression "to err is Truman," support the new and bold program?

The signs were not encouraging. One year earlier, on March 5, 1946, at Fulton, Missouri, with President Truman on the same platform, Winston Churchill had given his famous "Iron Curtain" speech in which he had drawn attention to the imposition of communist-totalitarian dictatorships on most of the nations of Eastern Europe. Britain's wartime leader had called for an Anglo-American effort to stand up to Soviet expansionism in Europe. But the reaction throughout the United States had been almost entirely negative. Truman had found it necessary to publicly dissociate himself from Churchill's message and claimed—falsely—that he had not known beforehand what his distinguished guest would say. Yet now, a year later, Truman was proposing that the United States, acting alone, assume a burden much heavier than anything Churchill had suggested.

The reason for this dramatic change in perspective was that during 1946 the president and his principal advisers—George Marshall, Dean Acheson, and others—had grown increasingly and genuinely alarmed by the expansionist tactics and hostile mood of the Soviet government. By the early months of 1947 they had reached the conclusion that the United States, acting in its own self-interest, had to prevent further Soviet gains. The conceptual basis of the view that, by its very character and needs, the Soviet Union threatened the entire international community and therefore the United States, was provided by a little-known American career diplomat and specialist on Russia, George F. Kennan. In his now-famous "long telegram," sent from Moscow on 22 February 1946, Kennan offered a masterful and convincing analysis of the deep historical, ideological and opportunistic roots of Soviet hostility toward the Western world. Having explained the problem he also provided the blue-print for its solution. Kennan advocated that the United States "contain" the Soviet Union by establishing around it a barrier of stable and democratic states which would frustrate Moscow's expansionist designs and force it to seek accommodation with the West. Prophetically, Kennan concluded that, if contained, the Soviet system would eventually collapse under the weight of its own internal weaknesses and contradictions. It was such a barrier of containment that the Truman Doctrine sought to inaugurate. In short, within one year (March 1946 to March 1947) the American response to Soviet expansionism had changed from confusion and indecision to a determination to stand up to the Soviet Union and its communist clients.

Thus, Truman's speech of 12 March 1947 was a declaration that the United States was prepared to take on the yet-to-be-defined burdens and responsibilities of the leader of the free world in order to oppose Soviet communism. As one of the president's speechwriters put it, the speech "marked our passing into adulthood in the conduct of foreign affairs." This bold and open-ended task is what prompted Secretary of State Dean Acheson to chose as the title of his memoirs *Present at the Creation*. All succeeding presidents would seek to define in their own terms and for their own times what Truman articulated in 1947. Indeed, since the end of the Cold War the underlying criticism of American foreign policy—criticism directed at Presidents George Bush and Bill Clinton—has been that no replacement has been found for Truman's strategy of containment.

The Truman Doctrine was a remarkable pronouncement not merely because it gave focus, direction and dynamism to American foreign policy in the wake of the Second World War. The choice of its first beneficiaries, and therefore its immediate geostrategic goals, was also unexpected and path-setting.

Before 1947, American policy planners had shown no interest in the Balkans. While trade activity with that region had always been modest, in the immediate postwar period Washington's relations with Greece and Turkey were normal but passive; contacts with the neighboring communist regimes ranged from hostile to non-existent. During and after the First World War, in which Turkey had fought on the wrong side, the massacres of Christians in Ottoman lands had earned that country the reputation of a barbarous and alien land. Turkey's neutrality in the Second World War had done nothing to improve its image in America. At the Yalta conference in February 1945, when Stalin complained that control of the Dardanelles gave Turkey a stranglehold on Russia's throat, President Roosevelt appeared to sympathize with the Soviet dictator. The president expressed the naive hope that the Russo-Turkish border might become as peaceful and stable as the U.S.-Canadian border. This despite the fact that, as the president's chief of staff, Admiral William D. Leahy, remarked, everyone at the conference knew that the Russians were eager to gain control of the Turkish Straits. For Roosevelt, who was preoccupied with much more important issues, Turkey's problems with the Soviets were not worth his attention and concern.

As for Greece, its heroic resistance to the Italian and German aggressors and the terrible suffering under the brutal enemy occupation had earned that small country much sympathy among Americans. And there was, of course, a traditional admiration for the world of classical Greece. Yet in the view of policy makers the interests of the United States remained unaffected by developments in Greece and in the Balkans generally. The region's reputation as Europe's perennial trouble-spot added to the desire of American officials to stay clear of the Balkans. As the end of the Second World War approached the American ambassador to Greece and Yugoslavia, Lincoln MacVeagh, tried repeatedly to warn Roosevelt that rivalry between Russia and Britain was bound to explode over the Balkans and spread unless the United States intervened. But Roosevelt made it clear that he was determined to keep the United States out of the Balkans. After a particularly frustrating meeting with the president, MacVeagh recorded in his diary: "The meaning of ... the short time he was willing to give me on this visit would seem to be that Pilate is washing his hands, or, to paraphrase Bacon, 'What are the Balkans? asked jesting Roosevelt, and would not stay for an answer.'"

Under the new president American officials had not remained totally indifferent to developments in Greece and Turkey. In April 1946 the battleship *Missouri* had paid a much-publicized visit to Istanbul. Although not intended as a deliberate warning to Moscow, the visit represented an expression of American support for the Turkish government. And in March 1946 the United States helped supervise the Greek national elections together with Britain and France, and provided modest relief assistance, mostly through United Nations channels. At the same time, however, the Department of State was opposed to any significant assistance to Greece.

In short, at the end of 1946 one could not foresee the dramatic change in U.S. policy contained in the Truman Doctrine, specifically as it related to Greece and Turkey. That change was the result of two factors. First, as already suggested, by the end of 1946 the Truman administration had pretty much decided that it had seen enough of Soviet expansionist moves in Europe and the Near East and that the time for action had arrived. Secondly, on 21 February 1947 the British government, which had been closely associated with the Greek and Turkish governments, secretly informed the United States that Britain could no longer provide assistance to Greece and Turkey. The British government asked if the United States was prepared to assume that burden. To quote again Truman's speechwriter, "Great Britain had within the hour handed the job of world leadership, with all its burdens and all its glory, to the United States." Such an exuberant statement was, of course, an exaggeration. In February 1947 Britain could not provide enough food and heating to its own people and was hardly in a position to hand over to the United States "the job of world leadership." But in human affairs perceptions are as important as scientific truth. For many of Truman's advisers, Britain's admission that it could not keep Greece and Turkey afloat amounted to an invitation to the United States to step forward as leader and defender of the free world.

The British diplomatic notes on Greece and Turkey triggered in Washington a wave of activity which today would be called crisis management. Under the direction of Dean Acheson, and after a series of consultations involving a variety of officials and agencies, the text of President Truman's speech was written, edited, and approved for delivery. Following congressional hearings in March and April "A Bill to Provide for Assistance to Greece and Turkey" passed the Senate on 22 April (by a vote of 67-23) and the House on 6 May (287-107). The first pillar of containment was now in place.

As a forceful declaration of a radically new strategy with nuclear and potentially global ramifications the Truman Doctrine has had its share of critics. They have ranged from prominent contemporaries such as George Kennan, Walter Lippmann, Henry Wallace and Senator Robert Taft to countless historians, political analysts and other students of American foreign policy and international relations. Such criticism has focused on a variety of arguments which concern the doctrine's assumptions, language and style of presentation, its impact on the East-West conflict and on its long-term consequences for the United States and for the rest of the world. It would be neither possible nor necessary to examine in these pages such diverse claims systematically and fairly. Instead, a few composite questions which critics of the Truman Doctrine have put forward over the years can be listed.

- Did the Truman administration, in its determination to gain congressional support, deliberately overstate the Soviet threat, thus contributing, however inadvertently, to the subsequent anti-communist hysteria and to McCarthyism?

By March 1947 Soviet pressures on Turkey and the resulting tension over the Straits question had subsided. There was therefore little reason to fear that Turkey might be attacked or forced to give in to Stalin's demands. As for a Soviet involvement in the communist insurrection in Greece, American intelligence reports and official perceptions were based on rumors, unsubstantiated evidence, faulty premises concerning Moscow's control over the communist parties of Greece and Yugoslavia, and the self-serving claims of the Greek government. American intelligence capabilities in the Balkans and communist Europe generally were in their infancy. Although it was not known at the time, Stalin had not encouraged the Greek communists to launch their insurrection and in 1948 he angrily ordered the Yugoslavs to stop their active support of their Greek comrades. In retrospect, the Truman Doctrine would have been on firmer ground had it been proclaimed in 1946, when the Soviets were openly and directly threatening to destroy the territorial integrity of Turkey as well as of Iran. But in 1946 Washington was not ready to take such a strong stand. Unfortunately for policy makers, they need to decide what is to be done without the benefit of hindsight.

- Did the Truman administration confuse the American public by declaring the enemy to be totalitarianism rather than Soviet power? Was ideology, whether totalitarian or communist, a serious threat to American institutions and the nation's interests? Without Moscow's power behind it could communism undermine the West? Conversely, if America's resolve was to defend democracy against totalitarianism (as the Truman Doctrine claimed) why not apply the same logic to the dictatorships of Spain, Portugal and much of Latin America?

Understandably the president and his advisers did not wish to provoke the Soviet Union and perhaps aggravate matters further by naming Stalin's regime and its official ideology as the declared target of America's new strategy. But the emphasis on totalitarianism and on ideology vaguely defined rather than on Soviet power introduced into the emerging conflict an element of ideological zeal and global crusading that once unleashed could not easily be reined in. By defining the threat in ideological terms the Truman administration set the stage for the chasing of enemies who were at times not worth the effort.

- Did the Truman Doctrine ignore the United Nations and condemn it to impotence rather than promoting it as the principal instrument for conflict resolution?

To be sure, President Truman paid no more than lip service to the newly created international organization. But it is difficult to see how in the late 1940s the United Nations could have produced a workable accommodation of the interests of the principal adversaries.

- Did the Truman administration, in its desire to prop up anti-communist forces, overlook the dire need for political and social reform of its client states? Did the cause of democracy actually suffer at the hands of many whom Washington supported? Did American policy overemphasize military assistance? Did Washington get into the habit of intervening and micromanaging the states it supported, thereby weakening further their institutions and their ability to stand on their own? Did foreign aid in the name of containment acquire a life of its own?

These and similar questions deserve careful scrutiny and dispassionate answers. That is the task of serious scholarship which in turn serves a vitally important purpose: a democracy's need for self-examination and open debate of the nation's interests and the government's methods in pursuing those interests.

The debate on the Truman Doctrine is certain to continue. However, in varying degrees the questions being debated are based upon the wisdom of hindsight. In the early months of 1947 the Truman administration was sure of one thing: if the Soviet Union was allowed to continue on the aggressive course it appeared to have chosen, much of the rest of the world would suffer and the international order which the United States had helped to build—most recently through the defeat of German, Italian and Japanese aggression—would be destroyed. Sizing up the new adversary through a confusing haze of facts, assumptions and calculations, President Truman and his advisers set out to meet the challenge. The Truman Doctrine was their trumpet call to action.   ☐

Origins of the "Greek Economic Miracle:" The Truman Doctrine and Marshall Plan Development and Stabilization Programs

JAMES C. WARREN, JR.

Politics and strategy in 1947, the survival of governments, the prospects of victory all revolved round the coming of the Americans.... and the breezes from the New World blew through the most ancient of Europe's civilizations.... they brought the prestige of limitless resources and an air of knowing how to put things right in no time.

Memories of a Mountain War
by Kenneth Matthews

When the Truman Doctrine mission went to Greece fifty years ago, its members were New Dealers—moderate social and economic reformers with a confident, can-do spirit. They were quite filled with a belief in the efficacy of a creative, reformist, leadership role for progressive government. And in that year, 1947, they had gone to the rescue of an Athens regime which, they were entirely convinced, was so incompetent and corrupt, so heedless of the needs of its citizens and so brutalizing of them in its methods that at least half the blame for the communist-led civil war rested with the "establishment," the political elite in the capital.[1] They were, in a word, reformers!

And what they found on the ground was appalling. The task of rebuilding from the World War II damages of a vicious Nazi occupation had hardly been touched. Moreover, the nation's foreign exchange earning capacity and its import needs (above all, food) were so badly out of balance (Table I) as to suggest outright bankruptcy if not imminent chaos and famine, or worse.

JAMES C. WARREN, JR., is an advisor to U.S. firms doing business in Greece. He served as chief, Import Program Office, the Marshall Plan Mission to Greece from 1950 to 1954.

1. There even developed amongst the Mission Americans a kind of special local demonology by which the ills of Greece were ritually (and semi-seriously) laid at the feet of, say, Mavromichalis or Bodossakis, the "Heaters" (American pronunciation for the political thugs known as the Xtes) or Maniadakis, perhaps the Greek cement cartel or maybe Zervas or Tsaldaris. By contrast, the figure of Varvaressos—who had been crushed back in 1945 by the combined hammer and anvil of the KKE (communist party) and the Enosis Viomichanon (Association of Industrialists)—was imbued with a kind of tragic nobility. These attitudes persisted right up through the '50s, and when the brilliant and aristocratic (parlor) socialist, George Kartalis, became co-sponsor of the Currency Stabilization Program in 1952, he was welcomed as almost the reincarnation of the dynamic Varvaressos—at least in the Metochikon Tameion Building.

TABLE I

GREECE

Balance of Payments—1948 (First Full Year of U.S. Aid)

			Millions of dollars
I.	Foreign exchange payments:		
	a. Imports		451.0
	b. Invisibles		18.7
		Total:	469.7
II.	Foreign Exchange earnings:		
	a. Exports		89.4
	b. Invisibles		57.5
		Total:	146.9
III.	Balance on Current Account:		−322.8

Source: See endnotes.

The Civil War added a further dimension of fear. An intelligence appraisal in map form (Figure 1) suggests the enormity of the security problem posed by the communist rebellion and civil war. There was hardly any part of the country which could be considered immune from guerrilla attack. Indeed, a very real question was just how to secure the physical safety of those who would be working on Greece's economic reconstruction.

The first AMAG (American Mission for Aid to Greece) personnel arrived in July, 1947. The bilateral treaties had been signed in June; the first aid cargo arrived in Piraeus in August. By November, the Americans on the ground had seen enough to put together the following statement of strategy and purpose:

1. The Mission recognized that without an end to civil strife and physical insecurity there would be no economic recovery;

2. But that military operations would have little chance of success unless efforts were made simultaneously to improve economic conditions;

3. And, to be successful, this two-way approach required much ancillary effort;

4. The mission therefore included divisions concerned with correcting inefficient and uneconomic government practices; controlling expenditure and augmenting revenues; regulating imports and stimulating exports; improving labor relations, public health and welfare.

THE NEW DEAL MISSION

The guerrilla war was indeed brought to an end in September 1949, two years later, but the economic task continued until mid-year, 1954. And it is the special quality of social and economic reform and structural, institutional change suggested in the strategy statement just cited that illuminated the history of the American adventure in Greece from beginning to end. This

FIGURE I

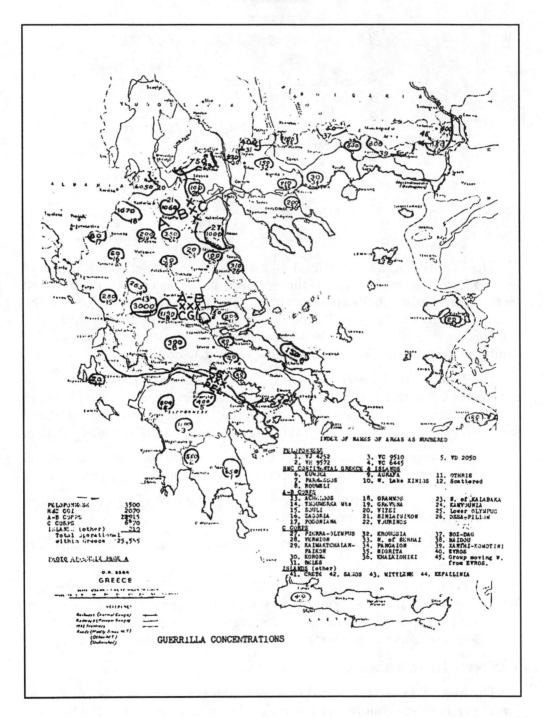

Source: See endnotes.

reformist zeal constituted a stubborn, real, sustained (and sometimes quixotic) element in this chapter of American foreign policy. The American Mission was enormous: at its peak there were 181 American specialists, advisors, and controllers and agents-of-change not only in all the major sub-sectors of agriculture and mining and industry; roadbuilding and ports and harbors; electric power and civil aviation—but also in civil service organization and method, in governmental decentralization, in labor union organization, in banking legislation and the progressive income tax, in public health and social security administration.

Three years later, these men were at the peak of their power. The fiscal year 1950/51 was also, not coincidentally, the peak year of American economic and development investment in Greece. They were pouring money and programs and ideas into Greece at a hectic pace. Investment expenditures were running at a level three times that which had been achieved during the Mission's first, emergency year when a crash program had been a necessity. And in their reform and development programs, these American specialists were lashed forward to strenuous endeavor by a mission chief of tough, demanding, mid-western, LaFollette/liberal/New Deal persuasion and galvanic, reformist energy—Paul R. Porter.[2] By November 1950, Vitsi/Grammos was a year behind them: the road was now open. And even the Korean War, then six months old, had little discernible effect on these New Dealers and their programs and projects in, and for, Greece. In a lengthy report to the head of the Marshall Plan in Washington, Paul Porter, in a personally authored document (not a paper developed and written by his staff) summarized accomplishments, analyzed Greece and its needs, and re-stated those reformist objectives laid down at the very beginning of the Truman Doctrine; the date was November 11, 1950):

> Results…have been impressive…in relation to the virtual chaos of three years ago…The Greek economy is no longer in a state of near-paralysis. Agricultural and industrial production have surpassed their pre-war levels…ports and railroads… repaired…highways…built, an ambitious electric power development program…is underway…Per capita food consumption is as high as it has been in modern Greek history.[3] Technical assistance in agriculture, industry, construction, transportation and public administration has already made an imprint on the attitudes of the Greek people which may fundamentally alter the course of their history.…
>
> Economic and political leadership comes mainly from a small wealthy class which, with some notable exceptions, is indifferent to its social responsibilities, is

2. Not to be confused with Paul A. Porter, who had been chief of the first (in fact, only exploratory) mission, January-April, 1947.

3. From the work of the Mission's Food Program Committee and, in particular, the efforts of Martha Tsongas Sismanides seconded to the Mission by the Food and Agriculture Organization of the United Nations (FAO): Caloric Content of Food Available for Human Consumption on a Daily Per Capita Basis: 1935-38 average 2,564; 1948-49 average 2,625; 1950-51 projected 2,520. (Per capita nutrition standards in Western Europe returned to the prewar level in 1951).

resistant to reforms, and is motivated by a mercantilist and rentier philosophy rather than a production philosophy...The tax structure is one of the most regressive in Europe, and tax evasion by many wealthy people adds to the inequality of burdens.

In a climate of distrust and discontent, political instability is both cause and effect. Since January of this year, seven governments held office—the longest for fifteen weeks. Following a bitter civil war which had divided families and has left deep wounds, a stable and competent Center government, imbued with a purpose of social reform, holds the best promise for unifying the people for constructive goals...but...the moderating advantages of a progressive Center government have not yet been realized. Proportional representation has proved to be a disintegrating factor....

Many of the political leaders, supposing that the basic interests of the nation are safeguarded by American economic and military aid indulge in the dangerous luxury of preoccupation with little things. Indeed, most ministers during the period of American aid have preferred to pass responsibility for difficult and unpopular decisions to the Mission.

Administration is highly centralized and is remote from the people. Local initiative has been stifled by the failure to hold local elections in more than fourteen years. Local taxing authority has largely disappeared. The relationship of the people to their Government has become that of petitioners, and the Government has become a petitioner to the world....

At the present time there is scant evidence that more than a few political leaders desire to be independent of American aid or believe that it will come to an end.

Probably the most difficult task faced by the ECA [Economic Cooperation Administration] Mission to Greece is to convince the Greek people that American aid will end in a few years and to induce the Government to prepare adequately for this event[4]....

"American aid...must be concerned with more than bridging the gap in the balance of payments, financing essential economic development and rendering technical assistance in the improvement of methods in production and marketing. American representatives are right to insist...for the benefit of the Greek people...that freely elected representatives of the Greek people should constitute a stable and efficient government, and that this government should be more responsive to the needs of the desperately poor, that it should...establish an equitable tax system...revitalize local government...foster competition in industry and trade... frame and execute a realistic plan of economic development....

...My colleagues and I have considered that our main efforts...should be...production...financial stability and inducing the Greek Government to reform its tax structure and to improve and decentralize the services of public administration... Despite a tendency of many ministers, viewing their own responsibility as a transient

4. Gunnar Myrdal, the economist/historian and at that time head of the United Nations Economic Commission for Europe, visited Athens a year later (December, 1951), and talked extensively with the Greek government and its officials. He went away disgusted, having noted that their preoccupation, to the exclusion of almost everything else, was discovering ways and means of insuring the continued flow of dollar grants from the United States.

one, to yield to any strong pressure, the price and wage line has been held reasonably well during the past year. It has not been pleasant to the mission to recommend a policy that represents so severe a degree of austerity for the great majority of the Greek people…Only a continued austerity in living standards will permit the execution of a major development program which will bring higher levels of consumption in the future…As production rises the workers and farmers must be enabled to enjoy a fair share of the increased national wealth….

That Greece can be self-supporting in 1954…depends [first] on…reduced trade barriers…in other Marshall Plan countries…The second is that the Greek Government will assume full responsibility for governing…and to act with a courage and firmness of purpose that becomes a proud and talented people.[5]

It is of course superficial to dismiss all this as mere "intervention" or "interference" in the internal affairs of a sovereign state.[6] When the Truman Doctrine mission came to Greece, it set up, in effect, a kind of substitute state. Perhaps even that term is not good enough, for there wasn't much of a state when the Americans arrived. There had been a massive failure of nerve, a near collapse of the state as a functioning organism. But the essence of what was going on was more complex than simply "filling a vacuum."

Of a certainty we had come upon a highly centralized mechanism of national governance, something resembling—when it was fully functioning, that is—the French tradition of *etatism*. But then the Americans grafted onto this theoretical, albeit dysfunctional, structure the methods and outlook of the New Deal: the welfare state whose principal engine was to be an enlightened, creative, leadership role for government services—from the Tennessee Valley Authority (TVA) to the Federal Reserve, from Social Security to the Wagner Act to Agricultural Extension Services and the Progressive Income Tax and Farm-to-Market Roads and the decentralization of government.[7] The

5. Although it is occasionally asserted that the Korean War marked some kind of special turning point for the American Mission policy in Greece—following which, according to this theory, the New Deal character of the Mission was extinguished—this extended excerpt from an important and official statement rather suggests otherwise, if for no other reason than its date. Incidentally, the style of the writing is revealing and indeed may hint to the reader that the real author of the so-called "Grady letter" of 31 March 1950 (which had bounced Venizelos out of office) was indeed none other than Paul R. Porter.

6. This is an area of scholarly research calling for serious endeavor: e.g., the American Director of the Foreign Trade Administration (FTA) within the Greek Ministry of National Economy is routinely described as having possessed (unqualified) veto power. Actually Law 480 establishing the FTA placed it under a seven-member Board on which the American Director had but one vote—and no veto. On the Executive Committee of the FTA, empowered only to issue regulations carrying out Board policies and decisions, the American director could only withhold his concurring vote to actions initiated by his two Greek committee members—and should he initiate action, he would have to carry with him at least one of his Greek ministry colleagues. The American director of the FTA used his Executive Committee concurring veto power once—and that was *at the request* of his two Greek colleagues (they had wished to be seen as voting for an action which, in fact, they knew they should oppose but did not dare).

7. Is it not curious that no scholar has yet attempted a comparison of the American program—and its actual results—with the rhetoric of PASOK?

centerpiece of the Truman/Marshall aid effort was, of course, the Recon-struction and Development Program—re-building and then expanding the Greek economy:

- For seven years the United States provided the fundamental resources to feed, fuel, and clothe the Greek nation. It was balance-of-payments support on a massive scale.

- For the first three of those seven years the United States also poured design and drive and investment monies into—and thereby rebuilt—the heavily damaged prewar economy of Greece.

- For four subsequent years the United States poured substantially greater investment into the expansion and further development of the Greek economy.

- Throughout that long endeavor, the United States also poured into the Greek ministries its advice, whether wanted or not; its restless energy, its stubborn reformism; its notions of both organization and method, on the one hand, and, on the other, simple economic growth. In a zero-sum society, the concept of enlarging the economic pie was nothing less than revolutionary.

TABLE II

GREECE

Investment and Development Expenditures Undertaken by the Truman Doctrine/Marshall Plan

Fiscal Period	Expenditures (in millions of $)[8]	Remarks/Context
1947/48	$53.5	first year start-up; civil war
1948/49	92.7	still full civil war
1949/50	131.1	civil war ends
1950/51	148.2	peak development phase
1951/52	86.5	stabilization program begins
1952/53	51.3	full stabilization program
1953/54	45.8	phase-out; the end of major aid

Source: See endnotes.

THE DEVELOPMENT PROGRAM

From a running start—indeed, the first year's efforts could very properly be described as an emergency program—the AMAG/ECA development and reconstruction effort grew very rapidly. Expenditures climbed by seventy per-

8. All dollar figures here and elsewhere in this paper are in actual dollars of the time. For an approximation of current (1997) values, multiply by seven.

cent in the second year; then an additional forty percent came on top of that second-year base. These were very large orders-of-magnitude changes, and the peak was not reached until the fiscal year 1950/51 (the year after the Korean War had broken out). Thereafter the program tapered off, as the Stabilization Program assumed priority (starting in the winter of 1951/52) and the investment mix began to favor, first, forced-draft, rapid progress on the national electric power program and, second, the completion of existing programs in other fields (industry, agriculture, transportation) rather than the inauguration of new projects. The BBC's correspondent in Greece, Kenneth Matthews, in his book *Memories of a Mountain War*, conveys a flavor of the American-financed reconstruction and development program as it developed in that first (emergency) year:

> American firms of contractors were out on the road, laying down a magic carpet to replace the gashed and pitted surface on which cars had broken their backs and motorists their hearts for long enough; and it was a revelation to see the American overseers at work. In weather which alternated blinding rain with meridian heat, they were up front with the labor gangs, encouraging, demonstrating; and the force of their example, the novelty and brute capability of the tools they used were having an extraordinary effect on the Greek laborers. They were refusing rest days...The new road was leaping forward a mile a day....[9]

> The Gorgopotamos. That much demolished viaduct, with its associated bridges, cuttings and tunnels had once more been reduced to ruins by the Germans on their retreat, and nothing had seemed more certain than that so dizzy a structure, so teasing a guerilla target, would not be raised again for the duration of the civil war. But the Americans thought otherwise. They had come to restore communications, hadn't they, to put Greece literally as well as figuratively back on the rails, and Jesus! They were not to be deterred by a few hoodlums!"

As the Development Program gathered speed, it also embraced a greater *breadth* and *balance*. In part this was a function of the increased security from the terror of civil war that was made possible, in the second and third quarters of the year 1949, by the advances of the Greek National Army as it recovered territory previously liable to guerilla raids (or even guerrilla occupation). To be sure, a heavy portion of the seven-year aggregate investment expenditure—$71.0 million out of the $127.4 million deployed to the social sector of hous-

9. AMAG's early emphasis on Transportation and Communication facilities (50% of the first year total of development expenditures while other major elements in 1947/48 were: agriculture 28%; industry 4%; housing/health/education 18%) is routinely ascribed to the priority of military exigencies and the Civil War and rather casually dismissed as having only marginal legitimacy in a "development agenda." It should be noted, however, that the United Nations' Food and Agriculture Organization, in its March, 1947, *Report of the FAO Mission to Greece* had emphatically declared (p. 7) that: "Restoration of the transportation system of Greece is perhaps the single most essential need to enable her economic life again to function normally." So strongly did these *agriculturists* feel, that they went so far as to recommend a kind of corvee: "A national emergency should be declared with respect to roads and a half-day personal service imposed each week on all male citizens over fifteen years of age."

ing/health/education—had to be devoted to the re-settlement of the 670,000 villagers who had been displaced during the civil war. They had to be equipped with mules and tools and seed and building materials upon return to their (more often than not) wrecked, even razed, former homes. But with increasing pace, the Development Program reached out to other sectors (electric power, mining, even tourism) whose reconstruction or expansion had been denied by the simple fact of their location-up country during the civil war. Industry and manufacturing, being mostly located in the cities of Athens, Thessalonike and Volos were not so constrained[10] and showed a rapid growth in investments under the Truman/Marshall program, doubling and tripling from year to year before phasing out during the last two years (1952/53 and 1953/54). Table III sets forth the seven- year aggregates by sector:

TABLE III

GREECE

Investment and Development Expenditures
Undertaken by the Seven-Year Aggregates (1947/48-1953/54)

Sector	Expenditure (in millions of $)
Industry and Manufacturing	$41.7
Tourism	5.3
Mining	22.2
Electric Power	99.6
Housing/Health/Education	127.4
Transportation and Communication	174.5
Food and Agriculture	138.4
Total:	$609.1

Source: See endnotes.

Among the major elements of this investment and development program were:

- the creation, for the first time in Greek history, of a national electric power system, a grid designed by American engineers and modeled on the TVA, with a quasi-independent, public corporate entity interlinking new hydroelectric generating stations at Ladhon and Agra and Louros with Athens Piraeus Electric Company (APECO) in Athens and a new thermal generating station based on the mining of lignite at Aliveri;

10. An exception (because of the availability of water power) was the textile industry of Naoussa in Macedonia—which had been raided and wrecked, by the guerrillas.

- the expansion and modernizing of Greece's traditional industries (cement, textiles, fertilizers) while promoting new ones: copper and aluminum fabrication, appliances, truck and bus bodies, diesel engines, farm equipment and tools, pharmaceuticals and paints;

- the re-opening and re-equipping of the chromite, bauxite and pyrite mines;

- the clearing and re-equipping of the nation's ports and harbors, and the Corinth Canal;

- the re-equipping of the fishing fleet and agricultural processing and storage plants;

- development of village potable water supplies, completing the anti-malaria program;

- modernization of hospitals and clinics;

- the re-building and improving of both highway and railway networks from Kalamata in the south to Alexandroupolis in the north;

- the building and repair of museums, archeological sites and hotels for the dream of future tourism, which still lay on the horizon.

FOOD AND AGRICULTURE

The most extensive program of them all was agriculture. Brice Mace, director of the American Mission's Food and Agriculture Division, reflected both Greek and U.S. priorities when he set forth this appraisal of agricultural strategies in Greece:

> War and occupation had cut off food imports on which Greece had come to rely. As thousands—somewhere between 400 and 500 thousand—died of starvation during the war, the consciousness of their agricultural inadequacy was seared into the souls of the Greeks, and they realized that balance of trade was no mere economist's catch-phrase—but instead meant life or death for the nation.

The American program of assistance to Greek agriculture brought to bear on Greek needs, talents and resources American agricultural extension agents from Kentucky and agricultural conservation service specialists from the U.S. Department of Agriculture and land reclamation experts from California—and more. Projects were set in train:

- to create and train a Greek force roughly equivalent to America's county agents—to bring new knowledge to the Greek village, to instruct in the use of fertilizers and pesticides, contour ploughing, seed selection and animal husbandry;

- to undertake large-scale land reclamation works—draining swamps, controlling seasonal flooding, preparing irrigation systems, reclaiming alkaline land;

- to supply the government's mechanical cultivation service and its well-drilling service with heavy equipment—tractors, draglines, rotary drills, bulldozers and trucks;

- to construct farm-to-market roads and link, for the first time in modern Greek history, formerly isolated villages to trunk and provincial highway systems and to market towns.

The result of these programs was an upsurge in agricultural production, and even more significantly, in productivity as shown in the following table:

TABLE IV

GREECE

Agricultural Production and Productivity: Year 1953 vs. Pre-war (1938/39)

Crop	Production	Yield Per Hectare
Wheat	+90%	+50%
Corn	+20%	+30%
Cotton	+100%	+60%
Potatoes	+200%	+65%

Source: See endnotes.

AND A MAN CALLED "PAPPOU" (GRANDFATHER)

Wheat, the staff of life in Greece, had been imported during the pre-war years at the rate of approximately 400,000 tons per year. By the fiscal year 1953/54, wheat imports had dropped to 75,000 tons. The most dramatic story, however, is that of rice—and of a man by the name of Walter Packard.

Walter "Pappy" Packard came to Greece in 1948 out of retirement and many years of service with the State of California land reclamation and irrigation agencies. He and his colleagues from the Ministry of Agriculture went to work sampling the soils of the country's alkaline river basins and deltas—areas of the country which had been barren literally since the time of Alexander the Great. And in the very poor village of Anthili, a hundred miles north from Athens, he persuaded the village elders to work with him, in an experiment: if villagers would contribute the manual labor, the American Mission would bring in the mechanical equipment, the bulldozers, pumps, draglines and pipe to convert the salt flats to rice paddies. The fresh water lying in the paddies, he explained, would leach the salts down and out and into the sea; five years hence, the villagers would be able to grow a variety of crops on the rejuvenated soil, but meanwhile they would enjoy a cash crop: rice. Their grandfathers' grandfathers had never seen anything grow on this land (but the Amerikanakia were rich and crazy, everyone knew that; so why not play along?).

The experiment worked! And the next year the project was expanded. Then it spread to other villages whose flatlands were alkaline. Pre-war Greece had imported an average of 25,000 tons of rice per year, but by 1953 Greece was not only meeting all of its consumption requirements from domestic production, it was, in addition, exporting 17,000 tons. The village of Anthili, where it all started, became rich. And in 1954 they erected a statue of Walter Packard in their village square. And if, today, one were to visit Anthili (it is not far from Thermopylae) one would see that statue of "Pappy" in characteristic bow-tie and rimless glasses, looking out toward the rice fields.

Less dramatic, perhaps, but even more revolutionary in its impact was the Mission's program for farm-to-market roads—for these truly transformed the face of Greece. Six thousand kilometers of these new roads, opening up what had been isolated communities, made possible the expansion of agriculture and its *transformation* from timeless patterns of subsistence farming—the traditional zero-sum society—to a flourishing trading basis. Pre-war, there had been a total of only 1,800 kilometers of these tertiary roads. By 1954, that figure had reached 7,600 kilometers while at the same time the so-called provincial road network, a step down from the major trunk arteries, was almost doubled. The last stage of this Marshall Plan program was the importation with U.S. funds of 48 mechanical graders and their allocation, one to each of the 48 *nomoi* (provincial administrative departments), for the maintenance of the new farm-to-market road system by local government services.

TURNING POINT

By the early nineteen-fifties, it had become clear that the dislocation of both World War II and the Civil War had been more than fully overcome. Indeed, it was evident that Greece was already operating at a national economic level which was well above pre-war standards (see Table V):

TABLE V

GREECE

Indices of National Consumption/Economic Activity: Year 1952 vs. pre-war (1938/39)

Sector	Percentage change
Consumption of wearing apparel	+37%
Energy consumption	+45%
Transportation	+107%
Metal working	+30%
Construction activity	+46%

Source: See endnotes.

Despite these significant advances, the Greek economy remained plagued by some very serious problems: the national budget was still badly out of balance; expansion of bank credit was far in excess of annual increases in national economic production; the artificial exchange rate was, in effect, penalizing exports while subsidizing imports; the black market for the dollar showed a premium of more than fifty percent over the official rate. And, most unsettling of all, the feverish demand for gold continued as if neither the civil war nor the reconstruction of the economy had become settled issues. The rush to convert drachmas to British gold sovereigns not only suggested a dangerous element of suppressed inflation, it was also a sign that the national currency was, in effect, being repudiated.

In the winter of 1951/52, then, the Truman Doctrine/Marshall Plan program in Greece turned to its final chapter—*economic stabilization* with its ultimate goal of *currency reform*. Given the pacification of the Civil War, the completion of the Reconstruction Program and the palpable success of the Economic Development Program, it was time to say that the *whole be judged as greater than the sum of its parts*, and to act in support of a national currency in which all of the Greek people could place their faith and confidence, rather than in this good investment project or that good development program. It was the same reformist spirit that had driven so much of the Mission's activity. But this time it was directed at a new and different, indeed a larger, target.

GOLD

Gold had been a festering problem throughout the post-war period, and in late 1951 and early 1952 the fever became dangerous. The gold sovereign had been the economic barometer in Greece; it was also a potentially deadly disease. And it had to be cured.

The disease had its origins during World War II. The British, working with the anti-Nazi resistance groups in the mountains, flew in supplies of arms, ammunition, military gear, medicine and food. They also flew in gold sovereigns.

The Greek mountains had never in their history been self-sufficient. Traditionally they had exported to the plains of Greece and the Balkans their meager accumulation of meat, or cheese, or hides, or wool—or human skills—and had exchanged these for food supplies (which were surplus to the more productive, arable plains). In the chaotic conditions of the occupation, however, even this hard-scrabble type of primitive exchange or barter (or land-based piracy) had broken down. Enter: gold.

The British with their gold sovereigns were able to secure for the guerrillas both supplies and a food allowance for their families who had remained in their villages. Originally one gold sovereign per month per guerrilla, the stipend was subsequently paid, in bulk in the case of ELAS, directly to the commanding officers. Two million gold sovereigns entered Greece this way, adding hugely to the approximately two million sovereigns which had been secreted away in mattresses and lock boxes over the previous one hundred years of modern Greek history.[11] The Nazis brought in another one million sovereigns to finance some of their operations.

And in the roaring inflation of the early post-war years, both illegal private imports and official Central Bank imports added another 2.5 million sovereigns to the pool. When the United States came to Greece in 1947, there were 7.5 million sovereigns, hoarded and circulating, in the country. By the end of 1951, there were 12.5 million. And the problem was getting worse, not better (see Table VI).

TABLE VI

GREECE

Gold Sovereigns Estimated National Stock

Period/Source	in thousands
Pre-war, approx.	2,000
WWII-British, approx.	+2,000
WWII-Germans, approx.	+1,000
1944/45-Bank of Greece	+150
1946 (fr.12 Feb.) Bank of Greece	+2,009
1947- Bank of Greece, net sales	+399
1948- Bank of Greece, net sales	+918
1949- Bank of Greece, net sales	+490
1950- Bank of Greece, net sales	+1832
1951- Bank of Greece, net sales	+1466
cumulative	12,264
MEMO: 1952: <u>Jan. and Feb. only</u>	+932

Source: See endnotes.

So nervous, so fearful of Slavic Bolshevism, so tinged by memories of runaway, hyper-inflation[12] was the entire Greek nation that the only real store of

11. Including of course those used in the annual Vasilopita (New Year's cake) and for the ritual decoration of Sarakatsani wedding costumes.
12. Few Greek citizens could forget the worthless banknotes that littered the sidewalks of Athens during the Occupation—or the so-called Svolos "Reform" of November, 1944 (upon the return of the Government-in Exile) when 50 *billion* drachmas were to be exchanged for *one* new drachmas, whose value in foreign exchange was then pegged at 150 dr. = $1. Nor could they forget that the ratio of 150:1 itself simply melted away and that by the time of the Truman Doctrine (June, 1947) the exchange rate had become 8,300:$1. Even that parity was eroded, if less severely, and by mid/late 1951 was effectively at about 20,000 to $1.

value had become the British gold sovereign. With a gold content (then) of just a fraction over $8 each, the sovereign was handy, recognizable and faithful, whereas a threatening world, a guerrilla war and a capricious government were "none-of-the-above."

The daily quotations for the sovereign became the barometer by which goods were priced—for example: olive oil or cotton. Dowries were established in sovereigns. Savings were held in sovereigns. An insurance policy was a cache of sovereigns. Major transactions, such as the purchase and sale of real estate, were of course negotiated in sovereigns. The gold sovereign was also a registry for domestic political and international events; it was not limited to just economic functions. When the Truman Doctrine was announced, the price of the sovereign fell. When Berlin was placed under Soviet blockade, it rose. When the Communist party in Italy was defeated in the important elections of the Spring of 1948, the sovereign price fell. When guerrilla attacks within Greece increased, so did the gold price. The outbreak of the Korean War forced the price up, as did the Chinese crossing of the Yalu River later that year (1950).

During the Great Depression and during World War II the world's stock of sovereigns had gravitated by and large to the United States. Illegal within the USA, they had to be exchanged officially, and so in the postwar years the principal inventory of British gold sovereigns was in the Federal Reserve Bank of New York. And it was from the Fed that the Truman/Marshall aid mission had to arrange for the Bank of Greece to buy these coins and to ship them by air to Athens.

We had to do so because we were stuck. We were stuck with the policy (which had been established in 1946) whereby the Greek Central Bank would meet all demand for gold at a specified ceiling price, a ceiling price established to give some credibility to the notion that the national currency, the drachmas, had a certain backing or validity. It was, in other words, a gold exchange standard. The sovereign was the safety valve for an overheated economy in a nervous corner of the Balkans.

In each year of the American major presence in Greece, from 1947 through 1952, we had authorized the exportation of gold sovereigns from New York and their importation and sale by the Bank of Greece, 5 million of them in all. We swallowed hard and rationalized the action as a kind of insurance premium: expensive, indeed unconscionably wasteful, but worth it by comparison with the feared alternative.

If a run on the Central Bank's gold stock were to start, the Cabinet would panic and we, the Americans, were fearful of a financial collapse. The Greek public had concluded that the only reason to hold the drachmas, even if only temporarily, was the implicit promise in the Greek/U.S. compact to keep open the gold window—to exchange paper drachmas for gold upon demand

and at an open market price which had an established ceiling, or maximum, price. Had that gold window closed; had the Bank of Greece been unable to meet the demand for sovereigns; had they run dry,[13] we fully expected that by nightfall all tangible goods throughout the country would disappear from sight and there would not be a store in all of Greece that would be selling its merchandise for drachmas. The price of the sovereign would go through the roof, and with it the price of everything else, including those basics for the least well off: olive oil, wheat flour and dried salted codfish. The price/wage spiral would then go totally out of control. Loans, frequently (and illegally) underpinned by a gold clause, would be called, driving the sovereign price still higher. Worst of all, we reasoned, that timid and tentative confidence in the future, that fragile sense that there were better days to come—which we had worked so hard to nurture—would be utterly shattered and, with it, all our hopes and plans for reconstruction and development, the cornerstone of our presence in Greece.

And so we paid the price, disgusted and hating ourselves for so doing. We allowed scarce and precious foreign exchange balances to be frittered away in the importation of sterile gold.

In 1945 and 1946, Greece was sliding into civil war, the government was playing a game of musical chairs, the establishment in Athens was dancing on the deck of a sinking ship—while the printing press was churning out banknotes and the Bank of Greece was ginning up additional credits for the merchants and industrialists and running down its previously husbanded foreign exchange reserves. Small wonder, then, that the public hastened to get out of flimsy, Romaic paper money into solid, international gold. Two million sovereigns were sold to Greek citizens in the year 1946.[14]

But by 1950/51 the Civil War was over and the Reconstruction Program had transformed the wreckage of WWII (and that of the Civil War) into a pro-

13. These gold crises were very scary, for they had an unpredictable quality to their intensity and duration, and the supply line was a long one. Clearing the exportation of sovereigns from New York, chartering a plane to carry them to Athens, getting that plane to Athens on time: these were time-consuming elements in a long chain of steps, any one of which could—and did—sometimes fail (see the telegram, Figure 2, for a particularly hair-raising example). Theatrical measures were, on occasion, required. The author recalls one gold panic (I tend to think that it was December, 1950) when the re-supply aircraft was down in Shannon with motor trouble. The gold window would have to close by mid-morning the next day unless something could be done. During frantic mid-afternoon meetings, involving the prime minister, the ambassador, and the key economic ministers, it was arranged that there be staged a fight between a Central Bank officer and the leader of the Bank of Greece employees union. That would cause the union leader to call a strike, and the bank would be closed—allowing enough time for the re-fitted aircraft to reach Athens with the sovereign re-supply. Fortuitously, someone discovered that the palace was to be visited by a royal cousin from England and so, on that specious account, a Bank Holiday was declared instead!
14. In this respect, the KKE was considered to be the richest, and best-endowed in gold sovereigns of any of the political parties in Greece.

FIGURE 2

By *N.W.D.* NARA Date *...*

EM~~BASSY FILES~~

TELEGRAM SENT

SECRET

To: SecState

Date: January 3, 1952

No.: 3014

Code: ~~SECRET~~ - Security Information

Charged to:

PRIORITY

Gold sales 2 January, 69 thousand; 3 January 72 thousand.

On hand 16 thousand with which to open tomorrow.

Charter plane due to arrive tomorrow morning.

Market opens at 10:30 a.m.

PEURIFOY

HRT.

HRTurkel/aca

SOURCE : See End-notes

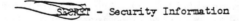
~~SECRET~~ - Security Information

~~SECRET~~

Source: See endnotes.

ductive society. The Korean War came as a political shock to the system, it is true. And with it came a run on the Central Bank's gold stock, but happily one that did not last overly long. It was summer. The Chinese crossing of the Yalu River, however, came near to the moment of peak, seasonal liquidity in Greece as the country approached Christmas and the New Year when, by tradition, the "thirteenth month's salary" was paid to employees. This run was serious. Paper money was really burning a hole in the nation's pockets. Sales of gold sovereigns in November and December 1950, plus January and February 1951, came to a four-month total of 2,237,643—worse than the whole of the calamitous year 1946.

And then there arrived the "September surprise," which continued into October 1951. The Greek drachmas was being repudiated by its owners, the Greek people. There is no other term for it.

Over the years, those living on the edge of the volcano called "gold sales" had become accustomed to, if never really inured to, a certain seasonality. It had become conventional wisdom that the demand for sovereigns went more or less hand-in-hand with the Christmas bonus, and one became used to seeing these heavy gold runs compensated for, at least partially, by Bank of Greece re-purchases in the open market during other, less liquid months of the year.

But in the autumn of 1951 this not very profound theorizing was shattered by some very rude facts. In September a run on the gold window started, and by month-end the net sales had reached 250,720 (on one day, September 21st, sales totaled 25,310 sovereigns!). There was no easing during October, when another 286,405 sovereigns were sold.[15]

THE BATTLE FOR CURRENCY STABILIZATION

This was the watershed. To maintain adequate stocks of gold sovereigns in the face of the September/October "surprise," Washington had to be asked for its assent to the gold export. And in a telegram at the end of October 1951,

---

15. This "contra-seasonal" gold rush was the result, in large measure of some naiveté on the part of the Americans whose good intentions were quickly bent by the Greek Cabinet for its own purposes—yet another example of the irony in the charge that the Americans "controlled" all serious issues in Greece. In early 1951, the Mission had developed a poorly thought out scheme to guarantee a basic ration of foodstuffs—in hopes of putting a lid on the price run-up generated by the Korean War and providing a measure of social equity. The scheme depended on a network of strategically located government-owned stocks of food products, some imported, others locally produced. The word "stabilization" is liberally associated with this new effort, and that fact has deceived some researchers who have used January/February, 1951, as the true inauguration date of the Stabilization Program—which it assuredly was not. The government quickly seized the opportunity afforded by this new program, buying peasant votes with puffed-up concentration prices, and thereby pumping vast quantities of drachmas through the so-called Supply Account and into the hands of the public—who equally promptly rushed their hot drachmas to the gold window, in September.

the Marshall Plan HQ gave its agreement—but conditioned it, in exception-
ally strong language, to the inauguration of a program of stabilization. *Greece's
Currency Stabilization Program began on 29 October 1951.*[16]

In that message, the HQ in Washington stated very bluntly that its
approval for the export of gold was to be "irrevocably the last (repeat last)
time gold will be sold"[17] and henceforth the "highest priority" was to be given
to the "containment of inflation." The cable noted that the growth in Greek
national production "had not been attended by a comparable decline in
requirements for external resources" and suggested that there was "increasing evidence of hoarding," which was "indefensible under the letter and spirit of the Mutual Security Act."[18] Lest there be any waffling, Washington drilled
home the message two weeks later—and this was the passage which had the
most profound effect upon the American Mission in Athens: "...Regardless of
intrinsic merits of any given program, it must be discarded, or at least shelved,
as long as its implementation has a net inflationary effect." The whole was
indeed to be considered as greater than the sum of its parts.

16. The date is significant. The problem for the researcher in going through American archival
   materials is the need to distinguish between what is no more than pious rhetoric on the one
   hand, and on the other, real policy that is put into practice. The truth is that the word "stabilization"—code for monetary and fiscal restraint in the face of inflationary pressures—
   appears in literally hundreds of messages flying back and forth between Athens and Washington. And this had been true in every year since the first days of AMAG, going all the way
   back to mid-1947. Yet in practice, this "policy" was violated left and right. It was not a case of
   outright insubordination. It is just that the word is too squishy. It left room for judgment
   and "best efforts" and these soft spots were too easily overwhelmed by the enthusiasm generated by and for new development projects. If one looks at the historical record—actual
   statistics for bank credit outstanding, the national budget, note issue, gold sales, the import
   surplus and counterpart releases—in no way can it be said that there had been in force a
   policy of "stabilization," at least until the winter of 1951/52.
17. In fact even Washington had the good sense to eat its own words two months later, for the
   consequences of sticking to that position before the Stabilization Program had really taken
   hold would have been catastrophic. In late December, 1951, a new gold rush broke out and
   this one was really a terror. Someone had leaked to the newspapers a closely held and
   exceedingly sensitive study prepared by an economist attached to the staff of Professor
   Zolotas, who was then a "technical expert" at the Currency Committee, in which a devaluation from 15,000 dr./$1.00 to 25,000 was recommended. The market went quite mad. On
   one day sales hit the unheard of peak of more than eighty thousand sovereigns, and the total
   for the period of one week from December 31 through January 7 was 433,394. See Figure 2
   on the perils of re-supply during the extended panic.
18. Note the title of the enabling legislation. The Marshall Plan had been promoted on the
   basis of a time-limited mandate; it was to expire in four years. But the work was not com-
   pleted and fashions on Capitol Hill had changed; therefore a new vocabulary was required.
   And in the alphabet soup so popular in Washington, the ECA (Economic Cooperation
   Administration) became MSA (Mutual Security Agency)—and eighteen months later FOA
   (the Foreign Operations Administration) and two years after that ICA (the International
   Cooperation Administration). The notion that the switch from ECA to MSA on December
   31st, 1951 meant the militarization of the aid program for Greece is without basis and,
   indeed, would strike anyone actually associated with the project (be he Greek or American)
   as absurd.

This passage struck, and with painful force, more at the operating divisions within the Mission itself than at the Greek citizenry. Each of the division heads (agriculture, mining, industry, transportation, public health, labor, etc.)—by and large good, progressive, active New Dealers, each with a sense of commitment to "his" program to "transform Greece"—rose up in righteous indignation. The Mission Chief himself came very close to resigning, and no one associated with this American adventure in and for Greece will ever forget his famous "firechief" cable of 11 March 1952 when, after battling so long and so hard, he finally caved in, saying: "Having received his directives, this Mission Chief has donned his firechief's hat, has sharpened his hatchet, and is now set to tear down as much of the house of Greece (which American aid has helped to erect) as is necessary to stamp out the fire-devil of inflation."[19]

These were not just bureaucratic skirmishings. The battle emerged from heartfelt beliefs. The Mission division heads felt very strongly that what they were doing for Greece—and that meant, specifically, *their* reconstruction and development and investment projects and programs for Greece—were being subverted by Washington bean counters who knew nothing of Greece itself, still less of Greece's "real" needs and the "better future" which these projects would bring "to the Greek people" (see footnote 19). It became very emotional. And in their dogged, long, and fierce fight—the issue was not resolved until May 1952, and it will be recalled that it all started at the end of October 1951—these American proconsuls of Greek agriculture, industry and mining, etc. found allies in both the Embassy and the State Department.[20]

The Embassy did not understand the Stabilization Program and its associated currency reform proposals; in a very real sense they were terrified by it, and their colleagues in State were equally uncomprehending. Together they did everything possible to scuttle the program. The ambassador himself even maneuvered to have the officers on the Greek Desk at the Marshall Plan HQ fired. The Stabilization Program prevailed.

19. It has been suggested that the members of the American Mission possessed only the perspective of the technician, the engineer, and that they were insensitive to wider social policy concerns and the welfare of the Greek people. Nothing could be further from the truth, as the record of the Mission/HQ conflict in the winter of 1951/52 demonstrates, and as is so poignantly illustrated by this passionate cable. Its author, Roger Lapham, millionaire retired principal of a West Coast steamship line and quondam Mayor of San Francisco, possessed no careerist, bureaucratic stake in the outcome of this battle; this was social commitment!

20. They even used back pressure on the Greek ministries themselves, their colleagues and partners in the money-spending process of development projects and programs. Minister of Coordination George Kartalis was forced to complain on at least one occasion that, while he and the American Mission's policy level were cooperating on the Stabilization Program, the Mission's division heads were giving worse than a mixed signal; they were actually trying to undermine the stabilization effort, promoting ministerial pressure on him through his fellow cabinet officers.

In a grant aid program such as this one, there is a gift of foreign exchange—but to the importer there appears to be no gift at all: he must put up the local currency to buy the dollars, or francs, or lira.[21] Thus the Central Bank accumulates local currency *counterpart* for that foreign aid. And the American government typically takes title jointly to this counterpart fund and may agree to disburse it for agreed investment or other purposes. The leverage of the new (and real) Stabilization Program lay precisely in this formulation.

Washington refused to release counterpart funds for further development expenditures beyond carefully controlled limits. A deflationary policy was thereby put in place, as importers, making their drachmas deposits to purchase foreign exchange, were in effect withdrawing currency from circulation. And the Marshall Plan HQ demanded that before counterpart be released, other inflationary phenomena be fully taken into account.

Washington warned that "counterpart accumulations should be sterilized against net increases in bank advances and the budget deficit:" expansion of bank credit to the economy and the use of the printing press to cover budget expenditures were to be offset by the withholding of counterpart releases for investment projects.

In a sense, none of this was new. Such exhortations (see footnote 16) had been a regular part of the HQ/Mission dialogue. In another and very real sense, however, it was indeed all new.

Messages of a similar character—inveighing against the pauperization of those least able to defend themselves against inflation; messages exhorting the Mission to put a stop to a gold hemorrhage which could only benefit the black marketers; messages seeking Mission action to get the Greek government to face up to its fiscal and monetary responsibilities—the filing cabinets were full of these cables, going back to the earliest days of the Mission.

Wherein lies the difference?

THE STABILIZATION PROGRAM

The difference was the invention of the Greek Desk in the Marshall Plan HQ. It was the so-called *Inflationary/Deflationary Balance Sheet*. And there is scarcely anything more important, in the history of the modern Greek economy, than this instrument. It was programmatic, in the sense that it looked forward, and it was a statistical record, in the sense that it could record accurately what had actually happened by comparison with the goals established. Above

---

21. In an effort to encourage the European economies and Greece's integration into Europe, 42% of America's Marshall Plan aid was given in the form of grants for Greece to buy in Europe. It had been, in fact, the author's job (heading the Mission's import office) to steer Greek procurement away from America and to Europe. The notion that the American aid program to Greece left Greece "heavily dependent upon American products" is pure fiction.

all, it was a quantitative, rather than simply pious, expression of intent. In it was summed up, on a monthly, quarterly, semi-annual and annual basis, the expected or allowable changes in key factors affecting Greek money supply.

- Imports: deflationary—in effect taking money out in circulation.

- Exports: inflationary—exporters cashing in their foreign exchange earnings and thereby injecting drachmas into circulation.

- Government tax collection: deflationary—money withdrawn from circulation.

- Government disbursements: inflationary—money pumped into the economy.

- Bank credit: expansion (inflationary) or contraction (deflationary).

- Gold sovereign sales: deflationary (in that they withdrew drachmas from circulation) but a dangerous double-edged sword.

It was a powerful tool, brilliant in its simplicity and discipline. Counterpart releases, or their opposite, counterpart sterilization, constituted the residual, the bottom line, in the equation. Thus, the Mission's Investment and Development Program became the swing variable: if the Government collected more income taxes, and they did,[22] while holding the line in budget expenditures, then there might be room for a greater volume of developmental investment—which every Cabinet minister wanted. If, on the other hand, bank credit was allowed to expand beyond the target set, then the release of counterpart for investment projects might have to be cut back—with the inevitable dislocation which the Cabinet ministers hated. *The sale to the public of gold sovereigns was no longer to be a principal method of counteracting the inflationary expansion of the money supply.* And in that sense the dynamics of the entire postwar Greek economy (1945 to 1952) were forever changed—from

22. The American Mission, from its earliest days, had been properly horrified at the extent to which the Greek government allowed its merchants, industrialists and black marketers to escape paying a decent, proportionate share of the tax burden—while at the same time the government squeezed its poorest citizens through a system of indirect sales taxes on items of essential current consumption. A constant in the Mission/Government dialogue over the years which span the American proconsulship was the AMAG/ECA/MSA/FOA (see footnote 18) program to make the progressive income tax a serious element of fiscal and social policy (refer also to Mr. Porter's November, 1950 statement quoted earlier). U.S. Treasury specialists were brought to Greece for this express purpose. Slow but steady progress had brought income taxes up to 21% of total tax revenues by 1950/51—and then, under the stimulus of the Stabilization Program's implicit system of rewards and penalties, that figure was pushed up to 25-26-27% during the next three years. And there it remained for the next thirty-five years, Papandreou rhetoric (pere et fils) to the contrary not withstanding.

late February 1952 there were no more sales of gold by the Bank of Greece.[23] It was the final, reformist act of a reformist American Mission.

The consequences of the Stabilization Program were quick to appear, dramatic in their character and lasting in their impact: the December 1951/January 1952 gold sovereign panic came to an end in February and reversed itself with such speed that the public, by March, 1952 was selling sovereigns back to the Bank of Greece at a price of 180,000 drachmas per unit, sovereigns which they had purchased less than two months earlier at the maximum ceiling price of 226,500: The major results were these:

- merchants and manufacturers, denied the luxury of ever-expanding lines of credit, actually had to sell their goods to maintain operating cash flow;

- prices, as a consequence, fell;

- so did the volume of imports, as goods previously hoarded in anticipation of inflation and price increases were sold;

- export receipts and the so-called "invisibles" (e.g. emigrant remittances) began to climb, a telling measure of the slowing of capital flight via black market channels;

- for the first time since 1940 and the beginning of World War II, the public showed that it was now willing to part with that which had been its constant companion during twelve long bitter years: the expectation of inflation;

- finally, in April 1953, the drachma was formally devalued, an action which this time (one is tempted to say, for the first time since WWII) was received by the public as credible. It had been well prepared for this action during the year and a half of rigorous stabilization.

BENCHMARKS IN THE STABILIZATION PROGRAM

CREDIT   Whereas total bank credit to all sectors of the economy (industry, agriculture, commerce) had expanded by a

---

23. Almost. But not quite. Most of the 12-13 million sovereigns did indeed flow back into the Bank of Greece during the '50s and '60s (as the Greek people found better, more profitable things to do with their money than to hold non-interest-bearing gold). But in the particularly fevered atmosphere of political maneuvering that characterized the latter part of 1965, Andreas Papandreou managed to use intemperate language of such inflationary potential that the Greek public (still shell-shocked by the prior history of hyper-inflation, still "blowing on their yogurt" [a Greek proverb: "Whoever is burned by soup will blow on yogurt." Ed.]) ran with their drachmas to the Bank of Greece's "gold window." There was a brief but heavy gold rush. To Professor Zolotas goes the credit of finally driving a stake through the heart of this vampire: after the panic subsided, he allowed the public to sell back to the Bank of Greece its sovereigns with no questions asked—but, on the other hand, if it was desired to purchase sovereigns from the Central Bank, then names and addresses had to be surrendered along with the drachmas. That did it. Finito la musica!

shocking 63% in the year 1949, an unacceptable 34% in 1950 and an excessive 22% in 1951, the Stabilization Program actually engineered a delicate contraction of 4% during 1952.

COUNTERPART

Counterpart withdrawals, which had been 2,100 billion drachmas in 1950, fell to 1,000 billion dr. in 1951; and in 1952, were throttled back to 400 billion drachmas.

AGRICULTURE

Agriculture production, meanwhile, was moving steadily upwards (refer to Table IV); twenty of the thirty principal products surveyed by the Ministry of Agriculture showed solid to strong increases.

INDUSTRY

The effects of the Stabilization Program on industry and manufacturing were a good deal less than one might have surmised from the high decibel complaints[24] generated within the Association of Industrialists and by its political allies. The overextended textile industry had massive, speculative, hoarded inventories to work off, and the Stabilization Program was eventually to help get this sector back to a healthier equilibrium—but not without a short, sharp decline in production, perhaps as much as 16%. But overall, the General Manufacturing Index declined by no more than one to one-and-a-half percent, and out of the twelve subsectors of that index, seven showed either no declines at all or, actually, quite sharp increases.

PRICES

The Athens/Piraeus Wholesale Price Index in January, 1952 (the moment of that particularly severe gold sovereign panic—refer to Figure 2, the re-supply cable) stood at 403.5 (the base year of 1938 on this index=1). By December, 1952, it had declined 3% to 391.6.

The "need," so-called, for American aid then simply fell away as agricultural and industrial and mining production rose, as hoarding ceased and capital flight not only slowed down but substantially reversed itself. An average of slightly over a quarter of a billion dollars a year in U.S. grant aid during the years since 1947 then dropped, in successive years to:

24. "Dhen exei lefta. Dhen exei pistoseis. Dhen exei dynami stin agora." Then, with gestures, "tha klisoume to ergostaseio—par ta klitheia! Na!" ("There is no money. There is no credit. There is no strength in the market." "We will close the factory—take the keys! Here!")

TABLE VII

GREECE

Marshall Plan Assistance—Aid Allotments

Fiscal years	Millions of $
1948/49	271.8
1949/50	282.4
1950/51	281.9
1951/52	179.0
1952/53	80.0
1953/54	21.0

Source: See endnotes.

In 1953—right in the middle of these dramatic changes—Bickham Sweet-Escott, an old Special Operations Executive (SOE) type who knew more than a little about Greece, was composing a very good little book entitled *Greece—A Political and Economic Survey, 1939-1953*, London, 1954. On page 162 he wrote:

> Nobody can seriously suppose that if American aid were to be withdrawn now, Greece could avoid a total economic collapse.

The passage is cited not to suggest that he was wrong (which he was) but to underline the rapidity and breadth and scale of the turnaround which stabilization had achieved for Greece. It surprised even the experts.[25] And so powerful were the effects of the Stabilization Program that its legacy endured for more than a dozen years thereafter. It was almost as if its principles had been tattooed on the foreheads of these who would go on to become the key Greek economic players of the fifties and sixties.[26]

And *on its own*, Greece went on to enjoy, over the next fifteen years, almost the highest rate of real per capita economic growth of any country in the OECD, save Germany and Japan. Historians and economists refer to this period as the Greek economic miracle and have documented the extraordinary, indeed revolutionary degree to which these national, aggregate economic

---

25. Sweet-Escott, a Briton, would have done well, as he was completing his MS., to keep in touch with the newspaper *To Vima's* Costa Hadjiargyris, to, whom no door in the American Mission was closed and who was, as a consequence, the best informed economic reporter in Athens. (But then, the Brits didn't like Costa). Hadjiargyris was quite well aware of the speed and direction of the change then taking place.
26. And there is little likelihood that they would agree with complaints that the Stabilization Program had trapped Greece into a multi-year, stagnating recession; or that productivity investments had been so postponed that the future outlook was one of no-growth. The basis in the actual record of events for such speculations is, to say the least, unclear.

gains were, in fact, translated into widely distributed and tangible benefits for previously neglected sectors of the population—the new, national wealth was not, as in the previous 120 years of modern Greek history, simply bottled up in the capital to be enjoyed by a small Athenian elite. The historian William Hardy McNeill in *The Metamorphosis of Greece since WWII* (The University of Chicago Press, 1978) said it best:

> The metamorphosis of human life that has been taking place is without historic parallel in Greece's past. It has affected the entire population within a single generation.

GEORGE KARTALIS

Ironically, the man who should be remembered today for his considerable role in Greece's turnaround, during the watershed Stabilization Program, is largely forgotten.

That man is, of course, George Kartalis, then minister of economic coordination, the most powerful ministry in the Center government which held office in 1951/52. Of a certainty he initially opposed, and opposed very strongly, the Stabilization Program. And he was not above making threatening noises to cut Greek defense expenditures as a form of bargaining against what he saw as the coming strictures of stabilization. (On the eve of Greece's admission to NATO, this device was bound to be a loser, which of course it was). Still he was obliged to fight back, for stabilization implied for him three things: first, it carried with it the suggestion of lower levels of American aid, and there was a pervasive, general public perception that the amount of aid signified America's love for Greece—and the principal economic minister of the day did not wish to be charged with the responsibility for having lost that love.[27]

---

27. Forty-five years after the fact, these notions appear absurd. Yet at the time, and for the political circles, they were very real. Almost the first act of Kartalis's successor, Markezinis—whose government, led by Papagos, had such a powerful electoral mandate that it could write its own ticket—was to make the pilgrimage to Washington to get more aid, that publicly understood symbol of love. Of course Athens' merchant/industrialist *kombina*, (establishment), the reformist American Mission's *bete noir*, knew better. They had understood from 1945, from the time of Varvaressos, that foreign aid—and the more the better—was a straight out substitute for income and excess profit taxes. (Who, after all, did indeed pay for the post-WWII Reconstruction? It was not the black marketeers). The newspapers, therefore, beat mercilessly on the *issue of aid qua* love, adding for good measure an additional mantra: that the aid was not really a geo-strategic or charitable gift but an inadequate repayment to Greece for the latter's noble sacrifices during WWII and thereafter, for being soldiers on the front line of the Cold War against barbaric Slavic Bolshevism. One is reminded of Mavrocordato's instructions to his commissioners who had been sent to London 125 years earlier to negotiate a loan with which to finance the War of Independence against the Ottomans: be pro-British and resolutely anti-Russian. Paul Porter, in the long 1950 document already cited, has written: "During most of the century and a quarter since their national independence from the Turks, they have balanced their national accounts by renting their strategic position in the Eastern Mediterranean."

Secondly, he was not happy about the prospect of having a smaller canvas on which to paint. That a New Deal conception of government and public works and infrastructure had been grafted onto a fundamentally etatist apparatus of governance had meant (in one sense) a great deal of pork barrel spread over a great deal of the country—a great deal of contracts and votes.

In addition to these factors, there was one more negative which quickly became apparent to Kartalis, who was a very clever man. It was not difficult for him to see what was coming in that portion of the Stabilization Program most intimately connected to the functioning of the private sector: monetary discipline. A credit squeeze would (and, in the event, did) produce the kind of political backlash that no minister would want to bring upon himself. (It is difficult to forget the screams, and crocodile tears, over the lack of credit (see footnote 24).

Still, Kartalis rose above that. He fought the good fight. But soon he could see that the entire apparatus of Washington was lined up in a solid phalanx against the perpetuation of the gold disease. He became the Center Government's almost sole spokesman for an economic policy prescription that was pure poison to the politician. He not only helped direct the program of currency stabilization, he became its advocate.[28]

The irony is that this man, virtually the first and only Greek economic minister since Varvaressos who showed both vision and determination, was about to be cut out, and by the very Americans whose new policy he had championed. Down the street from the Mission was the Embassy and there they were working to bring a conservative government to power with a strong majority in the Parliament. Ambassador Peurifoy had digested only too well the Mission's often expressed thought (see above, in the long statement by Paul Porter) that too frequent changes of government were inhibiting economic reconstruction and development.

Summing Up

In any event, and with Kartalis out of office, the Stabilization Program was capped by the currency devaluation of 9 April 1953, when the official

---

28. He was, of course, smart as hell. And he was also a fearful snob (more so than most Athenians, which is saying a good deal). Moreover, he did not, could not suffer fools gladly. I believe that, once brought into the logic of the Stabilization Program, once made a party to it as an intellectual construct, his own superior intellect positively embraced it. He admired the program for its intellectual rigor, for its quality as a seamless whole, and he quickly came to recognize that in Athens' political circles no one else really understood the program at all. (Mantzavinos, Pezmazoglou, Kyriazides, Zolotas—they knew of course, but they were technicians then and not yet players in the political world). Kartalis was not only a snob; he was an intellectual snob: he was now in almost exclusive possession of a tremendously powerful instrument which no one else in Parliament could understand. It became for him a kind of theoretician's *palouki* (club) with which he could knock about his opponents and make them feel small. He would just ride over them.

exchange rate of 15,000 drachmas=$1.00 was changed by decree to 30,000 drachmas=$1.00. A variety of gimmicks which had been in operation during the years of more or less multiple exchange rates had given the old 15,000: 1 parity an actual, effective rate of probably 20,000: 1—so the devaluation was not quite as radical as it appeared. Still, that calculation was for the sophisticated; to the wider public, the new rate had a shock value which gave a degree of confidence that it would last. Markezinis took credit for the difficult (and pioneering!) work done by Kartalis—and the myth persists to this day.

It took perhaps two years for the exchange rate adjustment to work its way through the economy in terms of prices and wages. But clearly, the major incentives became visible within twenty-four hours of the devaluation: exports and domestic production were now favored over imports—and both grew rapidly, as did invisibles; tourists began to show up on the streets of Athens in increasing (although still modest) numbers. The Development Program, moreover, far from being abandoned (as some have, without basis, alleged), continued to move ahead at almost the same scale as that achieved in its first, emergency, year back in 1947/48. And its principal focus, the new national electric power program, gave to the nation a visible sense of progress as the transmission line pylons began to march across the countryside. The writer recollects vividly the sense of confidence—and new, healthy independence— that was in the air in the year 1954.[29]

And, more or less *pari passu* with the decline in the size of the aid allotments (see Table VII), the roster of American Mission personnel shrank from its peak of 181 technicians and overseers and advisers to 169—to 134—to 62— to 11. American economic assistance continued, to be sure, through the '50s and up to the year 1962, when it did finally end. But these aid grants were modest in size, no longer of the massive, emergency, rescue, reconstruction and development character that had obtained during the years 1947-1954. And they were very closely matched by regular, annual increases in the Central Bank's foreign exchange reserves which suggests that, in the economic sense, if not that of the accountant, there really was no foreign aid accruing to the Greek national economy during these post-1954 years.

June 30, 1954, then, essentially marks the end of the American proconsular role in Greece, the end of America's reformist, New Deal adventure in and for Greece.

The Stabilization Program had been timely. This last chapter of America's pervasive economic presence in Greece catalyzed—and capitalized on—both

29. An unfortunate side effect of this palpable, ebullient new combination of national pride/accomplishment/security/optimism was the emergence of the singularly ill-timed drive for *Enosis* (Union of Cyprus with Greece), led principally by the monomaniacal and stubborn Alexis Kyrou.

of those elements of the Mission's program which had preceded it: the massive sustaining balance-of-payments support, on the one hand, and on the other, that part of the American effort which had been devoted to reconstruction and development investment. Here below, expressed in quantitative terms, is a comparison of the endpoint with the point-of-beginning, and it suggests the dynamics of the changes that had been wrought:

TABLE VIII

GREECE

1954 (last year of major U.S. aid) vs. 1948 (first full year of U.S. aid)

Structural Changes	Quantitative Changes (millions of dollars)
I. Expanded domestic production.................⇨import savings:	140
II. Expanded domestic production.........⇨new export earnings:	70
III. Currency stabilization......⇨dries up gold and black market:	80
Total positive swing:	$290
MEMO: U.S. economic aid in 1948 had been.............................	$288

Source: See endnotes.

It was a new and healthy equilibrium. And given a national currency in which its people could now place their faith (and which was even hoarded in the Balkans!), Greece went on quite literally to transform itself. Brice Mace, the director of the American Mission's Food and Agriculture Division, had expressed his admiration for those splendid Romaic qualities of adaptability and indomitable endeavor—and he alluded to the possibility that the best American ideas (not just American dollars and American machinery) might be combined with the best of the Greek spirit when he wrote:

> What would happen when the tractors and the new machinery wore out, when the draft animals died of old age, when America stopped sending fertilizer and seed and weed killer and engineers to Greece?

> Might the *ideas* which the Americans had brought to Greece remain long after the tractors and the engineers were to depart?

> And even poor old Kapitan Markos (Vafiades), returning after thirty years of exile in the Soviet Union, looked around in wonderment and confessed that what he saw in the new and deeply changed Greece truly represented the ideal for which he had once fought.

ENDNOTES

This is a memoir. The principal source in putting together these reflections on the occasion of the 50th Anniversary of the Truman Doctrine and the

Marshall Plan, has been the author's memory. Happily, it is possible to refresh memory with trips to the National Archives and the Truman Library, and I have taken liberal advantage of both these stimulating resources (the panic-stricken gold sovereign re-supply cable, Figure 2, is a product of the National Archives' splendid record-keeping). When it comes to numbers, however—and quite a few have been employed in this present manuscript—memory does not serve well. The numbers have, in fact, been drawn mostly from old Mission records and notes which have long been in my possession.

Among these I should single out two for special mention: *Greece—Statistical Data Book, Fiscal 1955/56 and Calendar 1956 Volume I*, by the Finance and Program Division of the U.S. Operations Mission/Greece, whose real author was the wonderful statistician who knew more about the Bank of Greece than the bank knew itself, Theodore Gennimatas (father of the late PASOK Labor Minister, George Gennimatas, and brother of the royalist general who, in ill health, was exiled by the junta to the island of Lefkas). This is an absolutely essential reference work for anyone who would understand this period of modern Greek history. The second treasury of numbers is *Greece—Import Data Book, Fiscal Year 1953/54, Volumes I and II*, also by the Finance and Program Division of the U.S. Operations Mission to Greece and of which the undersigned was author when he was a young man in Athens. □

Greece's Strategic Importance:
The Military Dimension

The Strategic Importance of Greece to the Balance of Power in the Mediterranean and Europe

LAWRENCE J. KORB

Let me begin by relating something to you that happened to me back in 1981 when I was in the Pentagon. I got a call at home one night from Rick Burt, who was then assistant secretary of state for European affairs, and he said he had a problem. He said that Reggy Bartholomew is negotiating for renewal of the base agreement with Greece and we need Richard Perle to sign off on the agreement and Richard is nowhere to be found. Richard is quite a bright person and has a lot of strengths, he said, but, one of them is not administration. We need to come to an agreement on wages with the civilian workers in Greece, he continued, so we can go ahead and complete the base agreement. He asked if I had the authority. I said I do not know, but go ahead and agree to it. The terms seemed to make sense to me, so he did and we were able to complete the base negotiations.

When my boss, Secretary of Defense Casper Weinberger, found out about it, he was very concerned because of the potential impact on other countries where we had bases. Because we paid the prevailing wages in the country, sometimes the raises for foreign workers would be more than we were giving our own workers. He said to me, how could you do something like that? This is going to set a terrible precedent. I said, it would be a much worse precedent if we do not have our bases in Greece. We need to project power in that part of the world. He said, *touché* and that was the end of the discussion.

That is what I want to discuss with you: the strategic importance of Greece to the security of the U.S. I thought the wages were pretty reasonable given what was paid to workers throughout Greece. It was quite a bargain having the bases in Greece.

In preparation for my remarks I was reading a number of books that dealt with this subject. One of them was Admiral Elmo Zumwalt's book *On Watch*. As you know, he was trying to get the U.S. Navy a home port in Greece and one of the figures he noted while trying to get this home porting concept

LAWRENCE J. KORB, Ph.D., is Director of the Center for Public Policy Education and Senior Fellow in the Foreign Policy Studies Program at the Brookings Institution.

through Congress, was that American vessels had called on Greece more than on any other place in the Mediterranean.

Let me put the whole subject into a context by going back to the time of the Truman Doctrine. I am not going to go into its origins, but in terms of the U.S. military, I think it is important to keep in mind that when World War II ended, the U.S. was the most powerful military nation in the history of the world. But within three years, our defense budget was down by 90 percent, and even though Bob Reichauer has said: "I do worry when we waste money," it was a little bit extravagant to cut our military spending by 90 percent and our armed forces from 12 million to a little more than a million. There was a tremendous desire in the U.S. to return to normalcy. People thought that with the end of World War II our obligations to the world in general and to Europe in particular would be over. As you know, the British understood the strategic importance of Greece and the Mediterranean and they tried to protect their interests and the interests of the U.S. until 1947, when in fact they could no longer bear the burden.

If you analyze what the British were spending in that area of the world and put it in today's dollars, it was quite a substantial amount, somewhere between 5 and 10 billion dollars depending on what deflator you use. When Britain could no longer protect the balance of power in that area of the world, the United States knew it had to pick up the burden. It did not dawn on us just in 1947. As Clark Clifford and David McCollum point out in their books, President Truman had already told our ambassador in Greece in 1946, that in fact, the U.S. would guarantee the security of Greece. President Truman knew we had to pick up the burden.

I would like to spend a few minutes talking about why it was important and why we did what we did and how important it was both for the future of that part of the world and for the winning of the Cold War.

It is obvious when someone asks about the strategic importance of Greece to the balance of power in Europe, in the Mediterranean, and in southeastern Europe, that the answer is the same one that any good realtor gives you when you are buying a house: location, location and location. If you take a look at a map, you will discover that Greece protects what the navy calls a line of communication through the Mediterranean to the Middle East and to North Africa.

It is no accident that the Russians have always tried to exercise their influence in that area. It is no accident that the British resisted a hostile power taking control of that particular area, and it is no accident that when the U.S., back in the '70s, was looking for strategic home ports outside the United States, the U.S. Navy settled on Athens as the place. Given the shrinkage in the military budget and given the fact that Francis Fukiyama [author of "The End of History," ed.] was not right, and the end of the Cold War was not the end of history, it would be good for the U.S., for the young men and women on the ships, to have a strategic home port and I could think of no better place to put it in than Greece.

It was also important for us to project our power in that area. Sometimes, because of the end of the Cold War in the late '80s and early '90s, we forget some of the things that occurred in the Middle East in the '70s; for example: the Jordanian Crisis and the Yom Kippur War. It was very important that we had bases there and we had somebody to allow us to use those bases and to use those forces to deal with these crises. In 1952, Greece joined NATO, thus insuring the southern flank would be intact to deal with Soviet communist expansionism. And of course, the 1953 military facilities agreement with Greece would not have been possible without the Truman Doctrine.

When you ask what were the motivations for the Soviet Union in this area, the answer is that it was not only the strategic location, but also the fact that Russians have always wanted warm-water ports, especially in the Mediterranean. By taking control of Greece, this would have fulfilled not only something strategically important to the Soviet empire but also the Russian dream to have warm-water ports. It would also have enabled the Soviets to circle the Middle East oil resources and the Western European democracies. Many people have written that had we lost Greece, we probably would have lost all of Europe.

So Greece was very critical not only for its location but also for its symbolism. And even today, even with the end of the Cold War, there still are a number of problems in the international system. The focus has shifted from Central Europe down to Southeastern Europe and the Balkans, and our relations with Greece and Greece's relationship to that area continue to be important. If we are ever going to solve the situation in the Balkans, Greece has to play a big role.

In addition to its strategic location, Greece is an important symbol. If Greece were not the birthplace of Western civilization and democracy, I doubt that President Truman would have been able to convince the Congress, dominated by the Taft wing of the Republican Party, to make that commitment and appropriate the funds.

If one had to pick a country to begin the stand against the Soviet empire, to begin the process of the policy that we now call containment, I can not think of a better place than Greece. In fact, in the speech that Truman gave to Congress in which he proposed what would later become known as the Truman Doctrine, he only got three applause lines. And one of his applause lines had to do with his statement that each dollar spent would count toward making Greece self-sustaining.

If you put yourself in Congress in 1947, less than two years after the end of World War II, with a president coming before you and asking for a momentous change in American foreign policy, you would not exactly be enthusiastic but, in fact, stunned. I think it was significant that, in that atmosphere, the Congress did applaud when Greece was mentioned.

It was also important that we were able to achieve our objectives in Greece without sending in American ground troops. Americans many times are criticized and described as being isolationist. There is a certain element of truth in that, but I think when it comes to the use of naval power and air power, that is not the case. It is only when the government sends in ground troops that Americans raise serious questions. For example, the big debate in this country about Bosnia did not occur when we were using air and naval power to try to deal with that conflict. It was only when we sent ground troops in that the American people and the Congress became very focused on it and were concerned about casualties. In Somalia in 1993, it was when eighteen Americans were killed that people demanded the U.S. pull out. It was important that we were able to achieve our objectives in Greece without actually sending in American ground troops; had we done that and had there been casualties, it is conceivable that the Congress would have said that what was happening in Greece is not our business and that as the most powerful nation in the world we do not need to be concerned about the rest of it.

One of the interesting things that I dealt with in government, and that Congress is always obsessed with, is burden sharing. Administration witnesses are always asked why we are spending so much of our GDP on the defense of other countries. The Japanese spend only one percent on defense and other countries in Europe are at two or three percent. Going back and looking at the percentage of GDP that Greece spent on defense during the Cold War, it was the highest in the alliance. This is a very important number. The very last thing I looked at right before the collapse of the Soviet Union in the late 1980s was that 7.1 percent of Greece's GDP was spent on defense, which was higher than in the U.S.

So when you went to testify before the Congress and they talked about the free-loaders of Europe, you could always point to Greece, as well as to Great Britain. That would help us maintain support for NATO with the Congress, which always thought that other nations were trying to take advantage of us. So Greece has been important because of its location, because of what it is, and because of the U.S. being able to achieve its objectives.

There is no doubt about the fact that Greece has a special role to play in the Balkans because of the situation with Former Yugoslav Republic of Macedonia (FYROM). It seems to me that we are never going to be able to bring a resolution to that crisis without the help and the intercession of Greece because Greece has a certain amount of credibility, particularly with the Serbs, much of which we lost because of the way in which we had to intervene in that country. So I think Greece is going to have a very critical role in the Balkans and certainly with Turkey.

If you take a look at stability in the world and particularly in the Islamic counties, it seems to me that Turkey will have a profound impact. There are two competing models for the future of Islam: the Turkish and Iranian models. If the Turkish model (the separation of church and state or a secular state as opposed to a religious state) succeeds it will be better for all. I think Greece can have a substantial role in helping the relationship with Turkey, seeing that its democracy succeeds, and helping to bring the Turks into the European family of nations.

I am quite familiar with all of the antagonisms. The first time I landed in Ankara on an official visit a couple of men showed up on the plane. They were wearing presidential type pins. I assumed they were Americans. They put me in a car and took me to downtown Ankara. On the way I realized they were not Americans; I looked closely at the pins and they were Jerry Ford pins. Reagan was President and I asked, where did you guys get that? Oh, Henry Kissinger gave it to us. He had been over there. I asked, where are you taking me? They said, you are going to see the defense minister, and I said, I am not scheduled to see him until tomorrow. They replied, we know that but he wants to see you now. The defense minister immediately started railing at me about the 7 to 10 military aid ratio; the fact that the Congress was giving 7 dollars to Greece for every 10 dollars they gave to Turkey, because of the disparities in the population of the two countries.

I finally asked, why are you doing this to me? I do not have anything to do with it. You ought to talk to my friend Rick Burt. This is his job. I know, he said, but you are the first American that showed up after this happened. I said to him, I think you ought to think about the image that you project to the U.S. and the way you run your government. At that time, they were under martial law. Americans do not look only at the strategic situation, but they also look at human rights, history and the principles it stands for.

So, my point is that if Greece and Turkey can work together and solve some of these problems, it would go a long way toward bringing stability to that part of the world and make the twenty first century a better century for all of us than the twentieth, which as you know, experienced four major wars. I am happy to conclude by saying that Greece fought with us on all four occasions.

The Strategic Importance of Greece from the Truman Doctrine to the Present

ADMIRAL HENRY C. MUSTIN, USN (RET.)

I am honored and delighted to be part of this most timely and important conference. Since many of the other speakers will address political and other aspects of Greece's role in the Mediterranean, I will concentrate predominantly on the military elements of the issue.

On a personal note, when I arrived in Athens in 1974 to command the U.S. destroyers homeported in Eleusis, I became aware of the legend of the temple of Poseidon at Sounion: If those who follow the sea do not pay the proper respects to Sounion, they face unfavorable winds, horrendous storms at sea, and death from sea monsters. Therefore, even though I am an Episcopalian, I made it a first order of business to visit Poseidon's Temple very early in my tour—with hat in hand. That visit paid off: while we had some unfavorable winds, they were few and far between, we had no horrendous storms, and we saw no sea monsters at all.

To set the stage for my remarks, I would like to offer a quote from Alfred Thayer Mahan: "Circumstances have caused the Mediterranean Sea to play a greater part in the history of the world, both in a commercial and a military point of view, than any other sheet of water of the same size. Nation after nation has striven to control it, and the strife still goes on." Those words, written in 1890, were true in 1947 and are true today.

Fifty years ago, when the Truman Doctrine was born, the fact that control of the Mediterranean had been in dispute for the first three years of World War II, with both sides at times having that control, was very fresh in the mind of U.S. strategic planners. Initially, President Truman asked for $400 million (about half of the cost of a single destroyer today) for Greece and Turkey. Ultimately, billions would be spent as U.S. and Greek security interests merged. Then, Greece entered the North Atlantic Treaty Organization in 1952. Winston Churchill had once referred to Great Britain as the free world's "unsinkable aircraft carrier" in the Atlantic, and NATO planners saw Greece through the same lens in the Eastern Mediterranean. Indeed, in recognition of the

ADMIRAL HENRY C. MUSTIN, USN (RET.), is a Defense Consultant. He serves as a trustee of the U.S. Naval Academy Foundation and vice chairman of the Amphibious Warfare Committee of the National Security Industrial Association.

maritime nature of NATO's southern region, a four-star admiral had been given command of all NATO forces in the south.

In 1953, the first defense cooperation agreement was signed between the U.S. and Greece, providing for U.S. military installations on Greek territory. There was close cooperation between our two nations in the fifties and sixties. Although NATO strategic planners believed that in a NATO-Warsaw Pact war the highest priority should go to the land battle in central Europe, they also recognized that protection of the territory of the members was the basic *raison d'être* of the alliance. Therefore, given fundamental force structure constraints, and including the nuclear backdrop, throughout the Cold War period the U.S./NATO strategy in the southern region was essentially maritime in nature, and the military emphasis was on keeping open the lines of communication in the Mediterranean. Even in the "cool" period of the 70's, in which Greece withdrew from the military wing (arm) of NATO in the wake of the Turkish invasion of Cyprus, the U.S. still viewed Greece as the key strategic anchor on NATO's southeastern flank. U.S. forces were still stationed there, albeit in reduced numbers. Greece returned to NATO in the early eighties and, despite some harsh rhetoric from Prime Minister Papandreou, his government signed a new defense cooperation agreement with the U.S. in 1983.

The collapse of the Soviet Union changed everything. Needless to say, those of us who have spent our entire adult lives planning to deter and/or fight the Soviets have had to re-evaluate our notions of security policy; we have had to recognize the new realities in Europe, and an essential part of that new reality is the role of Greece. I believe that there are three key elements of present-day U.S. and NATO security policy toward Greece.

First, the threat of a large-scale war with the Soviet Union has vanished. Now the southern region of NATO, not the central region, is where the action is (shades of Harry Truman). For fifty years, the central region, with its inevitable nuclear backdrop, was the dominant element of our defense planning. Today, the military action is in the southern region. Bosnia and the Balkans dominate American newspapers and Greece is at center stage. Greece's historical ties to Serbia and the other Balkan nations, as well as its geographical location, make it a key player in U.S. and NATO security policy in the southern region. Greece is in a unique position to influence the emerging democracies in the Balkans, to strongly support the NATO effort in Bosnia, and to serve as a staging point for other NATO operations in the southern region. The Clinton administration's firm commitment to the region is illustrated by the strong position of the U.S. that command of NATO forces in the region must remain in American hands.

Second, as if to echo the 1890 words of Alfred Thayer Mahan, the Eastern Mediterranean will remain strategically important to the West because of economic realities. Much of Europe's oil comes through the Mediterranean via the Suez Canal, and the Caspian Sea is an emerging source as well. As the U.S.

and Western Europe work to encourage democracy and free-market economies in the newly independent states in the Caucasus, economic links to the West will be critical for these states. In particular, their ability to open new markets will have a direct impact on their fledgling governments and in turn on stability in the region. From a strictly maritime viewpoint, the United States has a three-pronged role in securing sea trade in the Mediterranean, and Greece, still the "unsinkable aircraft carrier," is a key player in each prong.

- All hands have to perceive that U.S./NATO naval strengths are adequate to ensure continuity of sea trade with the U.S. and among its friends and allies, regardless of the combination of rival seapowers.

- U.S./NATO has to be visibly capable of maintaining the security of the sea-lanes in peace and in war, and this includes the safety of both ships and port facilities.

- U.S./NATO has to be prepared to support maritime trading partners in periods of crisis to ensure continuing economic and political viability.

It is no overstatement to assert that U.S. sea trade is such an integral factor in today's world economy that any disruption would adversely affect all of the maritime partners of the U.S. Or, as Themistocles said in 500 B.C., "He who commands the sea has command of everything."

Third, even more so now than in 1947, U.S./Greek security relationships must be viewed from the perspective of the entire region. The Middle East peace process, the Muslim fundamentalist movement, current developments in Turkey, and the ever present need for oil raise the tensions—and our security interests—in the region to new heights.

Greece has traditionally pursued a policy of friendship with the Arab states of the Middle East. There is a shared history with the Ottoman Empire, and a large proportion of Christian Arabs are of the Greek Orthodox faith. As a result, particularly during the difficult years of the seventies, Greece's strong ties with the Arab world enabled other Western nations, including the U.S., to use Greece as an interlocutor. Greece's important role has continued through the Middle East peace process. That process, although far from complete, has succeeded beyond anyone's expectations just a few years ago. Greece, through its presence on several multilateral working groups, has done much to contribute to this success. As we look to the year 2000 and beyond, Greece will remain a unique bridge between the West and this strategically critical area.

In recent years, a number of countries, including the U.S., have watched the spread of radical Islam with alarm. Western countries have pursued a policy of outreach to the moderate Arab states and none has done so more effectively than Greece. As but one example, in 1990, after Iraq's Saddam Hussein attacked Kuwait and tried to cloak his aggression in the name of Islam, Greece supported from the very beginning the multinational effort in Kuwait by carrying out air and sea surveillance, making airfields available to allied aircraft and deploying radars to its southeast sector. Airfields on Crete and Rhodes alone received over 3,000 U.S. aircraft from carriers in the Mediterranean.

Greece and Turkey are linked both historically and geographically; indeed, they are strategic twins. Recently, Greek Prime Minister Simitis said a stable Turkey is in Greece's interest. The reverse is true, and in spades. The impact on Turkey of an unstable or inimical Greece would have ripple effects on the entire military balance of power in the Eastern Mediterranean region. Thus there are new security imperatives for Greece and Turkey to move beyond their differences, and to work in consonance with the United States and NATO Europe to ensure stability in the region.

Finally, just a few short years ago, the energy crisis forced the world to search for alternatives to petroleum. Some optimists predicted that, by the turn of the century, oil would be a thing of the past. Today, we are merely thirty four months from the twenty-first century, and our dependence on oil is still a fact of life. As I said earlier, Greece sits astride the critical sea-lanes that link the Middle East with the industrialized world. Now the discovery of Caspian Sea oil and the talk of pipelines to bring it to Mediterranean ports only validates what strategic planners have known for years: Greece is critical to the free flow of oil from the Middle East.

Fifty years ago, President Truman stood in front of Congress in the midst of a changed world and courageously moved forward. He saw European and U.S. security policy in a new way. It was not easy: it required money, putting aside American isolationist tendencies, and a long-term commitment. Today, the United States and Greece are also standing in the midst of a changed world. Greece was an important Cold War ally, but when one considers the future of the Middle East peace process, the rise of radical Islam, Turkey, and the free flow of oil, the end of the Cold War has only increased Greece's importance to U.S. security planners. The United States, as an inland nation, looks in the twenty-first century to the nation that in 400 B.C. was the world's greatest sea power. Despite some zigzags, Greece has stood shoulder-to-shoulder with the U.S. throughout the twentieth century. The security imperatives of the future require that our partnership continues, and I am confident that the bonds formed in this century will be strong enough for the challenges that lie ahead. □

General James A. Van Fleet and the U.S. Military Mission to Greece

PAUL F. BRAIM

We celebrate, justifiably, the unique success of the Truman Doctrine in preventing the communist takeover of Greece early in the Cold War. Most historians give credit to U.S. General James Van Fleet for inspiring and guiding the Greek army, and its leadership, to military victory over the communist "bandits" (as the Greek government insisted on calling them). This decisive, clear victory in a long Cold War which, until its very end, saw mostly uncertain settlements, owes much to Van Fleet's leadership.[1]

I limit my praise of "Van" (his moniker), however, by acknowledging the fighting spirit of the Greek soldier, under the outstanding leadership of Marshal Alexander Papagos, and the aggressive leaders he selected. I also credit Tito's break with the Kremlin, and Stalin's apparent reluctance to continue to oppose British and American influence in Greece, for limiting severely the sanctuary and sustenance of the Communist Democratic Army of Greece (DAG) at the same time as a retrained and aggressive Greek National Army (GNA) launched its major offensives, although Van Fleet thought that closing the border was a minor action in the war.[2]

Some accounts credit Greek Queen Frederika for opening the way to Van Fleet's posting to Greece. General George Marshall, former chief of staff of the U.S. Army and U.S. secretary of state, in 1947, records Queen Frederika's appeal to him: "Greece needs a combat general…to train our soldiers to fight; you sent us a supply officer."[3]

PAUL F. BRAIM, Ph.D., Professor of American military history at Embry-Riddle Aeronautical University, is currently working on a biography of General Van Fleet.

1. Many statements on Van Fleet's ability by distinguished civil and military leaders are recorded in his *Official Biography*, published by Department of the Army, OCINFO, Washington, D.C., 1955.
2. Van Fleet's statement on Tito's closing of the border is made in a transcript of an interview of General James A. Van Fleet by Lieutenant Colonel Bruce Williams, on 3 March 1973, as part of the Senior Officers Oral History project of the U.S. Army War College, filed at USAWC, Carlisle, PA, pp. 57, 58.
3. Marshall told Van Fleet that Queen Frederika had stated her judgments about U.S. leadership in Greece, and requested a combat general from the U.S. (Unpublished autobiography of General James A. Van Fleet, hereafter called *VF Autobio*" p. 5.)

Marshall owed Van Fleet a major posting; during World War II, it was Marshall who had refused to promote Van to general's rank until late in the war, despite strong recommendations from the European Command, because Marshall had confused him with an alcoholic colonel with a similar name. President Harry Truman called Van Fleet the "finest combat soldier in the U.S. army" when he announced his posting to lead the U.S. Military Assistance Program in Greece. And there was general agreement among the U.S. army leadership that Van Fleet was the man for this new and difficult advisory task.[4]

Van Fleet's rise in combat leadership in Europe in World War II was phenomenal. From his aggressive command as a 52-year-old colonel of the 8th Regiment across Utah Beach in France on D-Day (June 6, 1994), Van Fleet rose to command III U.S. Corps, driving from the Remagen Bridgehead through Germany into Austria by the end of the war. Van could be described as a natural leader. An astute observer who served under him in World War II, Lieutenant Colonel (later Four-Star General) William DePuy said of Van, "He was a huge man, friendly but forceful; he expected to be obeyed—and he was!"

My study of Van Fleet (I met him a number of times during my military career) leads me to agree with DePuy. Van Fleet believed in himself and in his ability. He was certain he could inspire others to achieve victory. He regarded battle as the expected proof of his motto, "The will to win," which spirit he had developed and inspired in his men on the football fields from West Point to the University of Florida, and on the battlefields of World Wars I and II.

Like many big men (Van was 6'2" and 220 lbs.), he was self-confident without being assertive or demanding. He was not an intellectual; had not attended senior service schools. When selected for assignment to Greece, he was serving in his first major staff assignment (Operations/Training) in the U.S. European Command). Also, he had had no significant experience in working with allied military. But, he had had long experience commanding soldiers, in the field and in combat. He liked to be with his men, forward in battle, not at a command post, and he rose to the challenge of combat leadership enthusiastically.[5]

When General Van Fleet reported to General Marshall in his office at the State Department in late February 1948, Marshall, in his usual direct manner, asked the question, "Van, what can you do to help the Greeks beat the communists?" Van replied in general terms to the effect that the Greeks were a strong and proud people; if they had the will to win, he was confident he

---

4. *Official Biography*, p. 17; among the many leaders who commented upon Marshall's having confused Van Fleet with a Colonel Van Vliet, General Omar Bradley cites this reason for the delay in promotion of Van Fleet to general's rank in his autobiography, *A Soldier's Story* (New York: Henry Holt & Co., 1951) p. 283.
5. Van Fleet is discussed by DePuy in Romie L. Brownlee et al, *Changing an Army: An Oral History of General William E.DePuy*. Washington, D.C., U.S. Army Center of Military History, no date, pp. 66, 67.

could train them to do so. Apparently, this comment satisfied Marshall, for he grunted and nodded. He then advised Van to get to know their majesties King Paul and Queen Frederika, "and take them with you to the battlefront. The queen and king are very popular with the Greek people…let the people see that they stand behind you." Van thought that this comment from Marshall was the best guidance he got from anyone while he was en route to his post. Marshall also sent a personal and confidential letter to Queen Frederika, commending Van to her.[6]

Van met briefly with the British Mission in Washington, then stopped in London to confer with the British Imperial General Staff. The British had been fighting alongside, supplying, and assisting the Greek Army during and since World War II. Straitened economic circumstances required the British to turn over the advisory and later the supply task for the Greek Army to the United States. The U.S. advisory effort in Greece was under the overall direction of Ambassador Henry Grady, as the director of the U.S. Country Team for Greece; the U.S. Military Mission was under the Embassy's Assistance Program. The navy and air force also had supply and transport groups in Greece, and army engineers had a group operating there. These allied and U.S. elements were loosely coordinated.

During Van's first year in Greece, the organization of the country team, and the Joint U.S. Military Advisory and Planning Group, Greece (JUSMAPG) were brought into relative harmony; most military were responsive to (though not entirely under command of) General Van Fleet, in his role as director of the U.S. Military Mission. Of the approximately 400 U.S. military, 182 Army advisors were posted to the Greek National Army (GNA) down to division level; many accompanied Greek Army units on combat operations.[7]

General Van Fleet publicly announced that JUSMAPG advisors were to train and advise the Greeks; they were not to fight, therefore he and they would not carry weapons. This gesture was to show that the Greeks were in command of their forces, with the U.S. officers only there as assistants. Privately, however, Van was assured by Marshall, and by Greece's King Paul, that he had command authority and could give orders and direct the relief of those Greek officers who didn't measure up in combat. Van exercised this authority by strong recommendations for operations (including the relief of a dozen general officers), in the field and in the councils of the Greek army and state. He did not pass this command authority down his advisory chain; he did however, demand that his advisors press the Greek commanders to act more aggressively in the field, and he held those U.S. advisors responsible for the

6. Marshall's comment is recorded in *VF Autobio*, 7.
7. Organizational information is taken from a declassified memo from Gen. Van Fleet to Gen. J. Lawton Collins, chief of staff of the U.S. Army, dated 14 December 1948, pp. 1,2.

performance of the Greek units to which they were posted. This dichotomy, responsibility without command, became a feature of U.S. military assistance programs worldwide in this and later periods. As a matter of fact, JUSMAPG advisors did take command in combat on a number of occasions, and Van and most of his advisors did carry personal weapons, usually pistols.[8]

At the time of Van's arrival on 24 February 1948, the strength of the DAG varied around 20,000 in Greece, with an additional 8-15,000 in training in Yugoslavia, Bulgaria, and Albania. These were lightly armed, with a few mountain artillery guns. It was estimated that an additional 50,000 self-defense irregulars provided intelligence and support to the active fighters. At the height of the insurgency, in 1948, approximately 750,000 of the eight million Greek citizens were allied or sympathizers with the communists. Communist forces, under Markos Vafiadis (called "Markos") generally operated out of mountain hideaways, raiding the smaller towns for supplies and recruits.

Late in December 1947, the communists attempted to establish a seat of their Provisional Democratic Government in Konitsa (near the Albanian border; see map on following page). The GNA ejected the DAG from the area, but significant guerrilla strength remained active in the Grammos-Vitsi area on the northern border, in the Peloponnese, and in sufficient numbers in the center of Greece to carry out major raids—one of them only seventeen miles from to Athens. Despite about 20,000 casualties annually, the DAG maintained its strength by abductions of young Greeks and by recruiting in neighboring Communist countries.[9]

The Greek National Army (GNA) consisted of 146,000 active soldiers, bolstered by a National Defense Corps of 50,000 paramilitary, village-defense personnel. Although poorly trained, most of the soldiers were strong, inured to hardship, and willing to fight; most of them appeared to hate the communists for their atrocities in the villages. Leadership in the GNA was generally poor; much of the senior military leadership was over age for field duty, out of condition, oriented toward defense of population centers and headquarters, and non-aggressive. The GNA had not only been equipped and trained by the British; it had also been conditioned by the British to move cautiously, and to use firepower in lieu of maneuver rather than using fire to assist maneuver. Van insisted on, and secured, the relief of the slowest and most phlegmatic of the senior leaders, and set about training the rest of the army.

8. Information about advisors and their operations is taken from David Colley's article, "Hot Spot in the Cold War: American Advisors in Greece, 1947-49," published in *VFW* Magazine, May 1997, pp. 34-37.
9. Richard, A Clegg, *Concise History of Greece,* (New York: Cambridge University Press, 1992), 140,141; also Evangelos Averoff-Tossizza, *By Fire and Axe: The Communist Party and the Civil War in Greece, 1944-1949* (New York: Caratzas Bros, 1978), pp. 162-167.

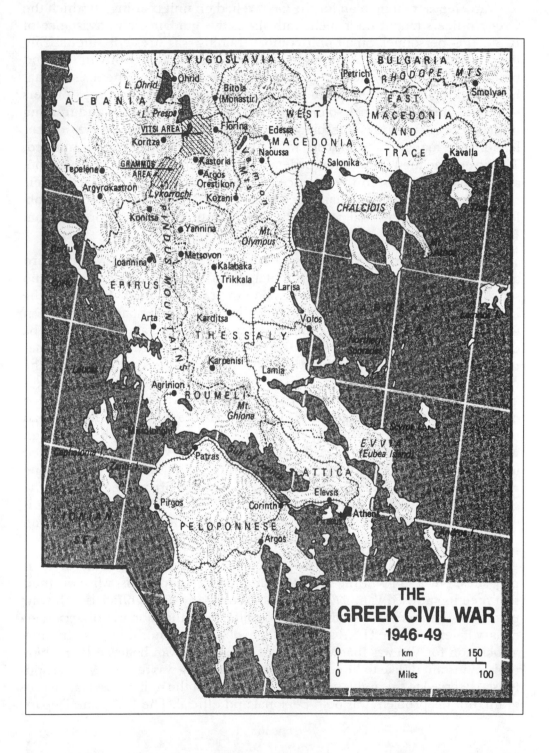

THE
GREEK CIVIL WAR
1946-49

Reprinted with permission from *"A New Kind of War:" America's Global Strategy and the Truman Doctrine in Greece* by Howard Jones (New York: Oxford University Press, 1989).

Van Fleet's training plan for the GNA relied on unit training, in which the Greek officers taught their men, with the active guidance and assistance of JUSMAPG personnel. Small unit combat training was stressed, emphasizing fire and maneuver. Van thoroughly enjoyed getting down on the ground beside the soldiers, to show them how to lay a machine gun; he insisted that his staff do likewise, often in the mud, and that they press the Greek officers to do the same. The Greek soldiers responded well, and morale and training improved concurrently. The biggest training problem for Van was officer leadership: many of the officers were, as stated earlier, defensive minded. They were inclined to question orders when these required offensive action, and to take no action in the absence of a direct verification of attack orders by a senior officer in their chain of command. JUSMAPG also had some problems replacing individual weaponry, which until 1949 was supplied from British stocks.[10]

Early in his tour, Van visited a battalion which had been deployed to guard a winery owned by a senior governmental official. From the winery, Van could see a strong communist defensive position on a nearby mountain, which the battalion commander disdained to attack because, as he stated, his mission was to protect the winery. The commander and his troops also appeared to be enjoying the products produced by the winery they guarded. The DAG, under no such self-imposed restrictions, visited the nearby villages and terrorized the citizens. On another occasion, Van escorted a group of senior U.S. officers and civilians to observe a Greek corps in an offensive which had been planned by JUSMAPG. Van was angered to discover that the corps commander had delayed the attack, while he launched a four-hour artillery bombardment on well dug-in enemy positions in the mountains. Van exploded; he explained loudly the use of artillery to assist the soldiers to advance by suppressing enemy fire as the soldiers attack. There was no enemy fire at the time, and the general was just wasting ammunition on a frontline enemy position which was well protected and difficult to strike. After getting the attack underway, Van returned to Athens with more names for relief from command.[11]

Van was given full support for his command actions, not only by their majesties, but also by Prime Minister Themistocles Sophoulis, who, on their first meeting advised Van, *sotto voce*, "Do not trust any Greek officials with your plans, not even me." The guerrilla radio called Van "the monarchofascist mercenary killer from the U.S.," among other sobriquets. Another not so friendly association for Van was that with Ambassador Grady. Van believed that Grady took an instant dislike to him, and for Van, the feeling was mutual. Van scrupulously deferred to the ambassador in his direction of the military assistance program, but his problem was both personal and official. The U.S. State Depart-

10. Williams interview, 14, 15; also Van Fleet memo to Collins, 2, 3.
11. *VF Autobio*, 23-36; also Colley, p. 36.13. Op. cit., 53-59.

ment and the U.S. Embassy in Athens publicly criticized the monarchist government of Greece for antidemocratic actions, such as the arrest and detention of political opponents. Van saw the Greek government's actions as necessary in a nation which was struggling with an insurgency of major proportions.

Ambassador Grady occasionally called Van to his office, then had him wait for some time in the anteroom. When Van came in and saluted, Grady would continue reading a paper as if he were too busy to acknowledge the greeting. He then would look up and criticize Van for some personal action such as hob-nobbing with royalty. Grady's correspondence with Van is peppered with demands for limiting military travel to social affairs; on a couple of occasions, he reprimanded Van for parking his chauffeured car in front of the Grande Bretagne Hotel (in which Van lived), and for misuse of the ambassador's official aircraft. A cooperative but difficult relationship for Van was with the British Mission and its senior officers. Although they were phasing out their presence, the British still insisted upon offering paternalistic guidance to Van, and if he refused it, to the Greek commanders behind Van's back.

General Van Fleet also had a friendly but cautious relationship with the Greek and international press; many of the reporters and their editors insisted on calling the insurgency a "civil war," this predilection due to their leftist leanings, according to Van. Reporters frequently tried to get him to criticize the Greek government, and just as frequently misquoted him. Van had a friendly relationship with the chief of the Supreme National Defense Council, General Yatsis. Yatsis accompanied Van to most of his inspections in the field, and approved, even deferred to Van's judgment, but it was obvious that he was physically unfit for the demands of his office and tired from long service.[12]

Some two years elapsed between the beginning of U.S. military aid under the Truman Doctrine and the achievement of combat effectiveness of the Greek National Army. Despite the failure of the communists to hold Konitsa, raids and seizures by the DAG were notably successful in 1948, and substantial assistance continued to come from the communist countries on the northern border of Greece. The guerrilla leaders and their bands were well trained in raiding; they had, of course, the advantages which inhere to a guerrilla force: the ability to strike anywhere, thus holding the initiative, while the National Army was trying to defend every major town and facility. The guerrillas were also good at using mines and booby traps to delay forces which were committed to engage them; they were also adept at luring National Army and some of the paramilitary National Defense units out of the towns, then doubling back to attack the defenseless citizens. These successes of the communist guerrillas forced Van to launch the GNA on the offensive while his program of training and invigoration of that army was only being initiated.

12. Op. cit. 50-52.

Early in 1948, Van directed the GNA to conduct mainly local offensives. The first of these was launched at a strong and active guerrilla force operating around Kurisa, near the port city of Salonika. The attack was launched despite snow and poor visibility, and the GNA defeated this force, and killed or captured 400 of the "bandits." (Here it might be noted that the GNA soldiers called the communists a name which is a derisive form of the word for goat!) The Kurisa operation was a morale boost for the GNA, while Van made much of this "proof" that the Greek soldier could beat any communist bandit on his own ground. Van next launched a larger offensive in the Rumeli Mountains (across the lower Greek mainland). This was a coordinated encirclement and concentric attack against an estimated 2,000 guerrillas. As GNA attacked, the guerrillas scattered and attempted to flee, and a good many of them succeeded in slipping away into the hills for a time at least. The twenty-day campaign netted a total of 1,400 killed, captured or surrendered. This was widely reported in the international press as a major defeat for the DAG. However, despite these local successes, Van was troubled by continued raids and terrorist acts by the DAG throughout Greece. He determined to strike at the major area of DAG strength and defenses: Grammos.

The Grammos mountains, extending south from the Albanian border, were the locus of the communists' "Supreme Military Council," what passed for a provisional government. DAG propaganda called their position "the impregnable fort;" studying the rough terrain, Van concluded that this was not an idle boast. Beginning in April 1948, Markos improved field defensive positions and brought reinforcements in from Yugoslavia and Albania. GNA intelligence reported that Markos intended to hold the five Grammos defenses "at all costs." It was hoped that failure of the GNA to destroy the DAG in these defenses would cause the Greek government to agree to an armistice and later a political settlement favoring the communists.

Van Fleet planned a concentric drive from the east, west, and south; he recognized, however, that the GNA could not entirely block the route of DAG reinforcement or escape along the Albanian border. Unfortunately also, the GNA was being pressed into action before it was combat effective.

The GNA launched the strongest offensive up to that time, with one division driving west from Nestorion, while another drove north. DAG resistance was strong, and the GNA moved slowly, cautiously, under heavy defensive fire. The Royal Hellenic Air Force bombed and strafed the DAG defenses intensively. As the GNA slowly advanced, Markos continued to reinforce, bringing about one-third of his entire armed strength into the region. In mid-August, a corps of the GNA seized the crown of the Grammos defenses, and Markos ordered a general withdrawal into Albania. The GNA had achieved a victory, but Van took little satisfaction; the combat leaders of the GNA, especially the senior leaders, had shown a marked lack of aggressiveness; most had remained on the low ground, too far from their advancing forces. Also offsetting the victory was the reappearance of the same DAG force crossing the Yugoslav border into the Vitsi area. In this area, the DAG set up strong defenses and blunted the weak attacks of the GNA until winter forced offensive operations to cease.[13]

The communists' withdrawal from Grammos ended Markos command; criticized by the secretary general of the KKE (Communist Party of Greece), Nicholas Zachariadis, for the Grammos failure, Markos was replaced by Zachariadis, who had argued for conventional operations rather than guerrilla raids. Markos had also supported Tito in his growing estrangement from Stalin. After the change of command and strategy by the DAG, it was soon obvious that their change to major conventional operations had been made too early. Now the strength of the GNA could be focused on the DAG in conventional defenses. (It should be noted that conversion of a guerrilla force to a conventional one is a most critical and difficult development, and that insurrectionist forces usually attempt to convert to regular-force status too soon.) A concomitant advantage accruing to the GNA was the opportunity to isolate some of the identified mountain defenses of the DAG, preventing egress from or access to their defensive positions. Receiving intelligence reports of Zachariadis's decision to fight conventional operations, Van announced that he was happy to accommodate him. The problem was that the GNA was not yet ready to "fight to win!"[14]

The communists were not the only force which saw a change in command. Seemingly by popular demand, General Alexander Papagos agreed to come out of retirement and take over the Greek National Army. Van found Papagos just the experienced and resourceful leader he had been seeking for the GNA. Van also got a lift from a visit by Secretary of State Marshall, who reassured the Greek government of continuing U.S. support, and, in private conference with Queen Frederika, from which Marshall had deliberately excluded Ambassador Grady, exchanged statements of confidence in Van's leadership. Marshall also smoothed the way for Papagos to become commander-in-chief of the Greek armed forces, without his having to report to the large National Defense Council. The council was trimmed to a small group, of which Papagos became the dominant member. Upon taking over, Papagos issued orders to the GNA, clearly and incisively stating:

> I intend total extermination of the communist banditry...I will spare no strong measure against those [leaders] who are afraid to fight...No troops will withdraw from their positions without direct orders of their superior officer.

Van was delighted with Papagos's instructions, which echoed his own military philosophy. He sent Papagos a number of terse, even abrupt messages

13. Op. cit., 53-59.
14. Op. cit., 59-63.

spelling out the deficiencies of GNA, especially a lack of aggressive patrolling and night operations. An atmosphere of mutual trust grew between Van and Papagos, and the GNA began to reflect their leader's vigor. In that new mode of confidence, Van and Papagos set JUSMAGP and the GNA into intensive planning for the offensives of 1949. Despite concerns expressed by some GNA leaders, Van also began a program of issuing rifles to the villagers for their self-defense.[15]

The first GNA offensive, launched in the winter of 1948-49, was a sweep through the Peloponnese, an area in which the communists had established a strong underground. The Greek government preceded the offensive by rounding up and detaining suspected communist sympathizers and supporters. Despite criticism of these arrests by the American press, and by the U.S. Embassy in Athens, the military operation was a complete success, and most of the suspects were released later. Guerrilla strength in the Peloponnese was reduced from about 3,000 to an estimated 250, scattered in small bands. This success was offset, in January 1949, by strong DAG attacks in the Rumeli area of southern Greece. These raids destroyed many towns, killed officials, and carried away recruits and supplies. JUSMAPG studies of the DAG offensives revealed that GNA commanders had failed to act on many intelligence reports indicating DAG buildups in the area.

However, Greek intelligence also revealed that the communists were in disarray as to their future actions in Greece, especially after Tito announced the closing of the Yugoslav border to the DAG. Van thought that Tito's action was of little significance, as the Yugoslavs couldn't close the long, mountainous border. However, it is my opinion that Tito's action, withdrawing support and sustenance, did signify a great political change in the region. Zachariadis denounced Tito, and vowed to continue the fight from his positions in the Grammos. He also announced agreement with Stalin's plan for an independent Macedonia, a pronouncement which angered Greeks of all political persuasions. General Van Fleet, after a flying visit to Washington, convinced the Congress, and the Truman administration to increase weapons and supplies for the Greek armed forces, including Navy Hell Diver aircraft for increased close-air support.[16]

In the spring of 1949, the DAG marshaled 8,000 troops in a defensive bastion in the Vitsi area, aware, as was most of the Greek citizenry, that a decisive battle was about to take place. The GNA, retrained, high in spirit, with aggressive commanders, was up for the battle. Van worked with Papagos this time to surprise the communists. The essence of their plan was for the GNA to mount an attack on the Grammos, and give all indications that this was the main attack. Then the main force would swing toward Vitsi, attacking east along the

15. Op. cit., 73-80.
16. Op. cit., 103-122; also Colley, pp. 36, 37.

border so as to cut off the defenders' line of communications and line of retreat as well. Another surprise: the attacks would be launched at night.

At midnight, on 10 August 1949, Greek commando units infiltrated enemy positions; at 5:40 A.M. the main attack began, supported by the Royal Hellenic Air Force, and by rolling barrages of artillery. King Paul, at an observation post with Van, became excited when reports came in that the offensives were succeeding in both the Grammos and Vitsi areas. The DAG leadership was in some confusion, as it became apparent that some GNA divisions were attacking along the Albanian border and cutting roads leading to both the Grammos and Vitsi positions. After some heavy fighting in the Grammos, the DAG withdrew, in disorder, into Albania and Yugoslavia. By the end of August, fighting had ceased. Estimates of DAG casualties totaled 5,500; the GNA lost 431. Tremendous dumps of arms, ammunition, and supplies had also been seized, including huge stocks of grain hidden away in caves. An amusing postscript: the Albanian government complained in the U.N. that Greek military forces were waging attacks into their country! Marshall Papagos, his fighting spirit overflowing, demanded the right to pursue the DAG into Albania; he was quieted down by his government, as Van, with difficulty, refrained from expressing his views, which agreed with those of Papagos.[17]

After this major victory, Greece returned to normal, with small, really insignificant communist incidents breaking out occasionally. The Greek economy improved swiftly, assisted by the Marshall Plan. Van wrapped up his reports, and visited many towns and gatherings. Messages of congratulations came from President Truman and many others. Greece had been saved from communism. General James A. Van Fleet had contributed greatly to that succor. His professional leadership, his drive, his will to win, and his empathy with the Greek soldier had brought victory.[18]

In May 1950, General Van Fleet was informed of his reassignment to the U.S., to be Commander of the Second U.S. Army at Fort Meade, Maryland. In his end-of-tour report, and in later summaries, Van stressed these points: This military advisory effort sets a pattern upon which U.S. military assistance should be based. The U.S. should study the Greek assistance program carefully; it will likely be repeated elsewhere in the struggle against communism. The U.S. army should restudy guerrilla and counter guerrilla warfare. We should provide guidance, assistance, weapons, training, and moral support for indigenous peoples to win their own wars against communist insurrection. Only the citizens of a nation can win its wars. The U.S. can help, but cannot win a war for other people! This last point was the major lesson learned from the communist insurgency in Greece; it was not, unfortunately, applied to the later U.S. assistance programs in Korea and Vietnam. □

17. Op. cit., 130-147.
18. Letter from Truman to Van Fleet, 22 May 1950; also Williams interview, 48-71, 13.

'Hot Spot in the Cold War,' American Advisors in Greece, 1947-49

Fifty years ago this month, the U.S. launched a military advisory campaign that helped achieve a clear-cut victory over Communism in the Balkans.

Few Americans have ever heard of Lt. Col. Seldon R. Edner or attach significance to his death. The thirty-year-old Air Force officer and advisor to the Greek air force was killed by communist guerrillas January 22, 1949, near Karpenision, Greece, after his AT-6 was downed over guerrilla-held territory at the height of the Greek Civil War.

Edner survived the crash, but was brutally murdered and mutilated by his captors. He was lynched, stripped, garroted, scalped, his head crushed and body mutilated. Communist propaganda then accused the Americans of strafing and bombing innocent civilians.

Edner's may have been the first American combat death of the Cold War in Europe. To be sure, GIs had been killed in incidents before along the Iron Curtain. But Edner was involved in a civil war where the guerrillas targeted American military personnel for death.

A NEW KIND OF WAR

New York Times reporter Anne O'Hare McCormick called Greece's civil conflict "a new kind of war"—a "hot spot in the Cold War"—and warned that the cradle of democracy must not become "another Czechoslovakia."

For Americans, Greece presented a new struggle that became the prototype of Cold War conflicts to come. It grew out of the ravages of the German occupation of Greece during WWII. When the *Wehrmacht* withdrew from Greece in 1944, fighting broke out between rightist and communist forces.

By 1947, the communists of ELAS (National Popular Liberation Army), also called *andartes*, or bandits, under the leadership of General Markos Vafiades, controlled most of the countryside while the government defended the urban areas. The British, historic protectors of Greece, supplied and trained

DAVID COLLEY, a free-lance writer based in Easton, Pennsylvania, has contributed ten articles to *Veterans of Foreign Wars* magazine's Cold War history series.

the Greek National Army (GNA). But exhausted by WWII, Britain began withdrawing its 15,000-man garrison from the conflict.

President Harry Truman faced a dilemma. Public opinion, military leaders and many in Congress opposed direct U.S. intervention in Greece. One general labeled the Alabama-sized county a strategic "mousetrap." Indeed, seventy five percent of Greece is covered by mountains.

Yet the U.S. could not stand by and allow this strategically located nation to fall to communism. Truman also realized that if Greece were lost, Turkey might fall and "confusion and disorder might well spread throughout the Middle East."

The president's solution became known as the Truman Doctrine. America would not permit the collapse of Greece or Turkey. The U.S. would "assist" the Greeks in defending themselves, through military and economic aid. Military advisors were part of the plan.

AN AMERICAN WAR

On May 24, 1947, the first U.S. advisors arrived in Athens. By December 1947, the U.S. activated JUSMAPG, the Joint United States Military Advisory and Planning Group. JUSMAPG's sole purpose was to assist the Greek army, but some advisors were assigned to the navy and air force. In February 1948, Lieutenant General James Van Fleet was named JUSMAPG commander.

JUSMAPG's peak strength during the conflict reached some 450 men in August 1949, about half of whom were advisors. Remaining members were mostly communications personnel responsible for sending daily reports back to headquarters in Athens. Army section advisors were assigned to field detachments at the 16 corps and eight division levels.

It soon became apparent that the U.S. was running the war. "This is not merely a Greek war, but an American war, it is the Americans who make it possible to fight it...Athens is almost like an Anglo-American (mostly American) armed citadel, and neither the Greek army nor government could survive ten days without aid—concrete military aid—from the United States," wrote John Gunther in *Beyond the Curtain* (1949).

One British writer observed: "Both on the ground and in the air, American support was becoming increasingly active, and the theoretical line between advice, intelligence and combat was a narrow one."

Advisors quickly found that this new war was fought under strange rules of engagement. They had orders not to carry weapons nor to partake in combat, even as many dodged bullets and shells. They were expected to lead, but often had to persuade or intimidate to motivate Greek commanders and troops. The war was said to be critical to the survival of the free world, yet some Greek troops hardly cared, or so it seemed.

Most frustrating of all, the enemy operated with impunity from sanctuaries in Yugoslavia, Albania, and Bulgaria. Pursuit of the guerrillas into these areas was forbidden. Moscow provided aid through Albania from August 1947 to April 1949.

All told, the Yugoslavs sent 35,000 rifles, 3,500 machine guns, 2,000 German bazookas, 7,000 anti-tank guns, 10,000 field mines, clothing for 12,000 men, and 30 wagons of food to Greece. They furnished all the supplies and equipment for one communist division, including five hundred draft horses, and operated three field hospitals in Yugoslav Macedonia for the wounded *andartes*. Yugoslavia was a ready sanctuary for guerrillas on the run.

TRAINING THE TROOPS

Never before had Americans been assigned such a role, as one advisor, Major Lee Hilliard, was to discover. Attached to the Greek 10th Mountain Division in Salonika, Hilliard accompanied it on missions into the rugged mountains. But guerrillas faded into the inaccessible terrain.

"Greek troops could chase the guerrillas up to the Greek border, but had to stop," Hilliard said. "And the guerrillas across the border would keep firing at us, but the GNA forces could only withdraw."

Major Morrell Sexton was assigned to the Greek 15th Mountain Division on the Yugoslavian border. He quickly noticed that GNA troops regularly broke for an afternoon siesta and had no confidence in their supporting fire, with good reason. They were more likely to be killed by their own artillery, mortars and machine guns than by the enemy's. Van Fleet was aware of these deficiencies. He was appalled to find one Greek battalion guarding the minister of war's winery in the Peloponnesse (southern peninsula). "The battalion was sitting there drinking the wine," Van Fleet recalled in his oral memoirs. "They were not allowed to attack the enemy in their stronghold five miles away."

Van Fleet quickly established training camps. Sexton was one of many pulled of the line after several months to train GNA infantry to work closely with artillery and heavy weapons fire. Cpl. Robert Watkins taught Greek troops how to use M-1s. His experience as a WWII infantryman made him an ideal instructor.

Advisors were required to be diplomats as well as warriors. Col. Everett D. Peddicord was senior military advisor to A Corps. "When the corps commander asked for advice I gave it. Otherwise, I kept quiet," Peddicord recalls. "That Greek general knew ten-times more about mountain fighting than I could ever dream of knowing." Peddicord's main job was to ensure that troops had sufficient supplies, particularly mules to transport munitions into the mountains.

But Peddicord was not averse to directing combat action. He once devised an attack plan when GNA troops couldn't break through a string of pillboxes in mountainous terrain in the Peloponnesse. Peddicord's plan was to approach from different directions as Greek air force Spitfires attacked the targets head-on.

The line between advising and participation was thin. Hilliard followed orders explicitly—most of the time—and refused to carry a weapon, even though the division commander assigned him several bodyguards and warned: "You know you will be killed if the guerrillas catch you."

TOO CLOSE TO THE ACTION

On one anti-guerrilla mission in the rugged mountains north of Salonika, U.S. Colonel Augustus Regnier approached Hilliard in an armored car. He urged him to take charge of a Greek infantry battalion while the colonel led the attack in the armored vehicles. "We'll make a great tank-infantry team," Regnier asserted.

Hilliard reminded Regnier of orders not to become involved. The colonel persisted. Finally Hilliard asked: "Are you ordering me to take command?"

"Take it as an order," Regnier barked.

Hilliard obeyed: "I took over from the Greek battalion commander, issuing orders through him to his troops. Away we went up the mountain with the colonel firing the 37mm gun personally."

Regnier boasted too loudly about his exploits and the incident was reported by CBS correspondent George Polk, who was later murdered by insurgents. Regnier was recalled to Washington for violation of orders and Hilliard was sent to Athens.

The reassignments were for show. Regnier was exonerated and Hilliard wound up as Van Fleet's personal aide.

Sergeant Harold Yamamoto, a communications specialist assigned to B Corps at Larissa, recalls that reports of U.S. advisors taking control of Greek units were common. Yamamoto remembers that dangers also lurked for rear-echelon personnel—he always carried a pistol outside of his headquarters base.

Still, American personnel were helpless against terrorist attacks. Yamamoto experienced one when a U.S. Army Signal Corps truck exploded at night on the street outside his quarters in Kozani. Guerrillas had blown up the vehicle.

Since the guerrillas controlled the countryside, supply of GNA outposts was by air. Cpl. Robert Stone was an Air Force crewman attached to the U.N. Special Commission on the Balkans, which made daily flights to various cities throughout Greece. Flying could be hazardous. Stone's plane was hit at least three times, once seriously enough to require repair in Germany. Sometimes landing strips came under fire and planes couldn't land.

Hellenikon Air Base, located five miles south of Athens, initially hosted a small U.S. supply unit to handle air shipments of Marshall Plan aid. From July 1948 to the end of the civil war, the 1015th and 1632nd Air Base squadrons were stationed there to assist the U.S. mission.

COMBAT ON THE COMMUNIST CURTAIN

By the end of 1948, guerrillas had been largely cleared from central Greece and the Peloponnesse, in part because the Americans demanded greater GNA aggressiveness. Combat shifted to the frontiers with Albania, Yugoslavia and Bulgaria, in the Grammos and Vitsi mountains and north of Salonika.

In spring 1949, the communist insurgency was on the ropes. The growing feud between Soviet dictator Josef Stalin and Marshall Tito prompted the Yugoslavs to close the border to Greek guerrillas. Albania and Bulgaria followed suit.

GNA was now better equipped and considerably larger. The armed forces had grown from about 168,000 men in 1947 to 263,900 in 1949.

The war also had taken its toll on the guerrillas. Never more than a force of around 25,000, the war had ground them down substantially. They reverted to the practice of abducting women to serve in their ranks. Increasingly, the communists became a motley crew, often without shoes and proper clothing.

In one decisive battle in the Vitsi area in August 1949, 50,000 GNA troops, with supporting air power dropping napalm, overwhelmed some 7,700 insurgents, who foolishly chose to slug it out. By October, rebel forces were shattered and either surrendered or fled into the Balkan communist states.

Total guerrilla casualties were horrendous compared to the GNA's. JUSMAPG reported 29,015 insurgents killed, 19,872 captured and 4,779 missing. Other sources put the number of rebel dead at close to 50,000. Their number of wounded is unknown.

Greek army deaths totaled 12,777, with 4,527 missing and 37,732 wounded, according to official Greek statistics.

Greek civilians suffered severely. Some 4,124 civilians and 165 priests were executed by the communists. Land mines claimed another 931 lives. More than 700,000 were made refugees, and nearly 30,000 abducted by guerrillas. Approximately 28,000 children were abducted and taken out of Greece for re-education in communist countries: only 10,000 were repatriated.

U.S. CONTRIBUTION TO VICTORY

At least three American lives were reported lost in the war, among them Edner Robert Watkins recalls an advisor assigned to his corps being killed in a jeep accident. And Lt. William O. Wagner, a U.S. pilot assigned to the U.N. staff, was killed in an accidental plane crash at Florina airfield in February 1949.

In the Adriatic Sea, at least three Navy fliers from Air Group 7 aboard the USS *Leyte* were lost at sea during show-the-flag exercises around Greece, reports Stanley Connell, the carrier's historian.

In the end, there is no question that U.S. resolve and $353.6 million worth of military aid saved Greece. Much of the credit must go to the few hundred American military advisors who learned to fight a new kind of war.

As Peter J. Stavrakis, author of *Moscow and Greek Communism,* wrote: "If the Soviets had been successful in displacing Western influence in the eastern Mediterranean, they certainly had at their disposal the basis of an expansionist policy." The Truman Doctrine was vindicated.   ❑

Reprinted with permission from the May 1997 issue of *Veterans of Foreign Wars* magazine.

The Military and Geostrategic Dimensions of the Truman Doctrine

LIEUTENANT GENERAL PHOTIOS METALLINOS (RET.)

On behalf of the Hellenic Institute of Strategic Studies, I thank you for the honor to call me to this stage. I will focus my remarks on the military and geostrategic dimensions of the Truman Doctrine and the Marshall Plan, as seen from Greece's standpoint. In this respect, I do not believe it would be enough just to give you moral satisfaction by referring to the precious contribution of the Marshal Plan to my country.

It is equally important to mention the right use of the American aid by Greece during the civil war, the Greek role in NATO and the West's defense system, and the congruity of Greek policy with common goals in the modern Euro-Atlantic system of collective security.

I will try to relate to you the kind of policy and concerns to which Greece, as a basic strategic factor in the Eastern Mediterranean and a European colleague, remains dedicated in its long-range political orientations, and its loyal support of Euro-American policy on stability and security issues in the area. It is a loyal policy that will survive any dramatic changes that could happen in the wider area.

The political surprise of the disbanding of the Warsaw Pact was welcomed as a happy end of a forty-five-year long European bipolarism. At the same time you are aware that major political surprises are not happy. The postwar history of the U.S. consists of a series of political reorientations and changes in American policy, especially in the Middle East area.

What characterizes the American presence in modern European history is a sincerity in its efforts to promote and secure collective interests within the framework of respect for the international justice. It is the kind of morality proclaimed first by President Wilson at the Paris Peace Conference, after WWI.

The Truman Doctrine was a long-range policy that had a decisive effect on the historical evolution of Euro-American relations in the last five decades, resulting in an integrated political and security entity.

PHOTIOS METALLINOS is a special analyst in International Relations, Hellenic Institute of Strategic Studies.

The Truman Doctrine is simple and practical in character, transparent in its political goals. Also bold and risky in the extent of its international implications. Generous to both war partners and former enemies, it was a clear political conception elaborated in the light of democratic institutions.

The basic political goal of Truman Doctrine, as stated by President Truman himself, was "to support free peoples, who are resisting attempted subjugation by armed minorities or by outside pressures."

Greece and Turkey were seen as key countries for the security of the Middle East, as well as of the European and American continents. Thus both Greece and Turkey were able to receive immediate aid to resist Soviet expansionism.

Greece had suffered a communist coup, while Turkey was under Soviet political pressure to relinquish control of the Straits to the Soviets.

At the end of WWII, Greece was at the most critical point of its modern history. While the rest of the European countries were trying to recover from the wounds of the war, Greece, although adjudged to be in the Western sphere of influence by the Yalta Conference, suffered a communist coup, an effort to force the country into the communist camp. To the ruins of the war were added those of a civil war.

After a heroic resistance against Italian and German attack Greece had suffered a four-year occupation by Italian, German, Bulgarian, and Albanian forces that caused, full devastation of the country. Greece lost eight percent of its population, about 1 million people, the most of all the belligerent countries. We had 360,000 starvation deaths. Fifty percent of the population were protubercular. 3,700 towns and villages were completely or partly damaged. 1,200,000 people were left homeless and 88,000 rural families lived in ruins. Despite this situation, people's participation in the resistance was whole-hearted.

By September 1946, the countryside was under communist control. The country was divided into two parts, with two different governments. 700,000 refugees from the countryside fled to the large towns to escape the terror of civil war. The country was in complete chaos; the legitimate government was not in control.

In the most critical phase of the civil war, on February 28, 1947 the British government informed the United States about its decision to stop financial and economic support to Greece after March 31, and to retire its troops. Greece turned for help to the American administration.

The Truman administration, and in particular Under Secretary of State Dean Acheson, the person who received the British note, understood the new international role assigned to the U.S.

The Marshall Plan, which was elaborated by the State Department's Policy Planning Group headed by George Kennan, was aiming for the economic, political and moral recovery of Europe. Greece received economic, technical and military aid to nourish its starving population and to resist its communist threat. Thus Greece was spared the communist socialistic misery of the Balkan countries.

America allotted to Greece $300 million and $100 to Turkey in urgent financial aid, for the period until June 30, when the Marshall Plan started.

Within the framework of the Marshal Plan's military aid, the U.S. took the responsibility of organizing and maintaining the Greek armed forces, starting April 4, 1947. On November 1st, 1947 the military material inflow to Greece started.

On July 15, Dwight Greeswald, the chief of American Mission for Assistance to Greece (AMAG) arrived in Greece. He was accompanied by 206 technical and military consultants. That number grew to 1,216 by next year.

On December 31, 1947 the JUSMAPG was established in Athens to run the Joint U.S. Military Assistance Program for Greece. General James Van Fleet, who arrived in Athens on February 21, 1948, was assigned to JUSMAPG command in parallel to the duties of the American Mission chief.

He was a distinguished and capable officer, a field commander of WWII with an excellent military record that helped him to rapid promotion in the military hierarchy. He was selected for the position by Secretary of State General George Marshall. General Van Fleet was a strong personality and an active officer devoted passionately to the duty of organizing and promoting the Greek Army. General Eisenhower described him as a "non-intellectual character, also straight and decisive."

Greek General Petzopoulos characterizes him as "a great friend of Greece." Tireless in following military operations, ignoring battle danger and field hardships, sharing the agony and pain of the Greek soldier, General Van Fleet was the friendly American figure carrying about everywhere the symbolic flag of the American presence and partnership.

Among the responsibilities of the chief of the American Mission was supervising the flow and utilization of military aid: supplies, materiel, weaponry, ammunition, etc. As an official military advisor he attended closely to and rather shared the monitoring of military operations.

With regard to exceptional responsibilities, the first were officially assigned to British General Scoby, who was appointed the High Military Commander of the troops stationed in Greece, by the Gazera Accords on September 26, 1944. The chiefs of military missions to Greece, first General Scoby and then General Van Fleet were engaged in high-level military decision-making. Due to the political instability of this era and loose political authority, with the Cabinet changing almost every two months, foreign military involvement in the Greek offices administration was inevitable.

By the end of 1947, Greece had received 174,000 tons of American military materiel, comprised of combat and training aircraft, cruisers, minesweepers, etc., valued at $40 million.

The American engineering unit under AMAG supervision carried out a full program of road and bridge construction, railway repair, airfield and harbor installations, irrigation project, etc.

By the end of 1949, based on the American ambassador's report to Congress, Greece had received a total of $2 billion in aid, seventy-five percent of which was American aid.

Despite the reorganization of the Greek armed forces, it was common knowledge, that the only missing thing was the spark of military leadership.

In October 1948 General Papagos was assigned the Greek armed forces command with field marshall authority. Military personnel were increased to 265,000. Under Papagos leadership successful operations against the communist guerrillas put an end to the civil war at the end of October 1949.

***

Coming to the geostrategic role of Greece in the Eastern Mediterranean, I will stress that the Truman Doctrine came about because Greece and Turkey were seen as the key countries for security in the Middle East and the protection of United States' interests there. Greek and Turkish territory is a unified geostrategic area, with both of the countries functioning as supplementary security factors. The immediate consequence of this strategic fact was the contemporaneous integration of both countries in NATO.

The control of the Straits was a corollary to the main Russian objective of unrestricted access to the Mediterranean. In 1945 during the Potsdam Summit meeting, Russia claimed the right to establish military bases in Thessalonike or Alexandroupolis harbor, as an alternative that would bypass the Straits.

At the same time, the Soviets exerted political pressure on Turkey, aiming at the revision of the Montreux Convention and seeking common control of the Straits with Turkey. (Proposals of June 22, 1946.)

The Truman Doctrine put the policy of containment and resistance against communist expansionism into effect, and was the basis of a long-lasting American policy with global dimensions. NATO, the American Joint Task Forces in the Mediterranean, Atlantic, Pacific communication and surveillance installations and facility bases, are the pylons of American global policy, as it is reflected in the Truman Doctrine and Marshall Plan. The American engagement in WWII had a total cost of $341 billion and 460,000 personnel losses. It was the greatest investment in peace and security the U.S had ever made in its history, and needed a long-lasting guarantee. The Containment doctrine was the answer to contemporary security concerns, far distant from the American continent. Greece's and Turkey's roles in the Marshall Plan and later in NATO would be key factors in Balance of Power system, along with European countries reinforced by the American military presence in Europe.

With American military aid Greece and Turkey upgraded their armed forces. A full network of military bases and facilities was organized within the framework of bilateral accords with the U.S., to support an integrated security system in the Eastern Mediterranean.

The early NATO era for Greece and Turkey was characterized by collaboration and mutual confidence. Our NATO roles were quite clear. Greece had its armed forces oriented to the north thus covering the main Soviet axis of attack flanking Straits, together with Turkey covering the axis against East Thrace and the Straits.

The strong points of the Greek contribution against Soviet threat was the Aegean islands area and Crete, affording the necessary depth to defend the Straits and the sea passage to the Mediterranean. The Aegean islands area, being part of Greek sovereignty, was under Greek operational responsibility as part of COMEDEAST. Additional major Greek contributions were American bases and installations on the Greek mainland and the island of Crete, in support of the American fleet in the Mediterranean. Crete represents a strategic point of a major importance in the control of North Africa and the sea lines of communications from and to the Black Sea, to the Middle East and the Indian Ocean.

Turkey, besides controlling the Straits, had to cover a wide front with the Soviet Union on Turkey's eastern borders as well as covering the southeastern front, bordering the Middle Eastern countries.

The first problems in the functioning of the NATO defense system arose from an antagonistic stance by Turkey and Turkish claims to exercise operational control upon Greek Thrace and the Aegean area. It was an early indication of Turkey's claims against Greek sovereign territory.

Relations of the two countries in NATO became gradually problematic. The NATO defense system in the area suffered. Turkey vetoed the integration of the Aegean islands into the NATO defense system. There was a dispute initiated by Turkey on the legal status of the islands, questioning signed treaties and Greece's sovereign rights that are based on international law.

Since 1973 Turkey has concentrated its efforts to force upon the Greek islands a regime of condominium, aiming at the exploitation of undersea oil deposits in the Aegean. The crisis in our relations reached its peak with the Turkish invasion of Cyprus in 1974 and the Greek withdrawal from the NATO military branch.

The U.S. position of maintaining an equal distance between Greece and Turkey impaired indirectly Greek sovereign rights in the area and encouraged Turkish claims, which sought an unacceptable negotiation of Greek sovereignty. The Imia issue was case in point.

Today's Turkish position is in direct dispute of the Lausanne Treaty and Montreux Convention concerning the legal status of the Aegean islands. Prime Minister Ozal during his visit to Athens on June 14, 1988, following the Greek-Turkish crisis of 1987 and the Davos talks, was quite clear in his attitude. He put relations with Greece on a new basis, departing from the signed treaties, which he characterized as "unsatisfactory."

The continued Turkish occupation of northern Cyprus impairs relations with Turkey. Greece considers Turkey to be the number one threat against its national sovereignty. Cyprus, is the key for the normalization of Greek-Turkey relations. As you know, Cyprus is an island of major strategic importance for the control of the Middle East area and the normal oil flow vital to the Western economies.

***

I shall make a brief reference to important changes characterizing the post-Cold-War era and the roles assigned respectively to Greece and Turkey in it.

The most important change is the new conception *of collective Euro-Atlantic security,* and the *multipolarity of the threats,* in the place of a bipolar East-West security system based on balance of power.

The new threats in today's security system are foci of instability in the Balkans, the Caucasus, and the Middle East, due to local independence conflicts, terrorism, and Islamic fundamentalism. The uncontrolled proliferation of nuclear weapons and guided missile systems are also threats to European security.

The perspective of a NATO expanding to the Eastern European area, widening its security institutions and its operational area outside its traditional borders is another innovation, with NATO now functioning in the framework of a Security Council mandate. The Gulf and Bosnian wars, where NATO was engaged (directly or not) were a new operational model supporting European security and peace. Today's NATO comprises a unique, organized multinational force, responsible for pan-European security.

This identification of new oil deposits in the Caspian Sea, deposits equal in volume to those in the Middle East is the new element upgrading the geostrategic importance of the wider area. At the same time, it enhances competition for oil exploitation and control of the maritime and terrestrial lines of oil and gas transportation.

In the light of these new realities, we have to reconsider the roles of countries in the Eastern Mediterranean area.

Balkan conflicts originating in Yugoslavia have been the focus of European and American efforts. The possibility of an uncontrolled instability in the Balkan region is a reality, testing the political and military peacemaking mechanisms. The Dayton peace accords remain only partially carried out.

You are aware of recent Albanian turmoil. There are more potential instability foci in the Balkan region, namely Kosovo, Bulgaria, FYROM, and always Bosnia. A new Marshall Plan type of initiative in the area is deemed necessary.

In the middle of a dangerous instability in the Balkans, Greece remains a unique oasis of stability and economic strength. Greece's efforts to mediate problems in the Balkan area are a function of its temperate and peaceful foreign policy. Greece has offered good services as a political mediator in the Bosnian and new Yugoslavian crises, and today also in the Albanian one, enjoying as it does the confidence of the Balkan countries. Greece is a model for the Balkans, with its stable democratic institutions, healthy economy, advanced technology, and military forces strong enough to support peace in the area.

It is equally important to recognize the beneficial role of Orthodox Christianity, as a supranational element for cohesion among the various nationalities in the Balkans.

Turkey sees its role in the new era, an autonomous power among Islamic countries of the Caucasus, Central Asia and the Middle East. The Islamic area of Central Asia is a priority target for Turkish political and economic influence. Turkey's political engagement in Caucasian conflicts, acting within the framework of a Panturkist ideal, caused an angry Russian reaction. Turkey's parallel effort to interfere in the Balkans, as a protecting power of Islamic minorities, was not fruitful.

The establishment of Black Sea economic cooperation, and the effort to attract oil transportation through Turkish territory is part of Turkish policy to upgrade its economic and political role in the area. As part of this effort, the application of excessive "environmental" constraints in the Straits had blocked Russian oil transportation and is thus a violation of IMO regulations.

Concerning the unstable Middle East area, Turkey seeks a role as a military deputy and supporter of American interests. Sharing a double identity as a West-oriented secular state and an Islamic country, it would like to be a political link between the Western and Islamic worlds, and a buffer zone bordering an unstable area.

The creation of the CFE Exempted Zone in southeast Turkey is positioned in the framework of American interests in the Middle East.

The political and military manipulation of the Kurdish issue by Turkey, parallel to the exploitation of the issue by neighboring countries, contributes to the high tension in the area. Iraqi animosity and its mutual economic interests with Turkey, Turkey's territorial differences with Syria in conjunction with excessive use of Tigris and Euphrates water by Turkey, Iranian economic and cultural rivalry in Central Asia, further complicate Turkish policy in the Middle East.

American policy makers tend to exaggerate the Turkish strategic factor[1]. Political and economic instability, the growing political and social role of the Islamic party, and the Kurdish issue represent some of the major Turkish problems. Demographic alterations in the coming twenty-five years, mainly in the Kurdish and Iranian populations will further complicate the Middle East problem.

War against the Kurds and the partial occupation of Cyprus are exhausting the Turkish economy. The long-lasting Cyprus occupation is a hard test of United Nations credibility and its ability to enforce its resolutions.

Despite American political efforts, Turkey's future in the European Union is quite uncertain. It is not Greece that blocks Turkey's integration. It is Turkey's bad economy, its violation of human rights and liberties, its arbitrary political methods and culture, its expansionist attitude. All of the above, together with Turkey's membership in OSCE and other European organizations create contradictory political swings between the Islamic and European worlds.

We prefer a more European and more collaborative Turkey, instead of an aggressive neighbor swinging between her domestic problems and imperial ambitions. A possible gradual transfer of the economic and political center of gravity of Turkey from West to East, would mean the definite solution of the "Eastern Issue" and endanger the European borders with Greece. Normalization of Greek-Turkish relations to the detriment of Greece's sovereignty rights would be a violation of the tenets of the Truman Doctrine and of international law.

Concerning Greece and Cyprus the main problem is the political containment of Turkish expansionism through the enforcement of U.N. resolutions on Cyprus. Any attempt to force a political solution of the Cyprus question based on a political compromise in favor of Turkish demands in the area would be a Pyrrhic victory for peace and American credibility, and a drastic break with Truman Doctrine principles.

Greece in the twentieth century offered much and lost too many in the battles for freedom and democracy. In no other period of its long history has Hellenism suffered such a great uprooting. Today's Turkey is built on Hellenic ruins: in Asia Minor, in Pontos, East Thrace and Constantinople, in Imbros and Tenedos islands, and now in the northern part of Cyprus.

Although history teaches us that the most convincing argument in international relations is that of power the greatest achievement of the political human being is the building of universal peace based on mutual confidence

---

1. In accordance with a Langley Foundation study, Turkey is among the sixteen "high threat" countries in the world, threatened with immediate collapse due to its major problems. ("Pontiki" 9-2-96)

and the consolidation of human rights and liberties. Thus was the wall of European bipolarity demolished and all Europe set on the road to peace. It is not only national power that has made the United States a global force, it is the trust of the people and human expectations for freedom and prosperity.

And now that the wars have come to end, I wish you to be happy in peace. Would all mortals from now on, live as one population, in conciliation, for a common prosperity. Consider the universe as your own country, with common laws, where the excellent will govern, independently of their race. I don't characterize people, as the narrow-minded do, as Greeks and barbarians. I am not interested in the descent of the people, nor about the race they are born to. I apportion them with only one criterion, virtue.

"For me any good foreigner is a Greek, any bad Greek is worse than a barbarian." Alexander the Great, town of Opi, 324 B.C.

Hellenism has honored President Truman by erecting his statue in Athens. As a free person I would like to express my gratitude for what the U.S has offered to my country.

Thank you happy citizens of the free and democratic American states. God blesses your country.   ☐

Bibliography

Ambassador Economou-Gouras: *The Truman Doctrine and Greece's Agony*, Athens, 1957.

M. Gen. D. Zaphiropoulos: *Anti-Guerrilla Struggle*, Athens, 1956

L. Gen. Alex. Tsigounis: *Athens's Post-War Division and Guerrilla War, 1945-1949*, Athens, 1966

L. Gen. Th. Petzopoulos: *1941-1850 Tragic March*.

Society for the Study of the Greek History (EMEIÓ): *The Sacrifices of Greece in the War, 1940 - 45*.

Charles M. Mee, Jr.: *The Marshall Plan*, New York, 1984.

Emanuel Wexter: *The Marshall Plan Revised*, London, 1983.

Lawrence Whitner: *American Intervention In Greece 1943-1949* (translation), Salonica, 1991. Columbia University Press, 1982.

Ambassador MacVeagh Reports: Greece, 1933-1947.

Henry Kissinger: *Diplomacy*, 1994.

The Greek Crisis and the
Truman Doctrine

The United States Role in the Greek Civil War

During World War II the seeds of dualism became evident in Greek politics. The political division that continued after the war had officially ended became an early scene of the new cold war conflict and contributed greatly to the interplay of Big Three policies in and around the Greek arena. The importance of Greece stemmed from the value of its geographical location in relation to the policies of the Big Three and on the emerging conflict between the Soviet Union and Great Britain, with the United States gradually supporting Britain's Greek policy.

The objective of Great Britain was to keep Greece outside the orbit of the Soviet Union. To achieve its objective, Great Britain in October 1944 concluded the well-known agreement with the Soviet Union. In the agreement Rumania and Bulgaria were allotted to the Soviet sphere of influence, Greece to the British. As a result of this agreement British troops landed in Greece in mid-October 1944. These British troops were to maintain the territorial integrity of Greece from threats by outside foes.

In 1944 the official policy of the United States regarded Greece as being primarily a British responsibility and gave support to British policies. Both powers, however, desired to neutralize the Greek left through a center-right coalition. They believed that Greece's problem was due to a combination of internal weaknesses of great proportions and external pressures. These two factors made Greece the classic example of how a country could collapse unless outside help was supplied. Between the communist uprising in December 1944, and Truman's offer to help Greece in 1947, the United States, under the stress of events due to deteriorating relations with the Soviet Union, shifted from a passive policy of political idealism to an active realistic role in Greek affairs. This transition did not occur overnight. American interest in postwar Greece had mounted quickly after 1945. This was manifested in visits of American warships to Greece, in the decision to send observers to the Greek elections, in defending the Mission's report against Soviet criticism, and in supporting Greece in the debates in the Security Council, in February,

---

BASIL KONDIS, Ph.D., is Professor of Modern History at the Aristotle University of Thessalonike and Director, Institute for Balkan Studies, Thessalonike, Greece.

September, and December, 1946. The decision to help Greece in 1947 was the next logical step in the policy followed by the U.S. in its relations with the Soviet Union in Greece.

The United States perceived the crisis in Greece as a part of a Soviet plan to turn Greece into a people's republic. Moreover, the decision to aid Greece was a crucial prerequisite for stability in Turkey. If the communist guerrillas succeeded in seizing control in Greece, Turkey would have been threatened because of the strategic position of the Greek mainland and islands. World War II had shown that with the Germans in possession of the islands, the Allies had lost control of the Eastern Mediterranean. The same would have been true had the Soviet Union taken them over.

During the period after the December uprising the internal conflict in Greece was linked with the rivalry between the Soviet Union and the Western powers in the Balkans, thus giving great international importance to the political struggle in Greece. The deterioration in Greece posed a dilemma for the United States. The Americans had either to avoid further involvement with Greece and run the risk of seeing the country become a people's republic, or become more involved in Greek domestic affairs by pressuring the Greek government to take immediate and energetic measures to solve its economic difficulties. The U.S. government was fully aware of the grave difficulties facing Greece. It hoped, however that Athens, by taking firm action and at the same time being confident of outside assistance, would be able to lead Greece on the road toward economic recovery.

By the fall of 1946 the State Department had formalized and underlined its growing interests in the Eastern Mediterranean and had shown that Washington regarded the oil resources in the Middle East and the strategic location of Greece and Turkey of vital importance.

Although economic aid continued to be discussed during the fall of 1946, there were numerous indications that the United States was willing to consider military as well as economic aid to Greece. In early October, at the Paris Peace Conference, Prime Minister Constantine Tsaldaris met with Secretary of State Byrnes. The American secretary told Tsaldaris that the United States would send an American economic mission to survey Greek economic conditions, that Greece would get a liberal share of post-UNRRA aid, and that the American government would do what it could to make surplus military equipment available to Greece.

By mid-October, the military and economic situation in Greece had become very serious. Refugees from the countryside fled to Athens and Thessalonike, foreign exchange was exhausted, and a deep sense of panic had infected the country. Because of rising military expenditures the cost of living was increasing. The British government, confronted with the Greek request for more arms in order to increase the strength of the army, refused to comply;

Britain could not undertake the obligation to support a larger Greek army. On the other hand, the United States sent eight American army officers to Athens to join the staff of the military attaché. *The New York Times* reported that the sending of these officers to Greece indicated the growing American interest in the worsening situation in northern Greece.

At this point the American government was very much concerned with the political situation in Greece, and was looking for ways to counsel the Greek government to pursue a policy of moderation. It was thought that the best thing to do was for the American ambassador to have a conversation with the King. Indeed, on October 11, MacVeagh visited the king and suggested that he should provide personal leadership, insist on the political leaders getting together to form a broadly representative government, promote widespread tolerance, justice and mercy, permit difference of political opinions, prosecute nobody except for definite commission of crime, and finally free all those imprisoned for political crimes. If such a program were put into effect, MacVeagh stated, seventy percent of the existing "banditry" would disappear.

The State Department, having reevaluated its general policy toward Greece, thought that it should be made clear to the king and Greek government officials that active American support of Greek independence and territorial integrity was based on the assumption that Athens would repudiate its aggressive policies, and that the extreme right would inevitably move toward the center. That the security of Greece was of vital importance to the United States was stated in a letter from President Truman to King George. The letter mentioned that to enable Greece to fight for its independence and the preservation of its territorial integrity, the United States was prepared to grant substantial aid and supplies. The president suggested that the Greek government should help persuade American public opinion that the rulers of Greece constituted no oligarchy of reactionaries, that democratic institutions were fully functioning, and that the entire Greek people, except the communists, were united.

Should the American people be so convinced, they would be prepared to submit to the new economic sacrifices that aid to Greece would entail. President Truman suggested that the best way for persuading the American people was to broaden the Greek government, to avoid excesses, and speedily to reorganize the army. Thus, by the end of October 1946, the United States intended to give direct aid to Greece, going beyond mere moral support and a show of force through naval visits. The Greek ambassador reported shortly after Truman's message that the defense of Greece was indeed a concern of the United States. The Americans had assured the Greek government that the integrity of Greece was a basic point of American policy in the Eastern Mediterranean. This policy's implementation would become more effective if Greece formed a government of national unity. The Americans thought that the conditions which favored the growth of communist strength would disappear if economic and political reforms were undertaken by a coalition government of centrists and social democratic parties.

Throughout this period the problem that was greatly complicating the international situation in Greece was the matter of the South-Slav federation of Yugoslavia and Bulgaria. An added complication was that it was generally supposed that one of the federated states would be a greater Macedonia which would have included certain territories of Greece thereby violating the territorial integrity of that country. An important aspect of the Greek civil war has always been the relation of the Greek Communist Party (KKE) with the Soviet Union. In recent years, "revisionist historians" reject as unfounded the American fears about a Soviet plan to take over Greece. They argue that there was no danger from the Soviet Union, and that Stalin opposed, from the start, the Greek communist attempt to seize power.

Generally, there is no evidence to suggest that in 1946 Stalin wanted a communist take-over in Greece and that, in preparing for the "third round", the Greek communists were following Soviet instructions. There is, however, a definite possibility that the Soviet Union did not object to a KKE bid for power in the summer 1946, although it was not willing to make the Greek problem a major aspect of Soviet foreign policy, since it wanted to exploit the Greek civil war for its propaganda value, especially when Britain and the United States criticized Soviet policies in Eastern Europe. Stalin changed his attitude toward the Greek civil war only after the announcement of American aid. It is known, for example, from the works of Djilas, Dedijer, and Kardelj that in February 1948 Stalin told the Yugoslavs that the "uprising in Greece has to fold up." Neither Djilas nor Dedijer state anywhere in their studies that Stalin opposed the Greek uprising in 1946, nor that he told the Greeks to stop the armed struggle. Indeed, when Zachariadis learned about the Moscow talks from the Yugoslavs, he was not alarmed, as Stalin's views were not expressed directly to the Greek communists.

Moreover, when, in September 1949, Zachariadis asked Stalin about the information given to him by the Yugoslavs, the Soviet leader denied having said anything to them. It is evident that the lack of sources makes it very difficult to clarify Soviet policy in 1948. In any event, we have contradictory statements. In March 1949, Stalin, discussing the Greek problem with the Albanian leader Enver Hoxha, stated: "As for the Greek people's war, we have always considered it a just war, have supported, and backed it wholeheartedly...." Also, the meeting with Stalin in January 1950 of Hoxha, Zachariadis, and Partsalidis gives added evidence that the Soviet leader did not oppose the Greek civil war. At that meeting Zachariadis' position that he would never have started the armed struggle if he had known in 1946 that Tito would betray the KKE was severely criticized by Stalin, who pointed out that there was Bulgaria and Albania, and that the Greeks had to fight for the freedom of the people, even when they were encircled. Moreover, he criticized the Varkiza agreement, noting that the Greek communists should not have signed it and should not have laid down their arms.

The conversations of Stalin with the Yugoslavs and the Albanians do not indicate in any way whether or not Stalin opposed or supported the Greek civil war. One can say that the Soviet Union permitted the Greek communists to go ahead with the revolt, the latter assuming full responsibility, and the Soviet Union avoiding any official connection with the KKE. Should the revolt be successful, all the better for the Soviets. If it were a failure, then the Soviets could maintain their non-involvement.

At this point in December 1946, Greece was in danger of losing the war without having fought it. The country was faced with danger from within and from without. These two dangers were interlocked; if one were realized, the other also would be realized. In order to prevent the threat of being crushed by outside forces, Greece sought the assistance of the United Nations Security Council in restraining Greece's three northern neighbors from aiding the guerrillas. And, to avert a collapse from within, the Greek government appealed to the United States for economic and military aid.

According to Secretary Byrnes the American government was sympathetic toward Greece, and had a strong desire to contribute to Greece's economic recovery. However, President Truman could not help Greece avoid collapse and communist control without authorization from Congress.

Early in 1947 the question was either to give massive American economic and military aid to Greece or let the country be turned into a people's republic. The prospect of a communist Greece, outflanking Turkey and the Middle East and thus endangering the security of Western Europe, forced President Truman to go before Congress on March 12, 1947 and ask for the allocation of $ 400 million in aid to Greece and Turkey.

The American government used the occasion of the British withdrawal from Greece to enunciate a policy which it had been thinking about for a long time. There was nothing surprising about Britain's departure from Greece. What really shocked American officials was the abruptness with which Britain forced the issue. No one had expected the British to withdraw by the end of March. The Americans needed three or four months to lay out the details of their new policy toward Greece; the British withdrawal, however, had a catalytic effect on American planning.

Besides the strategic considerations of the Truman Doctrine, the economic factors were very important. American officials looked at Greece and Turkey and the entire Mediterranean region as the key to insuring the flow of raw materials and thus maintaining American economic power. The oil resources of the Middle East and the economic interests of the United States in the Mediterranean area, namely the "open door," were of vital importance.

The American objective in Greece was not to reconstruct the Greek economy but only to hold inflation to the point where there could be no adverse effect on political stability and on military efforts to defeat the insurgents. An important aim of the aid program was to rebuild the confidence of the Greek people in their economy and provide an incentive to stimulate their own efforts toward recovery.

Throughout the civil war period, the Greek government had no economic policy at all. It gave special favors to a favored few in order to permit them to make huge profits. The Americans, being aware of the inadequacies and shortcomings of the Greek officials, and seeing that the security situation in Greece was having a direct effect on the economy, were inclined to concentrate on the establishment of internal security first as a necessary prelude to, and basic prerequisite of economic and political reforms and economic rehabilitation.

The immediate problem the Americans had to face right after the proclamation of the Truman Doctrine was the military problem. The first officers of the military mission arrived in Greece on May 24, 1947. The basic objective of the mission was to assist the Greek military, by furnishing it with supplies and equipment, so that it could restore order and security within the state and enable the vital processes of reconstruction to proceed unhampered. Beyond the immediate tasks of determining what supplies and equipment were needed and assisting in their receipt and distribution on arrival in Greece, it was also necessary for the United States military mission to undertake the instruction of Greek personnel in the operation and maintenance of American equipment, with which they were unfamiliar. It soon, however, became evident that the problem of supply and training were too closely integrated with those of the strategic, tactical and political aspects of the Greek army for them to be maintained altogether as a separate undertaking. By the fall of 1947 the American officers had become quite naturally involved in the problem of developing the Greek army into a more effective fighting force, and recognized that eventually they would have to assume a major planning role in Greece. The use of American combat troops in Greece was considered, but rejected as unnecessary.

The great needs of the Greek army were revivification of its offensive spirit, freedom from political interference and release of its units from static guard duty. More than one-half of all infantry battalions were dispersed for the protection of villages and towns, thereby making it impossible to organize striking forces for a real offensive against the guerrilla forces. A major change in the tactics against the guerrillas took place in the spring of 1948, after the arrival in Greece of General James Van Fleet. The general, as director of the newly established Joint United States Military Advisory and Planning Group, had great powers and managed to convince the Greek General Staff to take the initiative and undertake operations against the insurgents in the Pindus and Grammos mountains. However, at this point a most effective step was undertaken by the Greek army, namely, the policy of evacuating peasants from the border villages. This policy, suggested by the Americans, had a twofold objective. First, the communist Democratic Army would not be able to find men to recruit and second, the guerrilla forces would not be able to find food supplies in the villages. This policy proved to be very successful as the Democratic Army had a shortage of manpower in 1949, while it had plenty of weapons. The Greek communists had planned to increase the strength of the Democratic Army from 20,000 to 60,000 men with the objective of taking control of western Macedonia.

By the end of June 1949 and before the final defeat of the guerrilla forces in August 1949, a total of 396 ships had delivered, since the beginning of the aid program to Greece, 520,000 tons of military supplies and equipment from the United States. This massive military aid enabled the Greek army to defeat the guerrillas. During this period the Americans controlled the Greek state apparatus, facilitated the dominance of the right in the country and brought about Greece's political dependence upon the United States. ◻

Greece and the United States

THEODORE A. COULOUMBIS

The Greek civil war, to which the Truman Doctrine was deeply attached was a tragic period. The history of the Greek civil war has been written in three waves. The first wave was written by the victors of the civil war. I call it the orthodox school of thought. The second school of thought comes much later, after the fall of the dictatorship, after 1974, when a whole array of books and articles were published. I call it the revisionist school of thought, because it was told mostly from the perspective of the vanquished in the civil war.

This presentation will fall into the third school of thought, which I call post-revisionist. This school of thought emerged only with distance and time, the healing of the war's wounds and also the bankruptcy of the Soviet system. It views the civil war as a tragedy, where the heroes of both sides are flawed and where, in the end, the American presence (through the Truman Doctrine and the Marshall Plan) enters in the form of *apo mixanis theos* or *deus ex machina*, to pick up the pieces and create a new order out of chaos.

The third school of thought, interestingly enough, includes books and articles written by the victors as well as the vanquished with a self-critical orientation. In fact, one of the most touching books I have read is by Hronis Misios, an ex-communist. The book is titled *At Least You Died Early*. From Misios' perspective, even after its defeat, the communist opposition was equally as, if not more oppressive than its capitalist adversary.

If you go these days to Athens and visit Klafthmonos Square, the Square of Tears, you will find a beautiful statue symbolising the reintegration of Greek society. It depicts the torn body of Greece, cut in half, with a third part putting its arms around the two and bringing them together into a single and reunited society.

But let us briefly relive the experiences of those times. In early 1947 the Greek civil war began assuming large-scale proportions. This was happening at a time when the British had given notice of their inability to support the Athens government beyond March 31, 1947. Simultaneously, Greece's Balkan neighbors were vilifying and propagandizing against the allegedly fascist and

THEODORE A. COULOUMBIS, Ph.D., is professor of International Relations, Department of Political Science and Public Administration, University of Athens, Faculty of Law, Economics and Politics and president of the Hellenic Society of International Law and International Relations.

authoritarian measures of the Greek government. The economy was in a state of near paralysis following the terrible legacy of war and occupation. The non-communist politicians still nursing old, traditional grudges appeared unwilling or unable to coordinate their activities. Most of rural Greece was in E.A.M./E.L.A.S. hands and the situation was deteriorating fast. At this most critical bend of Greece's post-war tragedy, British interference ran out of steam and the United States was invited to fill the vacuum. The transition policy was named the Truman Doctrine and presumably signalled a radical turn in the traditionally isolationist and non-interfering policy of the U.S. It is important to illustrate the near complete dependency of the Athens government on external British and later American support. The late '40s were not a time for Greek politicians to worry about the niceties of autonomy or even its outward appearance. This was a time where political survival was at stake and they were not likely to bite the hand that fed them. No one has captured better this condition of total dependency than former U.S. Secretary of State Dean Acheson, one of the competing fathers of the Truman Doctrine. In his memoirs he wrote:

> All this time Greece was in a position of a semi-conscious patient on the critical list whose relatives and physicians had been discussing whether his life could be saved. The hour had come for the patient to be heard from. On March 3 with the support of friends and their guidance of a feeble hand, the Greek Government wrote, asking for help—financial, economic, military and administrative.[1]

Apparently the diplomatic hand of Greece was so "feeble" at the time that even the request for American help had to be drafted in Washington by U.S. officials.

The Athens government understood very well that American help would mean limitations to its national sovereignty. The minister counselor of the Greek Embassy in Washington, Mr. Economou-Gouras, reported to the Athens home office that "Although the U.S. government had no desire to intervene in Greek internal affairs, it recognises, nevertheless, that the full implementation of the proposed plan could not but involve *some kind of interference in these affairs.*" A bit later Gouras added: "...the U.S. Plan will be accomplished by a limitation in some measure of the sovereign rights of Greece."[2]

While the Athens government (and that is part of tragedy that I am trying to convey) was clinging desperately to Washington's support for survival, the communist insurgents were looking for Moscow's support in their badly thought-out quest for power. In Moscow's case however, guidelines, slogans and aphorisms abounded, but tangible material support was not forthcoming. It is now generally argued by analysts that Stalin and the Soviet Union were opposed from the start to the Greek communist bid for power, which

1. Dean Acheson, *Present at the Creation,* (New York: 1969), p. 221
2. Quoted in Joseph M. Jones, *The Fifteen Weeks,* (New York: 1964), pp. 77, 146.

was viewed as impotent, as well as quixotic and destabilizing of the post-war balance of power in the Balkans.

Professor Basil Kondis, in his presentation, mentioned the Moscow percentages agreement between Churchill and Stalin (Moscow, October 1944) which, if you read in Churchill's memoirs, was kept faithfully throughout the period of the Greek civil war. Stalin's clearest illustration of his attitude vis-à-vis the Greek communist guerrillas emerged in a conversation he had with Milovan Djilas. Assessing the Greek communists, Stalin argued that they had no prospect of success at all. "What do you think", he said to Djilas, "that Great Britain and the United States—the United States the most powerful state in the world—will permit you to break their line of communication in the Mediterranean Sea? Nonsense, and we have no navy. The uprising in Greece must be stopped and as quickly as possible".[3]

The Greek communist insurgents managed, however, to secure substantial assistance from their Balkan neighbors, especially from Yugoslavia. But this assistance might have been extracted at the expense of a promise that a slice of Greek territory would be, "restored to Yugoslavia."[4] Also illustrative of the foreign dependency of the Greek communists was their split into pro-Titoist and pro- Stalinist factions after the Soviet Yugoslav dispute surfaced in 1948. The Stalinist faction promptly purged the Titoists, thus insuring the loss of the main source of tangible, external support for the E.L.A.S. forces.

The civil war which afflicted Greece for nearly four years was bloody, damaging, and costly to the nation and its people. Estimates of battle casualties are staggering for a country of such small size, which had just emerged from the devastating effects of World War II and the occupation, during which 550,000 people (eight percent of the Greek population) perished.[5]

Instead of concentrating on reconstruction and development and competing within the bounds of the democratic process, Greek elites (both communists and non-communists), penetrated by external parties, sought to substitute violence for politics in their competition for the reins of power. The results were predictable: according to Greek government figures, the communist guerrillas, between June 1945 and March 1949, suffered 28,222 killed, while 13,100 were taken prisoner and 27,931 surrendered. The estimate of those wounded was twice as high as the above combined.[6] The Greek national army suffered 10,927 deaths, 23,251 wounded and 3,756 missing, while about 4,000 civilians had been executed, murdered, or lost in combat-related accidents.[7]

3. Milovan Djilas, *Conversations with Stalin,* New York), pp. 181-2.
4. Richard J. Barnet, *Intervention and Revolution,* (New York : 1968), p. 126.
5. Constantine Tsoukalas, *The Greek Tragedy,* (Harmondsworth, England, 1969), pp. 91-92
6. Edgar O' Ballance, *The Greek Civil War,* New York, 1966), p. 192.
7. *Ibid.*

One analyst, Edgar O'Ballance, estimated the total cost in human life alone of this bloody exercise to have been over 158,000 dead, of whom about half were armed communists and the rest were government troops, security forces, police and civilians.[8] Beyond these casualties there were an estimated 700,000 refugees who were displaced from northern Greece, mostly to the Athens area, hoping to avoid the effects of the civil war. It is instructive to read on this point the outstanding book by William Hardy McNeill, *The Metamorphosis of Greece,* which presents the story of the rapid emptying of the villages and the resultant urbanization of Greece, a tragedy which ultimately created the demographic infrastructure upon which a stable democracy was to be built after 1974.[9] One should also consider the loss to Greece of 50,000 to 100,000 able-bodied men and women who fled at the end of the civil war to the various countries of Eastern Europe and to the former Soviet Union. By the end of the civil war, the communist insurgents—having been decisively defeated—retreated mostly to Albania and Bulgaria, as well as to other East European countries and the Soviet Union. They promised, unrealistically, that someday they would return to claim the victory that had eluded them so narrowly.

In retrospect, the Greek civil war appears to have been politically pointless, in the sense that the superpowers had quietly pre-empted its outcome. If one were to judge the people who fought and died on both sides, one could say that they carried their quest for political power beyond the limits of prudence. In the case of the Greek communist leadership, one should add political obtuseness, in the sense of this group's inability to read Stalin's subliminal signals regarding the futility of their struggle. Both sides in the civil war demonstrated a strong propensity for foreign associations and dependencies, much in the tradition of modern Greek history. We should remember here that political parties in Greece, after independence from the Ottoman Empire, were called the British, French, and Russian parties. And those were their official names.

Finally, one could add that in this battle amongst extremists it was the center, progressive and pragmatic forces of the country which were by-passed in the stormy political process. The nearly total eclipse of Greece's centrist forces was probably a function of the neutralization of the moderate political leadership as a result of protracted years of persecution under the Metaxas dictatorship and the Axis occupation, followed by the blunt and destabilizing policies of the British during the war and early post-war years.

We can conclude safely that, perhaps without the massive (over $2 billion dollars) U.S. military and economic aid, Greece would have been placed under

---

8. *Ibid,* p. 202
9. William Hardy McNeill, *The Metamorphosis of Greece Since World War II,* (Chicago, The University of Chicago Press, 1978).

a form of communist rule which would have evolved into a political system somewhere between the former communist systems of Bulgaria and Yugoslavia.

In conclusion, some telegraphic conceptual and counterfactual thoughts that might probe some discussion: The long-term consequence of the Truman Doctrine is that Greece avoided the fate of a Soviet satellite and developed into a viable democracy and market economy, even though it took some years. Had Greece avoided the civil war, had the Left and Right played by the rules of the parliamentary game (with which Greeks had had long experience in the nineteenth and even in the twentieth centuries), Greece would have matched developments in countries such as Italy and France. For those who still think in territorial terms, Northern Epirus might have been part of Greece, preventing the difficulties the Greek minority is facing in Albania today. The Cyprus issue also would not have deteriorated the way it did, thereby bypassing the most damaging experience in Greek foreign policy since World War II.

In the past, I used to be fascinated by concepts such as influence, interference, intervention and penetration and I paid little attention to variables such as socio-economic backwardness, poor and populist leadership, and painful historical memories of the two major schisms between royalists and republicans and communists and nationalists in the twentieth century. All these variables came to a head in April of 1967, when the dictatorship was imposed on Greece, leading Americans and West Europeans to consign the country to the category of an unstable democracy in the "praetorian zone."

Since 1974, Greece has come a long way! It has bridged the gaps of the two major schisms of the twentieth century. It has developed a viable two-party system, or a bi-pentapolar party system. It has entered the E.U.'s greenhouse of democracies; it is steadily meeting the stringent criteria for membership in the hard core of post-Maastricht Europe, and it is firmly anchored, in terms of security, in the Euro-Atlantic family of nations. But Greece's major problem, as we all know, is its neighborhood. Very often I keep telling my students that we are like Pompeii and our neighborhood has a couple of mountains called Vesuvius and Aetna, and we cannot be towed away. The key to Greece's future is to consolidate further its democratic institutions, to protect them, to remain in the region of stability and interdependence, to continue steadily improving the economy, and, with respect to its neighborhood, to avoid becoming part of the problem by yielding to nationalistic temptations, but to remain part of the solution. ☐

Truman Doctrine:
A Fiftieth Anniversary Reassessment

VIRGINIA TSOUDEROS

Fifty years have elapsed since President Harry Truman addressed the U.S. Congress and asked its approval to aid Greece and Turkey. It marked a new era in U.S. foreign policy. The U.S. took the leadership of the western camp. Its primary aim for the next forty years was to contain the expansion of the Soviet Union. And while the policy of containment ended with the fall of the Berlin Wall in 1989, the impact of this policy on countries like Greece and Turkey, which had found themselves on the frontiers between East and West can still be felt. What was the impact on Greece and how did the U.S. decision influence Greece's development since 1947?

There are two aspects to the Truman Doctrine and the Marshall Plan as seen from the Greek point of view. First, the impact it had on Greece's political, economic and social development during these past fifty years. It suffices to mention the opportunities given to Greece to develop free institutions. Second, the impact it had on Greece's position as related to its neighbors, be it to the west, north, or east.

There is no doubt that the Truman Doctrine gave Greece the opportunity to live in freedom and develop its democratic institutions. It was up to the Greek people themselves, the Greek government and opposition and the political world as a whole, to take advantage of opportunities offered, and to establish a democratic system of government, based on the principles of free elections, free expression and respect of minority opinion.

Even before the end of the war it was apparent that the unnatural but temporary wartime alliance between the West and Soviet Union was coming to an end and was being replaced by confrontation. This was to mark not only changes of alliances between states but also between parties within each state.

Within Greece the political scene was confused for two main reasons: The unnatural but temporary wartime alliance between the Western democracies and Stalin's communist regime which gave a false message to many young idealists who little did they realize the existence of political cynicism. Added to this was the repugnance felt by the majority of Greeks for the pre-war Metaxas

VIRGINIA TSOUDEROS served as Deputy Foreign Minister of Greece from 1991 to 1993 and Member of Parliament for nineteen years (1974-93). Ms. Tsouderos also worked at the International Monetary Fund and was a journalist.

dictatorship (1936-41). The King and his British supporters were held responsible for the later.

All of this did not allow for clear thinking. The end of the war led to unnatural alliances, which became an easy object for mutual vilification between right and left. As a result, supporters of the Western ideals of freedom and staunch opponents of the communist system, found themselves in the same camp with collaborators of the Nazi and Fascist occupation forces and the followers of the Metaxas regime. Similarly, for exactly the opposite reasons, Greek communist forces, especially in the north, found themselves giving cover to, or accepting in their ranks, entire battalions of collaborators of the Germans, Italians, or Bulgarians. The communists in Greece did not understand that the panslavic aims identified themselves with the communist regime as they had done before with the tsarist one.

To this confusion was added the different goals of foreign missions in Greece. The British government, expert on disputes in the area, cared little to help dissipate the confusion. Its interest was to reestablish the pre-war status quo, while British officers in the field followed, more often than not, a different policy. Their aim was to damage the military power of the enemy with any forces available, regardless of political affiliations and future implications. No wonder that the Truman Doctrine by itself could not solve the problems brought about by all this confusion of political ideals, new social needs, and clashes of great powers' interests in controlling this vital political area.

Truman gave Greece and Turkey the opportunity to construct Western-type pluralistic democracies by defending those countries against the Soviet threat. And this in itself was a great gift. Luckily at the time, the vital interests of the U.S. coincided with those of Greece to protect itself from a new form of dictatorship.

By 1946, the great alliance imposed by the vagaries of war had come to an end, and the dawn of the Cold War was in sight. New, unnatural alliances were formed on all sides. Wartime enemies became allies, and friends of yesterday became suspicious opponents. While it is a relatively easy thing for states to shift alliances with each other, such shifts are much more difficult within societies and social groups.

On the other hand the American officers who replaced the British in 1947 were primarily responsible for the implementation of the Truman Doctrine, and had little concern for internal politics. Nor should we have expected this from the U.S. representatives in Greece, although quite often officials in the field interfered in Greek political affairs, leading them to misuse of power well beyond their authority. Having said that, I consider that although democracy in Greece, in the first post-civil-war years, fell far short of what it should have been, this responsibility lies largely with the Greek governments as well as the short sightedness of the opposition forces and the communist leadership. The same situation in other European countries was dealt with in a less detrimental way, perhaps because there was no confusion among the aims of the resistance groups during the occupation. On the whole the communist leadership in Greece had as its priority the preparation of the social revolution and forceful takeover of power after the end of the war. Fighting the Germans came second and was a good excuse to recruit young freedom loving Greeks.

Thanks to Truman, Greece in 1989 was the only Eastern European country with well established, free democratic institutions and a per capita income one hundred fold of that in countries of the former communist bloc. Greece, thanks to the Truman Doctrine, is the only member of the European Union in the Eastern Mediterranean. However, there were serious limitations to the policy due to its stopgap character. We cannot resist wondering how things would have been if greater attention had been given to policies which took into account the merits of each case separately, and not just that of the global containment policy.

Now I shall turn to the impact the Truman doctrine had on the balance of power between nations in the region and stability—short and long term—in the Eastern Mediterranean. The Truman Doctrine was primarily about democracy through the containment of the Soviet Union. As the well-known columnist Walter Lippmann said in 1943: "The U.S. chose to support Greece and Turkey because they were a strategic doorway for us to the Black Sea and the heart of the Soviet Union."

The U.S. was concerned about Stalin's intention to succeed where the tsars had failed. It was obvious that the Soviets at the time considered the moment propitious to impose on the "Evasive Neutral" (as Professor Weber called Turkey) a new regime in the Straits, thus allowing the U.S.S.R. to become a Mediterranean power. From the Soviet's viewpoint, suspicion of Turkey was absolutely justified. We should remember that during the most critical days of the Battle of Stalingrad, Turkey helped the Germans form an army of 200,000 composed of Muslims from the occupied Soviet territories. Turkey's policy during World War II, detrimental as it was for the allies, was of no concern. Now the U.S. containment of communism was of uppermost concern.

However there were serious limitations to the policy due to its stopgap character and one and only goal. We cannot resist wondering how things would have been if greater attention was given to policies which took into account the merits of each case separately, and not just that of a global containment policy.

Turkey's policy creates a permanent sense of instability in the area. If we seek stability, then a policy of containment of Turkey is needed. In this sense, the policy of equal distance, initiated in Truman's days, has had a negative impact on the Greek-Turkish relationship. If attention had been given to the development of democratic institutions and respect for human rights, perhaps today the stresses in the Aegean might have been less, or nonexistent. The implementation of the Soviet containment policy, without taking into account the merits and the specific character of certain special cases, created problems. These problems, although not quite clear at the time, have now emerged to bedevil all parties concerned.

Two such examples are of absolute concern to Greece. The last phase of the Greek civil war, 1946-49, was to a large part fostered by Tito's plan to create a new federal state in his version of a Greater Yugoslavia. It reflected his ambition to expand the borders of Yugoslavia to the Aegean. While Tito was on good terms with the Soviets, his support of the communist army in Greece coincided with Soviet interests and made him an enemy of the West.

The whims of history are most unpredictable. Suddenly, the leader of the world democratic camp, a staunch believer in human rights, free elections and the rights of minorities, found itself receiving with open arms the deserter from the Stalinist camp. It was an unexpected gain in the difficult struggle to contain communist expansion toward the vital region of the Middle East that contains the sources of energy for the West. While the global responsibility of the U.S. dictated a policy of encouragement to Tito's new orientations, Greece's special concern focused on his insistence in pursuing his so-called "Macedonian" policy.

Fifty years ago, while U.S. officials recognized the validity of Greece's concern with Tito's irredentist claim on Macedonian heritage, Greece was pressured not to raise the issue, as the priorities of the time were to stabilize and secure Tito's position outside the Soviet camp. It was argued that there was no danger to Greece's national security since the claims were unfounded. Fifty years later, Greece was asked to accept an agreement which in fact gave credence to Tito's policy. This was based on the acceptance of a Macedonian identity other than a Greek one. As a result, the Greek identity of Macedonia, which most serious scholars accept as a fact, is put into question in the name of political expediencies. By ignoring at the time the special merits of the question, a precedent was created that serves destabilizing irredentist claims in the area. Greece is now saddled with a problem which has created incipient claims on its national integrity, with all that this means for the Balkans. Let us not underestimate the fact that, although this newly founded state (FYROM) is perceived to have problems mainly with Greece, the real danger to its existence and regional stability comes from its other neighbors, Albania and Bulgaria. By undercutting and weakening Greece in this area, the only country linked by cultural and economic interests to the West, this vital region may one day offer an easy prey to radically hostile forces. So, while in 1947 the global policy approach dictated tactics aimed at cajoling, or a least not disturbing Tito, the fact that the special issues of Greece's case were not addressed is to a large extent responsible for today's problems in the region.

In the second example the same shortcomings can be identified concerning the impact of the Truman Doctrine on Turkey's position in the Middle East. No doubt, the threat from Soviet expansionism faced by Turkey and Greece was similar, but there existed serious differences in outlook and goals in the relationship between the two countries. Since Kemal's time, Turkey only tenuously adhered to the 1924 Lausanne Treaty with Greece—of which she had imposed the conditions as a victor—using it instead as an instrument for further claims. Greece's adherence reflected a policy of peaceful coexistence implemented by Prime Minister Elevtherios Venizelos in 1932. The occupation of Alexandretta (Syria) by Turkey, the disregard of the provision for self-rule of the islands of Imbros and Tenedos, near the Straits, the invasion of Cyprus in 1974, recent claims on Greek islands and Thrace are but a few examples of Turkey's post-Lausanne policy. Turkey needs little encouragement to show disrespect of international agreements and the rule of law.

Turkey's policy, creates a permanent sense of instability in the area. It needs no encouragement. To ensure stability, a policy of containment of Turkey is needed. In this sense the policy of equal distance with complete disregard of Turkish scorn for the rule of law initiated in Truman's days, had a negative impact on the Greek-Turkish relationship. If attention was given to developing democratic institutions and respect of human rights, and fighting poverty, perhaps today the stresses in the Aegean might have been less or non-existent.

The "evasive neutral," while an object of attention by all parties during the war, could not have expected in its wildest dreams that soon after the end of the war it would receive the same economic assistance as Greece. Turkey had fared well economically in World War II, while suffering no material or human losses. Moreover, Turkey had sold its raw materials at quite advantageous prices to the Axis. Ankara conveniently declared war against this good customer a week before its collapse. Pragmatism at the time dictated the need to strengthen Turkey economically and militarily, in view of the desire expressed by the Soviets to control the Straits and become a Mediterranean power.

Unfortunately for Greece, the U.S., as Kissinger points out in his well-known recent book *Diplomacy*, is averse to implementing a policy based on the principles of the balance of power. U.S. foreign policy was then based purely on one issue: containment. Other merits in a case such as dictated by the wisdom of history and the dangers created by the imbalances between allies, do not seem to have played any major part in the implementation of the Truman Doctrine. In certain quarters, one could even detect the notion that they viewed this as one geographical area, ignoring the characteristics of the two different countries and the interests of the people.

I fully understand and even admire the position of the new U.S. secretary of state, that the U.S. cannot be "a prisoner of history, but a shaper of history." I cannot but ponder on the fact that, more often than not, policies which do not take into account their long-term impact can have negative repercussions on the ends they were meant to serve. History can be very vengeful against those who snub it.

The Truman Doctrine created a reality which it imposed on an already existing balance of power architecture. One cannot hold responsible for unexpected developments those who conceived of the Truman Doctrine. The fact remains that, as one of your distinguished diplomats and experts in the area recently said in an interview on Cyprus television, "as long as the U.S. has a global role to play, Turkey will be important to the U.S." Turkey is important while it does not get out of hand; just as Iran was and can be important as long as she does not get out of hand. Turkey's demands never end. This is something that the British understood. This is what makes Turkey a destabilizing center in a troubled area. When all its demands are met, Turkey proves arrogant and insatiable. When contained, Turkey can become a cooperative neighbor. Those of us who live in the area know that when hard to get balances are disturbed, hell is let loose.

What is called the moralistic approach to international policy may not be regarded as serving the purposes of a great power. Responsibilities are of such magnitude that the pragmatic approach is considered more efficient. The pragmatic approach always is part of any foreign policy whether of a large or a small country. In democratic societies, however, pragmatism must be tempered by moral considerations and legal codes, otherwise public opinion may react in a way as to neutralize the effects of such pragmatic policies.

The history of U.S. foreign policy is replete with examples. U.S. policy has always tried to provide moral justification. For example, President Roosevelt presented U.S. participation in the war not as an effort to save the British Empire, but to build a world based on principles of the Atlantic Charter. The human rights campaigns led by the U.S. were to a degree responsible for the downfall of the inhuman Soviet regime.

Encouragement of regimes for purely pragmatic reasons and, supplying them with sophisticated deadly weapons' systems while disregarding their contempt for the rule of law and international agreements, assures disaster sooner, rather than later. In this regard I feel compelled to mention the U.S. sale to Turkey of the ATACM missile system aimed at "command and control structures" and personnel. Its range is meant for use against targets within 150 km. In the case of Turkey, these targets are largely Greek and Cypriot ones with high civilian concentrations. This may serve the needs of Turkish policy makers, for such a threat is a more efficient way to force populations to leave their homes (the Turkish Army used mass terror to accomplish this goal in the past in Cyprus and in Kurdistan). But providing instruments of ethnic cleansing and mass murder does not conform with American values. Why should U.S. policy makers be surprised and disturbed when anti-missile missiles are obtained by Cyprus, in an effort to defend its population from these deadly weapons? The Cypriots, by their purchase of the S-300 system, are going a long way toward restoring the balance of power, which can only augur well for the stability of the region.

In conclusion, we cannot forget that the timely assistance given by the U.S. to the government of Greece, saved the Greeks from experiencing Soviet-style totalitarianism. It is unfortunate that wisdom comes only too often with hindsight. I am sure that many responsible Greek politicians on both sides of the battlefield would have agreed, if asked today, that they would have evaluated the circumstances of the post-war era differently, and would have used the opportunity given to us by American assistance to build sooner a more just and stable democracy. It took us another twenty-five years to reach a more balanced outlook on internal politics and accept the realities of the international interplay of power.

It seems to me equally just to point out that Greece has paid, and is paying, more than her full share for global policies aimed at the peace and security of mankind. It is time to take into account certain special conditions which in the past presented and are again present, serious causes of unrest and undermining of stability and peace in the Eastern Mediterranean region. We can only hope that the day will come when the goals and general principles for which Truman worked and in which he believed will guide all of us to build a more stable and just world. □

The Truman Doctrine:
Impact and Legacy

The U.S.-Greek Strategic Relationship During the Cold War and Beyond

MONTEAGLE STEARNS

The fiftieth anniversary of the Truman Doctrine means the fiftieth anniversary of the occasion on which the United States first declared its special concern for Greek independence. We sometimes forget that the occasion might have been celebrated more than a century earlier—in 1823—in the form of the Monroe Doctrine, which was originally conceived by President Monroe. As a strong declaration of American support for Greek independence, it was Secretary of State John Quincy Adams who converted the Monroe Doctrine into a warning to continental European powers against further colonization in the Western hemisphere. This is a reminder that American foreign policy can be diverted from its intended course and that doctrines are not always what they seem to be. Even the Truman Doctrine has had unintended consequences.

One of these involved Cyprus. We know that the immediate effect of the Truman Doctrine was for British influence and responsibility in Greece to be transferred to the U.S. A result of that transfer of power and influence was to untie the hands of Greek conservatives in the Papagos government in seeking *enosis* with Cyprus. Cyprus at the time was a British crown colony and union between Greece and Cyprus was beyond the hopes and dreams of Greek foreign policy as long as Greece was dependent on British assistance to check the rise of Greek communism. With that transfer of responsibility to the U.S., it is no coincidence that Greek support rose for the idea of *enosis*. And it was, as you remember, when Anthony Eden gave his famous "never" to Marshall Papagos, that the situation in Cyprus became critical, because Greek Cypriots and Greeks were convinced that nothing short of violent opposition to British rule would be successful.

Out of the tumult of those years of struggle came the ill-fated London Tripartite Conference of September 1955 among Britain, Greece, and Turkey, and the Turkish anti-Greek riots in Istanbul and Izmir during that conference. The Turkish anti-Greek riots resulted in the deterioration of Greek-Turkish relations, which has never been reversed. Greek-Turkish relations never recovered from those terrible days in September 1955. Cyprus is still the

MONTEAGLE STEARNS, Ambassador to Greece (1981-1985)

victim of that train of events. In a sense, when Cyprus achieved independence in 1960, it was a consolation prize for Greek-Cypriots who would have preferred union with Greece, and also for Turkish-Cypriots, who would have preferred that Cyprus remain a crown colony or that the island be divided.

What this means to me is that the Truman Doctrine had an effect, not only on internal developments in Greece, but also on the balance of power in the region, posing for us the question: What kind of regional balance should we be seeking after the Cold War? The Cold War abbreviated our terms of reference when we addressed regional problems, since we were convinced that blocs were more important than regions and that a balance of power, when it did not exist in a given region, could be imposed by the two superpowers leaning against each other from outside the region.

We in the U.S. and in Western Europe discounted the importance of regional problems. After the promulgation of the Truman Doctrine, the U.S. did not really develop a Greek policy or a Turkish policy. We simply tried to fit Greece and Turkey into our Soviet policy and the fit was never a very comfortable one. But, this had another effect that was even more uncomfortable. It meant that we discounted the importance of problems—the problem of Cyprus, the problem of the Aegean, the problem of Greek-Turkish relations generally—because we believed incorrectly that when Greece and Turkey were admitted into NATO in 1952, their ultimate security aspirations had been achieved. Everything else was of lesser concern. And this was, of course, far from the truth. Particularly as the Cold War turned into a frozen war, Greek preoccupations and to some extent Turkish preoccupations with regional issues became much more important in the two capitals.

Not so in Washington. The mistake that the United States government made in this period—the post-Truman Doctrine period—was a peculiar American mistake. It was to regard Greece and Turkey as components of a strategic equation, rather than as products of their own historical experience. With the Cold War behind us, we must dismiss from our minds blocs and strategic equations and begin to approach regional problems on their merits.

It is clear, first of all, that the importance of southeastern Europe has increased since the end of the Cold War. Averell Harriman wrote to U.S. Ambassador to Greece Lincoln McVeigh in July of 1946 that even if the Soviet Union were to occupy the region of the straits of the Dardanelles, the Greek islands would represent an important barrier to the extension of Soviet influence into the Mediterranean itself. If that was the case then, it is no less so now, not because the Aegean islands are a barrier to the successor states of the Soviet Union, but because the Aegean islands can serve as a guarantor of free passage, of innocent passage, and a guarantor that no hostile power can occupy the Aegean itself.

How long will the U.S. regard the Mediterranean and the Aegean as important geostrategic areas? It was a fellow speaker, Admiral Henry Mustin, who pointed out that the Clinton administration has made clear in rejecting French attempts to transfer the southern command of NATO in Naples from an American admiral to a European officer, that the U.S. continues to believe that the Mediterranean and the Aegean are vitally important areas for the U.S. and for U.S. security. In this connection, it is important to remember that the U.S. today may be the only remaining superpower in the world, but is in fact more dependent on the rest of the world than it was immediately after WWII.

When I say that the U.S. is more dependent on the rest of the world, I mean that in 1945 the U.S. was responsible for producing roughly 52 percent of the world GDP, but was responsible for only 10 percent of the world volume of trade. Today, the U.S. economy is responsible for 25 percent of the world GDP, but 30 percent of the world volume of trade. Roughly three out of ten American jobs are dependent on either foreign investment or foreign trade. And when we study the Gulf War—and hear some American commentators say that it demonstrated the supremacy in military terms of the U.S. in the world after the Cold War—we must remember at the same time that the diplomatic effort that was organized to help pay for the Gulf War was as intense and, in the end, as effective as the military campaign it had supported. In other words, the U.S. had to go to others. We could project power but we could not pay for the projection and we did not wish to pay for the projection.

Greece, Greek space, and Greek security have to be of continuing significance to the U.S. Admiral Mustin referred to the strategic importance of the Souda Bay naval base in Crete. No one could operate in the Eastern Mediterranean without taking Souda Bay into account. It is still the only harbor in the eastern Mediterranean which could, if necessary, shelter the entire U.S. Sixth Fleet. As long as freedom of passage through the Eastern Mediterranean matters to U.S. policy makers, Souda Bay and its support facilities will matter.

The Greek seacoast, including the Greek islands, is about as long as the American coastline, if you subtract Alaska and Hawaii. So Greece is by definition a maritime power. And the U.S. has a maritime tradition dependent more and more on trade, which means it depends more and more on assuring free lines of communication, including notably, sea lines of communication.

Thus, Greece continues to be a very important friend for the U.S. And as the action in NATO moves from northwestern Europe, which we used to call NATO's central front, to the southeastern flank of NATO, that will add to the need of the U.S. to pay more attention to the area.

What does paying more attention mean? I think it means that the U.S. is going to have to develop a Greek policy, however relatively. It is going to have to develop a Turkish policy. It has to take a much more active interest in Cyprus than it did in the past. We were very reluctant to recognize the importance of Cyprus and the Cyprus problem. Right from the beginning, as long as Cyprus could be treated as a British problem, we were delighted, and later after Cyprus became independent, when we paid attention to the problem of Cyprus, it was in spasms of crisis diplomacy—the George Ball mission, the Clifford mission, the Vance mission, the Matt Nimetz mission. These missions, on the whole were well intentioned, but they tended to be, with the possible exemption of the Nimetz mission, fire-fighting operations. When the danger of an armed conflict between Greece and Turkey over Cyprus had been eliminated, Washington went back to its other preoccupations. We never developed an independent view of what was right or wrong for the Cypriot people. Now that has to be done.

We know the Clinton administration has committed itself publicly to a new Cyprus initiative. My wife Toni and I were in Cyprus in late November and early December 1996 and did not come away from that visit optimistic. We toured the north for most of an afternoon, and it is a desolate region, Kyrenia an abandoned port. You have the sense of walking through a wax museum. We had lunch in Kyrenia and were virtually the only people there that day. The bill came to so many Turkish liras that we paid in dollars. Occupied northern Cyprus has inherited all of Turkey's economic and fiscal problems, along with some others that it made itself. Contacts between Greek Cypriots and Turkish Cypriots are almost nonexistent and, as you know, the situation has been complicated by massive immigration from the mainland. A great many Turkish Cypriots have departed. It would have been easier for Greek and Turkish Cypriots to reach an agreement, even with Turkish Cypriot leader Rauf Denktash, than it is likely to be in the future with the unknown effect created by Anatolian immigration. Some of those Anatolian settlers are not even Turkish in ethnic terms, including the Lat people from the Black Sea coast. They tend to be the least educated and the least westernized of the Turkish population.

The Clinton administration is committed to making a new effort and, by implication, also committed to evaluating the Cyprus problem on its merits and not simply as a weight in the superpower balance. Frankly, however, they have very little to work with. I myself have felt for many years that progress on Cyprus is going to be impossible until there is progress in improving Greek-Turkish relations. That was hard enough when Westernizing influences where unchallenged in Turkey during the Cold War. The emergence of powerful Islamic political forces necessitates a reappraisal of Turkish policy.

Are we seeing the birth of a new, post-Kemalist Turkey? I think, rather, we are seeing a partial rebirth of pre-Kemalist Turkey. I served many years ago as a young officer in Turkey, when I was working in the information program of the State Department. I had the chance to travel in eastern Turkey near the Soviet border and to southeastern Turkey, in the region of Diyarbakir, where at night you heard gunfire along the border because Kurdish unrest was perfectly evident, even then. There had been a large-scale Kurdish uprising in the 1930s.

What is happening now is not new. This is the old Turkey reasserting itself. I would conduct these field trips and would return to Ankara and participate in staff meetings at the embassy and realize that my colleagues in the political or economic section were talking about a totally different Turkey from the one I had been traversing. The well educated, diplomatically astute governing class of Turkey talked a language that Western diplomats invariably understood. It was only when you went out beyond the range of that elite, that you began to see that there was a completely different Turkey existing alongside it.

Bizim Koy—my village, in English—is a fine Turkish novel published almost fifty years ago. It describes the misadventures of a young Turkish villager traveling from eastern Turkey to Istanbul to sell the turkeys he has raised. In the course of the journey, he loses them all. Some are stolen, some are killed, and some are eaten by wolves. He eats one or two himself to survive and ends up in Istanbul with nothing. That dimension of Turkish life is real. With the demographic changes that have occurred in Anatolia over the last twenty to thirty years those Turks (and Kurds) who live in it are beginning to find a political voice.

When I talk to Turkish specialists I find they do not consider the "new" Turkey to be a passing phenomenon. They think that if there were to be Turkish elections tomorrow, the Islamicists would probably get a larger percentage of the vote. This does not mean that Turkey is going to turn into Iran. Turkey and Iran are as different in their way as Turkey and Greece are. But it does mean that the Turkey that the West and Greece came to take for granted is probably not going to be the same again. This poses problems not only for American policy but also for Greek policy.

It is in Greece's long term interests that the Westernizing influences in Turkey be nurtured, that Turkey become more European. It is certainly a fact that even if Greece today would become an advocate of immediate admission of Turkey into the European Union, the economic objections would be overwhelming from the Western Europeans themselves. Under no circumstances is Turkey, within the foreseeable future, going to become a full member of the European Union. But to the extent that Greece helps Turkey become more European, Greece's security and Western security will, I think, be enhanced.

When we talk about security in the post-Cold War, we are not only talking about military measures. We are also talking about the political and economic health of the region of southeastern Europe and of the Balkans. And here, Greece's influence can be enormously constructive. Already, economically, Greek investment in Bulgaria is second only to that of Germany, and it is fair to say that the drachma has become the reserve currency of the Balkans. If Greece has not been able to do even more economically, it is because Greece has been far too timid and cautious both in its diplomatic and economic policies. From a political standpoint, Greece, after all, is a member of both the European Union and NATO, as well as the Western European Union.

Greece's alliance system is the most effective of any country in the region and Greece is a functioning democracy, which having ended its own nightmare of civil war, now has political parties which represent genuine alternative approaches to the organization of its society. They do not have to be called the Russian, the British or the French parties. They are Greek parties. Greece no longer needs patrons. It now needs allies and it has them. The bolder and more imaginative Greek policy becomes, particularly toward its neighbors, the less defensive it is, the more constructive its effect will be and the less dangerous the neighborhood that it lives in will become.

And it is certainly in the interests of the U.S. to promote that process to the extent possible. The most important way in which the U.S. can help to maximize Greece's stabilizing and developmental influence in the region is to do what we can to make Greece more self-confident. Athens has every reason for greater self-confidence. Greece is in a strong position and should not conduct its foreign policy as though it were in a weak position.

So, to strengthen the strategic relationship of Greece and the United States after the Cold War, I see a need for careful review by both sides. On the American side, we need to develop a clearly focused Greek policy to replace our earlier Soviet-focused policy of containment. On the Greek side, is the need to recognize the strength of the Greek position in the region and to make the most of it. I hope we can work together to make that happen. ❑

Greece's Vital Role in the Triumph of the Democracies

PAUL R. PORTER

I am not the Paul Porter whom President Harry Truman sent to Athens in early 1947 to appraise the dire consequences of the sudden withdrawal of British aid to Greece and whose report led to the creation of the Greek-Turkish aid program. His middle initial was A. Mine is R. The near identity of our names was confusing to many people when I went to Athens in 1949 to administer our aid.

I arrived in Athens for the first time at 5:00 A.M. on an all-night flight from Geneva. At the Grande Bretagne hotel, I was assigned its best suite. I was shaving when the general manager knocked at my door to welcome the Paul Porter he knew. His beaming face froze when he saw me. Concluding that I was an impostor, he informed me that the suite of rooms had been reserved for another party. I should move to a single room. I had just repacked my bag when he returned, apologizing profusely. He had just seen the morning papers, he said, and learned that there were two Paul Porters. The suite had been reserved for me, after all.

During the civil war, then nearing its end, the Greek government had made special security arrangements for my two predecessors, former Governor Dwight Griswold of Nebraska and John Nuveen, an investment banker from Chicago. Each day, a soldier accompanied me to my office and sat just outside my door with a revolver in his lap. The house I inherited as mission chief was patrolled day and night by soldiers in colorful evzone costumes. The security arrangements were vivid reminders of the communist-led civil war that had raged for four years. Some 670,000 citizens among a population of 7.8 million were forced into refugee camps. Without American economic and military aid, Greece would have spent the next forty years on the wrong side of the Iron Curtain.

To appreciate the critical role that Greece played in the ultimate collapse of the Soviet Union, I draw attention to two historical epochs of singular

---

PAUL R. PORTER held three positions in the Marshall Plan: chief of its mission to Greece (1949); its assistant administrator (1950); and was appointed to its No. 2 post, the Acting United States Special Representative in Europe, based in Paris (1951).

importance. The first was the epoch of the world's first democracies in the Greek city-states. The high point of that epoch was surely the defeat of the mighty Persian empire by Athens and its allies. It was followed by the creation of the Confederacy of Delos, a mutual-security association of democratic states that had no parallel until the creation of NATO. Unfortunately, the confederacy did not survive. In time, Athens itself fell to the troops of Philip of Macedon, father of Alexander. Democracies disappeared from the face of the earth for more than two thousand years.

The second historical epoch of which I speak began with the First World War and lasted until the collapse of the Soviet Union six years ago. The bungled peace that followed the First World War planted the seeds of the second. Among the unhappy consequences of the peace was Turkey's drastic venture in ethnic cleansing that drove a million Greeks from sites in Asia Minor that had been the homeland of ancestors since ancient times.

In the Second World War, the Greek army held Italian invaders at bay, whereupon the Germans intervened with a brutal conquest and occupation. When they surrendered, the British provided emergency economic aid and military support against a communist uprising. However, by early 1947, Britain itself was in a desperate plight. Its government informed General George Marshall, then our secretary of state, that it could no longer give aid to Greece. He promptly informed congressional leaders that "we are faced with the first crisis of a series which might extend Soviet domination to Europe, the Middle East and Asia."

On March 12, President Truman addressed a joint session of Congress. His talk lasted only 18 minutes—an example I will follow. Greece, he said, was in desperate need and it should be our policy to give financial aid to help its people preserve their freedom. He asked the Congress to approve $250 million for Greece and $150 million for Turkey, which was also threatened by the Soviet Union. The Congress voted by a three to one majority to meet his request.

Encouraged by the favorable public response, General Marshall on June 5 proposed aid to other European countries willing to join together to achieve their recovery. When the Marshall Plan began in May 1948, the Greek aid program was merged into it. I will try to give you a few glimpses of the obstacles we faced and how the aid mission and the Greek people responded to them.

On the Saturday before Labor Day in 1949, Averell Harriman, who as United States Special Representative in Europe occupied the No. 2 post in the administration of the Marshall Plan, told me in his office in Paris that he and Paul Hoffman, the administrator, wanted me to become chief of the mission to Greece. My predecessor, John Nuveen, was being transferred to Belgium and on Tuesday evening would be on a TWA plane from Washington that would pass through Geneva, where I worked for the State Department. Harriman wished me to join Nuveen on that flight. Between Geneva and Athens, Nuveen instructed me in my new job.

He and Griswold had chosen a staff of exceptional ability. At the peak, the mission employed 181 Americans and 48 Greeks—the latter as interpreters, special assistants, typists, drivers, and two as legal advisers. Most of the Americans provided technical assistance in agriculture, manufacturing, mining, road building, electric power, finance, export development, and public administration.

Greece is poor in the raw materials needed by industry. To this natural disability was added a situation described by the *Sunday Evening Post* as "Left in ruins by the German occupation and ravaged by four years of civil war, this small, rugged country had to be rebuilt stone by stone." Many of the refugees from the Turkish ethnic cleansing were still in temporary quarters when I was in Greece. Their plight added to the poverty and political instability that gravely hampered the nation's recovery from the Second World War.

Election by proportional representation made it difficult for Greece's political leaders to maintain a governing majority. During fifteen months I dealt with seven governments. There were times when we disagreed with the government or important elements of Greek society. The government wanted us to finance a steel mill and an oil refinery. We declined. The proposed investments could not have provided steel or petroleum products as cheaply as they could be imported. When prosperous ship owners were delinquent in taxes, we pressed a hesitant government to deny needed shipping documents. It did and the taxes were quickly paid.

Almost every week I met with the prime minister and other ministers to discuss how to deal with the many bottlenecks in the aid program. Every two weeks our treasury expert and I met with the chairman of the Greek equivalent of our Federal Reserve Board to review the performance of the nation's economy. Every day, I met for half an hour with our ambassador. I was fortunate to have a cordial relationship with all of them.

I hated to leave Greece. My wife and I had made many friends among the Greek people. On my way to work it was an inspiration to raise my eyes to the top of the Acropolis and see the marble Parthenon gleaming in the rays of the morning sun. However, after I had been there 15 months, I was asked by William C. Foster, who had succeeded Paul Hoffman as administrator of the program, to join him in Washington as assistant administrator. My last act before leaving Greece was to persuade our military authorities who administered our aid program in Germany to stop financing imports of tobacco from the United States and to substitute tobacco from Greece, which traditionally had been a major supplier of the German market. Restoring that practice meant a double saving for the American taxpayer. We stopped spending Marshall Plan dollars for tobacco to Germany while Greece's new export earnings reduced its need for American aid.

During the first week in my new job I was visited by five United States senators from tobacco-raising states. They were not pleased. They asked me to revoke the new arrangement so that American exports of tobacco to Germany would continue. I told them that we would not pay for any tobacco exports unless directed to do so by legislation.

The aid program, which continued until 1954, was a major success. With our help, Greece rebuilt its war-damaged economy, established new industries, resettled the many people displaced by the civil war, built roads that linked isolated villages to markets, created a national electric power network, reclaimed unproductive land, improved public health, stabilized its currency, and raised both agricultural and industrial production to levels never attained before. It resumed its role as an exporter of tobacco and became also an exporter of rice, frozen fish, cement and textiles. It became a member of NATO and the European Union and during the long Cold War played an essential and honorable role in the eventual collapse of the Soviet Union.

We do not know what name historians may give to the epoch that began with the First World War and culminated with the Soviet collapse. I choose to call it *The Time of the Trials and the Triumph of the Democracies.* In the time since the triumph, both we and our allies have become so immersed in the squabbles of the day that the vision and the common will that produced the triumph have faded. Hence, the question: Can the triumph be maintained, or will it come apart like the Confederacy of Delos? We may not know the answer for a generation or so, but I remain optimistic. If the United States and its allies can preserve and extend their well-earned triumph, the years we have known will be remembered as one of the great periods in all history. ☐

The Impact and Legacy of the Truman Doctrine: The Clinton Agenda in View of the History of U.S.-Greek Relations

VAN COUFOUDAKIS

Let me congratulate Gene Rossides for sponsoring the first event in Washington, D.C. commemorating the proclamation of the Truman Doctrine, which was a turning point in post-World War II American foreign policy.

Over the last day we have paid homage to one of the greatest presidents in the history of our country, a man who rose to the challenge of a new and dangerous era, and mobilized the nation in pursuit of the objectives he defined in his address to Congress on March 12, 1947.

In the time available to me, I will comment briefly on the challenges facing American relations with Greece in the absence of a doctrine or of a clearly formulated direction in our foreign policy in this momentous period described as the post-Cold War era.

Greece fought valiantly in the Second World War from October 1940 to May of 1941. Greece was devastated during the Axis occupation. Liberation brought civil unrest, political instability, and dependence on outside powers. Britain's collapse drew the United States into the Greek crisis because President Truman recognized the strategic and political importance of Greece for American interests in Europe. Greece in 1947 was vital for regional stability, much as it is now.

Throughout the Cold War Greece supported the United States, despite negative public perceptions of American policy in Greco-Turkish relations and the problem of Cyprus. Dependence led to the manipulation of Greek politics by the United States. However, I must emphasize that Greek political and military elites were willing participants in this process. As you know, it "takes two to tango." In 1967, a military dictatorship was established in Greece; its only international support came from Washington. This madness culminated in the coup against the government of Cyprus and in the Turkish invasion of Cyprus, with Kissinger's toleration and support. These events inevitably undermined the relations of Greece with the United States.

VAN COUFOUDAKIS, Ph.D., is Dean of the School of Arts and Sciences, Indiana University-Purdue University, Fort Wayne and Professor of Political Science.

The restoration of democracy in Greece in 1974 marked a fresh start in American relations with that country, as bilateral relations moved from dependence to interdependence.

The end of the Cold War brought a sense of optimism, with the decline of the nuclear threat and the anticipation of greater reliance on the rule of law in international relations. The international community, however, was unprepared for the rapid changes that followed the end of the Cold War. The United States and NATO attempted to define a new role in this rapidly changing international environment which was filled with new sources of instability.

Greece encountered a new threat from the north. This time the threat did not come from a hostile ideological system, but from the revival of irredentism and nationalism that followed the demise of communism and the collapse of Yugoslavia. Instability was also caused by the rapid and simultaneous economic and political transitions that the former communist Balkan countries were going through, and by Turkey's involvement in the affairs of those countries. However, the major threat facing Greece in the post-Cold War era came from the east. Turkey's revisionist policies that began in 1974 in the Aegean and Cyprus have now culminated into a full-blown challenge of the status quo that was established by international agreements since 1923.

In 1947, President Truman acted decisively in Greece because he concluded that instability in southeastern Europe would have an adverse effect on the rest of Europe, and thus for American interests. Today, Greece *is* the source of stability in the region. Greece and the United States share a common and enduring interest in Balkan stability and in the continued peaceful economic and political transition in the former communist countries of this region. In contrast to its neighbors to the north and to the east, Greece *is* politically stable, with established and functioning democratic institutions and processes. Most importantly, however, Greece *is* a status quo power with *no* revisionist objectives and with *no* territorial claims against any of its neighbors. Greece will protect its borders but, in contrast to many of its neighbors, it does *not* look beyond its borders to satisfy its national sentiments. Greece supports the status quo established by international agreements, such as those of Bucharest in 1913 and Lausanne in 1923. Greece is also the only European Union member located in the Balkans. In contrast to its neighbors, Greece has made a political, economic, strategic, and cultural commitment to an integrated Europe. The activism and successful performance of the Greek private sector in Bulgaria and Romania shows that Greece has the entrepreneurial know-how and the ability to contribute to the transition to free economies of the countries of the region and to their economic development.

Finally, in view of the strategic threats facing southeastern Europe and the Eastern Mediterranean, Greece continues to occupy a most important strategic location vis-à-vis the Balkans, Northeast Africa and the Middle East. Much like during the Cold War, Turkey would be strategically isolated and unable to perform the role it now claims for itself without a strong Greece on its west.

While Washington and its European partners share goals such as stability and peaceful change, they disagree on specific policies, institutional roles and policy priorities. Examples include the role and expansion of NATO, NATO's out-of-area operations, Turkey's role in the post-Cold War era and its relations with Europe. America and Western Europe are often competing for political, strategic and economic influence rather than cooperating in southeastern Europe.

The United States played a pivotal role in bringing about a short-term resolution of the crisis in the former Yugoslavia. Despite policy disagreements with Greece, the United States did assist in bringing about an interim agreement between Greece and the Former Yugoslav Republic of Macedonia (FYROM), and in improving the conditions for the Greek minority in Albania. However, the relations of Greece with the United States will continue to be affected by the American response to human rights issues in Albania and FYROM's attempt to claim a denomination appropriating Greece's historical and cultural heritage.

In the final analysis, the foremost priorities of Greek foreign policy are Greco-Turkish relations and Cyprus. These issues will actually provide the critical test for the relations of the United States with Greece in the post-Cold War era. Washington has become Ankara's silent partner in pursuit of the late president Ozal's vision of Turkey "from the Adriatic to the China Wall." Greece is *not* asking the United States to abandon Turkey, but to recognize that the common goal of stability in southeastern Europe and the Eastern Mediterranean cannot be attained through revisionism and through violations of international law. Issues affecting Greco-Turkish relations directly affect American interests. Respect for international treaties, the sanctity of internationally established borders, and the renunciation of the threat or the use of force have been and remain fundamental principles of American policy. These are also the issues underlying Greco-Turkish relations today.

Under Secretary of State Dean Acheson, in his testimony to the Senate Committee on Foreign Relations, described Turkey as a "proud and independent country" that would not accept interference in its politics or policies. Today, this perception of Turkey has become a self-fulfilling prophecy and a rationalization for U.S. unwillingness to confront Turkey over its revisionist policies and the threat posed to American interests by the rise of Islamic fundamentalism in Turkey. It has also allowed Turkey to manipulate American policy without fear of consequences for its gross violations of human rights, its recent violations of American laws regarding dealings with terrorist countries such as Iran, Iraq, and Libya, its continuing occupation of Cyprus, and the threat to use force in the Aegean and Cyprus.

Throughout the Cold War the United States recognized the strategic interdependence of Greece and Turkey, but placed greater strategic value on Turkey because of its geographic location, its control of the Straits and the size of its armed forces. These assessments were wrong then because, without a strong, pro-Western Greece, Turkey would have been isolated and its control of the Straits would have been meaningless if someone else controlled the space from Crete to the Straits. This is true today, especially with the unstable conditions in the Balkans and the rise of Islamic fundamentalism in Turkey.

Greece is a member of the European Union, NATO and a close ally of the United States. In the absence of a common European defense and foreign policy, and the American activism in the Balkans, Greece has cooperated with the United States in pursuit of common objectives in the region and in defusing problems in its relations with Albania and the FYROM. Greece also recognizes that the United States can play the most significant role in moderating Turkey's revisionism. The alliance of Greece with the United States may be tested in the future by another development, i.e. the emergence of a unified Europe. This may create a dilemma for Greece in view of its commitment to European integration, the significant role the United States will continue to play in the region, and the frequent divergence of European and American interests and policies. The hope in Greece is that this will not present an either/or choice in its foreign policy. The future challenge for the European Union and the United States will be the compatibility of their interests and their ability to pursue together common objectives in an interdependent international environment.

In view of these comments about the challenges facing the relations of the United States and Greece, what are some guidelines for the Clinton administration?

a) Do *not* take Greece for granted *or* treat Greece as America's stepchild. The days of the late 1940's, the '50s and the '60s are behind us.

b) Do *not* isolate and condemn Greece as was done during the Yugoslav crisis. This will lead to a siege mentality in Greece and will prove counterproductive to the common interest in regional stability.

c) Do *not* expect that Greece will sacrifice its vital interests in order to appease unstable regimes such as those of Berisha, Gligorov, or Erbakan.

In turn, these three guidelines require that the Greek political leadership needs to incorporate in Greek foreign policy the consensus that emerged in post-1974 Greece on foreign policy issues, and *not* allow personal political ambitions and partisan interests to undermine the long-term national interests of Greece. It also requires that Greece promote its *long-term* interests through multilateral European institutions, where, on the eve of the twenty first century its future lies.

Americans of Greek origin need to project the common values and common interests that have guided and bonded the relations of the United States and Greece throughout this century. The Truman Doctrine defined America's relationship with Greece during the Cold War. The common threats that the United States and Greece confronted then are long gone. It is time to redefine American relations with Greece on the basis of the common values and long-term interests the two countries share in the region, and for Washington to show sensitivity to the special security needs of Greece that emanate from the dangerous neighborhood Greece is located in. ☐

The Truman Doctrine and the Value in Developing a Special Relationship with Greece

EUGENE T. ROSSIDES

Greece's defeat of the communist insurgents during the Greek Civil War (1946-1949), with military and economic aid from the United States under the Truman Doctrine, was an historic turning point in the Cold War containment of communism and in world history. Stopping the communist takeover of Greece, including Crete, prevented Stalin's and Tito's domination of the Aegean Sea and Eastern Mediterranean and the strategic encirclement by the Soviet Union of the Middle East oil resources, including the Persian Gulf area.

The seeds of the civil war were sown during the Greek national resistance to Nazi Germany's occupation of Greece. Greece's famous *OXI!* (NO!) on October 28, 1940 to Mussolini's ultimatum, and its defeat of Mussolini's fascist forces in Albania for a period of several months (October 28, 1940-April, 1941), forced Hitler to divert valuable troops and arms to invade Greece on April 6, 1941 and delay his May 15, 1941 timetable for the invasion of the Soviet Union. Greece's fight against the German invasion, the fierce resistance in Macedonia and Crete, further delayed Hitler's timetable. Because of the seven weeks it took Germany to conquer Greece, the start of Operation Barbarossa, the invasion of the Soviet Union, was delayed until June 22, 1941. That delay overturned German plans to occupy Moscow before the onset of the heavy Russian winter and was a turning point in World War II.

That delay has been credited by military experts and historians as one of the main factors that prevented Hitler's defeat of the Soviet Union. Karl E. Meyer, in a *New York Times* editorial footnote, stated that Hitler believed that the several weeks it took Germany to subdue Greece was responsible for his losing the war against the Soviet Union. (*N.Y. Times*, April 16, 1944, A20, col.1)

But Greece's actions in World War II did not end there. During the harsh Nazi occupation, Greece's national resistance activities forced the Germans to

EUGENE T. ROSSIDES, ESQ., is senior counsel in the international law firm of Rogers and Wells. He served as assistant secretary of the U.S. Treasury Department (1969-1973) He is the president of the American Hellenic Institute Foundation and a member of the board of directors of the Eisenhower World Affairs Institute.

retain a large number of troops in Greece, which otherwise could have been deployed on the eastern front and in North Africa, and could have tipped the balance in both those campaigns. Six hundred thousand Greeks, nine percent of the population, died from fighting and Nazi Germany's starvation policy. Greece's merchant marine and navy played a significant role in World War II.

The Greek national resistance was a people's resistance. Of the two main groups, EDES and EAM, the largest was the communist-dominated EAM. In December 1944, on the heels of the German retreat from Greece, EAM made an effort to take over the government in Athens but was stymied by British intervention. It was EAM which, in 1946, started the Greek civil war.

While the rest of Europe was rebuilding following World War II, Greece was forced to fight a civil war against communist insurgents supported by Stalin and Tito and supplied primarily by Tito from the Skopje area of Yugoslavia. Tito's aim was to get control of Thessalonike, the main port in the Balkans for access to the Aegean and Mediterranean Seas. Stalin wanted control of Greece in order to gain control of the Eastern Mediterranean and encircle Middle East oil.

The decade of 1940-1949 is one of extraordinary accomplishments by the Greek people and is a continuum climaxing with the Truman Doctrine and the defeat of the Greek communist insurgents. Greece's heroic resistance and its influence on the outcome of World War II as well as the containment of communism in the Cold War, are little known or appreciated outside of Greece.

American policymakers in the White House and State and Defense Departments made a serious mistake in not developing after 1949, with the defeat of the communists in Greece, a special relationship with Greece to the mutual benefit of both countries. It should have been obvious then, as it should be today, that Greece is the key for American interests in the Eastern Mediterranean, in the Aegean Sea and in the Balkans.

Why do I say that it is obvious that Greece is the key in the area for American interests? First, because of Greece's location. Souda Bay in Crete is one of the finest harbors in the world. Its value in controlling the Eastern Mediterranean and in projecting American power in the region was dramatically demonstrated during the Persian Gulf War.

Greece's control of the islands in the Aegean was adequate for U.S. and Greek naval vessels to block any Soviet threat coming through the Dardanelles.

Greece, located on the Balkan peninsula, is a member of NATO and the European Union with a vibrant and stable democracy. It is therefore, key to the efforts of the U.S. to bring democratic reforms, economic progress and stability to the Balkans.

And Greece, is a reliable ally that, with Britain and France, has fought alongside the U.S. in four wars in this century.

If we had developed a special relationship with Greece from 1949 on, we would have achieved greater and earlier results in our Cold War containment policy against the Soviet Union, our primary national security concern at that time.

Unfortunately, U.S. policymakers made the mistake then of coupling Greece with Turkey in responding to the Soviet threat, and continue to do so today without the Soviet threat. The history of our relations with Greece and Turkey over the past five decades has amply demonstrated the error of that policy. We should have had a Greek policy and a Turkish policy—not a joint Greece/Turkey policy vis-à-vis the Soviet Union, as Ambassador Monteagle Stearns stresses in his essay (pp. 164-169).

There are several examples of mistaken policy decisions because of the failure to have a Greek policy and a Turkish policy. The following is a partial list:

- The decision in September, 1955 by Secretary of State John Foster Dulles to send identical letters to the prime ministers of Greece and Turkey following Turkey's organized pogrom against the Greek community in Istanbul, which devastated that community. The Turkish government was the perpetrator of the crimes against its Greek minority. The Greek government was an innocent bystander. Yet the letters, in effect, said to stop quarreling, and that the common danger for both countries was from the Soviet Union.

- President Eisenhower stopped and reversed the aggression against Egypt by Britain, France and Israel in late October 1956, and enunciated the Eisenhower Doctrine: "There can be no peace without law. And there can be no law if we were to invoke one code of international conduct for those who oppose us and another for our friends." Cyprus was used by the British as their key base for the invasion of Egypt. Thereafter the United States, which had taken over responsibility for Greece and Turkey from Great Britain in 1947, should not have allowed the British to play off the 18 percent Turkish Cypriot minority against the 80 percent Greek Cypriot majority to prevent majority rule on Cyprus and the end of British colonial rule. Also, we should have objected to the terms of the 1959-1960 London-Zurich Agreements, which gave the 18 percent of Turkish Cypriot minority a veto over all government decisions.

- In 1974, following Turkey's aggression and invasion of Cyprus on July 20, 1974 with the illegal use of American-supplied arms and equipment, Secretary of State Henry A. Kissinger violated U.S. laws and his oath of office by failing to halt immediately all arms shipments to Turkey. Turkey's invasion of Cyprus violated the U.S. Foreign Assistance Act of 1961, as amended, the U.N. Charter, Article 2 paragraph 4 and the North Atlantic Treaty Preamble and Article 1. Kissinger also refused to condemn Turkey's invasion of Cyprus and actually encouraged the second phase of Turkey's aggression on August 14, 1974, when Turkey seized 33 percent of Cyprus to add to the 4 percent seized in the initial invasion.

- On January 31, 1996, a crisis erupted between Greece and Turkey over the islets of Imia in the Aegean Sea. While the Clinton administration acted strenuously and succeeded in defusing the crisis, it failed thereafter to apply the rule of law to the situation. It failed to state that the treaties and agreements involved, i.e. the Lausanne Treaty of 1923, the Italy-Turkey Convention of January 4, 1932, the Italian-Turkey Protocol of December 28, 1932, in which Imia is specifically named as belonging to Italy, and the Treaty of Paris in 1947 in which the Dodecanese Islands and adjacent islets were ceded by Italy to Greece, clearly established that Imia is sovereign Greek territory. The executive branch applied a double standard on the application of the rule of law to Turkey, which put Greece's sovereign rights in the Aegean at risk for the first time.

Fundamental to a special relationship is the support of democracy, the rule of law, majority rule with protection of minority rights, and the basic human rights and values set forth in our Constitution and Bill of Rights that Americans and Greeks fought for in World War II.

Unfortunately, the White House and State and Defense Departments have not changed their policies toward Greece and Turkey despite the end of the Cold War in 1990. They continue to apply a double standard on the rule of law for Turkey and excuse Turkey's numerous violations of law and horrendous violations of human rights. And they continue to fuel an irresponsible arms race between Turkey and Greece.

Greece today is still the key for U.S. interests in the region in protecting the sea-lanes in the Eastern Mediterranean and Aegean Seas for the transportation of oil, natural gas and trade goods generally, and in promoting democracy, economic progress and stability in the Balkans. The U.S. has an important opportunity today to further American interests in the region by developing a special relationship with Greece, with mutual benefits to both countries. We should do everything possible to seize the opportunity. ☐

Appendix

80TH CONGRESS } HOUSE OF REPRESENTATIVES { DOCUMENT
1st Session } { No. 171

RECOMMENDATION FOR ASSISTANCE TO GREECE AND TURKEY

ADDRESS

OF

THE PRESIDENT OF THE UNITED STATES

DELIVERED

BEFORE A JOINT SESSION OF THE SENATE AND THE HOUSE OF REPRESENTATIVES, RECOMMENDING ASSISTANCE TO GREECE AND TURKEY

MARCH 12, 1947.—Referred to the Committee on Foreign Affairs, and ordered to be printed

MR. PRESIDENT, MR. SPEAKER, MEMBERS OF THE CONGRESS OF THE UNITED STATES:

The gravity of the situation which confronts the world today necessitates my appearance before a joint session of the Congress.

The foreign policy and the national security of this country are involved.

One aspect of the present situation, which I wish to present to you at this time for your consideration and decision, concerns Greece and Turkey.

The United States has received from the Greek Government an urgent appeal for financial and economic assistance. Preliminary reports from the American Economic Mission now in Greece and reports from the American Ambassador in Greece corroborate the statement of the Greek Government that assistance is imperative if Greece is to survive as a free nation.

I do not believe that the American people and the Congress wish to turn a deaf ear to the appeal of the Greek Government.

Greece is not a rich country. Lack of sufficient natural resources has always forced the Greek people to work hard to make both ends meet. Since 1940, this industrious and peace-loving country has suffered invasion, 4 years of cruel enemy occupation, and bitter internal strife.

When forces of liberation entered Greece they found that the retreating Germans had destroyed virtually all the railways, roads,

2   RECOMMENDATION FOR ASSISTANCE TO GREECE AND TURKEY

port facilities, communications, and merchant marine. More than a thousand villages had been burned. Eighty-five percent of the children were tubercular. Livestock, poultry, and draft animals had almost disappeared. Inflation had wiped out practically all savings.

As a result of these tragic conditions, a militant minority, exploiting human want and misery, was able to create political chaos which, until now, has made economic recovery impossible.

Greece is today without funds to finance the importation of those goods which are essential to bare subsistence. Under these circumstances the people of Greece cannot make progress in solving their problems of reconstruction. Greece is in desperate need of financial and economic assistance to enable it to resume purchases of food, clothing, fuel, and seeds. These are indispensable for the subsistence of its people and are obtainable only from abroad. Greece must have help to import the goods necessary to restore internal order and security so essential for economic and political recovery.

The Greek Government has also asked for the assistance of experienced American administrators, economists, and technicians to insure that the financial and other aid given to Greece shall be used effectively in creating a stable and self-sustaining economy and in improving its public administration.

The very existence of the Greek State is today threatened by the terrorist activities of several thousand armed men, led by Communists, who defy the Government's authority at a number of points, particularly along the northern boundaries. A Commission appointed by the United Nations Security Council is at present investigating disturbed conditions in northern Greece, and alleged border violations along the frontier between Greece on the one hand and Albania, Bulgaria, and Yugoslavia on the other.

Meanwhile, the Greek Government is unable to cope with the situation. The Greek Army is small and poorly equipped. It needs supplies and equipment if it is to restore the authority of the Government throughout Greek territory.

Greece must have assistance if it is to become a self-supporting and self-respecting democracy.

The United States must supply that assistance. We have already extended to Greece certain types of relief and economic aid, but these are inadequate.

There is no other country to which democratic Greece can turn.

No other nation is willing and able to provide the necessary support for a democratic Greek Government.

The British Government, which has been helping Greece, can give no further financial or economic aid after March 31. Great Britain finds itself under the necessity of reducing or liquidating its commitments in several parts of the world, including Greece.

We have considered how the United Nations might assist in this crisis. But the situation is an urgent one requiring immediate action, and the United Nations and its related organizations are not in a position to extend help of the kind that is required.

It is important to note that the Greek Government has asked for our aid in utilizing effectively the financial and other assistance we may give to Greece, and in improving its public administration. It is of the utmost importance that we supervise the use of any funds made available to Greece, in such a manner that each dollar spent will count

RECOMMENDATION FOR ASSISTANCE TO GREECE AND TURKEY   **3**

toward making Greece self-supporting, and will help to build an economy in which a healthy democracy can flourish.

No government is perfect. One of the chief virtues of a democracy, however, is that its defects are always visible and under democratic processes can be pointed out and corrected. The government of Greece is not perfect. Nevertheless it represents 85 percent of the members of the Greek Parliament who were chosen in an election last year. Foreign observers, including 692 Americans, considered this election to be a fair expression of the views of the Greek people.

The Greek Government has been operating in an atmosphere of chaos and extremism. It has made mistakes. The extension of aid by this country does not mean that the United States condones everything that the Greek Government has done or will do. We have condemned in the past, and we condemn now, extremist measures of the right or the left. We have in the past advised tolerance, and we advise tolerance now.

Greece's neighbor, Turkey, also deserves our attention.

The future of Turkey as an independent and economically sound state is clearly no less important to the freedom-loving peoples of the world than the future of Greece. The circumstances in which Turkey finds itself today are considerably different from those of Greece. Turkey has been spared the disasters that have beset Greece; and, during the war, the United States and Great Britain furnished Turkey with material aid. Nevertheless, Turkey now needs our support.

Since the war Turkey has sought financial assistance from Great Britain and the United States for the purpose of effecting that modernization necessary for the maintenance of its national integrity.

That integrity is essential to the preservation of order in the Middle East.

The British Government has informed us that, owing to its own difficulties, it can no longer extend financial or economic aid to Turkey.

As in the case of Greece, if Turkey is to have the assistance it needs, the United States must supply it. We are the only country able to provide that help.

I am fully aware of the broad implications involved if the United States extends assistance to Greece and Turkey, and I shall discuss these implications with you at this time.

One of the primary objectives of the foreign policy of the United States is the creation of conditions in which we and other nations will be able to work out a way of life free from coercion. This was a fundamental issue in the war with Germany and Japan. Our victory was won over countries which sought to impose their will, and their way of life, upon other nations.

To insure the peaceful development of nations, free from coercion, the United States has taken a leading part in establishing the United Nations. The United Nations is designed to make possible lasting freedom and independence for all its members. We shall not realize our objectives, however, unless we are willing to help free peoples to maintain their free institutions and their national integrity against aggressive movements that seek to impose upon them totalitarian regimes. This is no more than a frank recognition that totalitarian regimes imposed on free peoples, by direct or indirect aggression, undermine the foundations of international peace and hence the security of the United States.

4 RECOMMENDATION FOR ASSISTANCE TO GREECE AND TURKEY

The peoples of a number of countries of the world have recently had totalitarian regimes forced upon them against their will. The Government of the United States has made frequent protests against coercion and intimidation, in violation of the Yalta agreement, in Poland, Rumania, and Bulgaria. I must also state that in a number of other countries there have been similar developments.

At the present moment in world history nearly every nation must choose between alternative ways of life. The choice is too often not a free one.

One way of life is based upon the will of the majority, and is distinguished by free institutions, representative government, free elections, guaranties of individual liberty, freedom of speech and religion, and freedom from political oppression.

The second way of life is based upon the will of a minority forcibly imposed upon the majority. It relies upon terror and oppression, a controlled press and radio, fixed elections, and the suppression of personal freedoms.

I believe that it must be the policy of the United States to support free peoples who are resisting attempted subjugation by armed minorities or by outside pressures.

I believe that we must assist free peoples to work out their own destinies in their own way.

I believe that our help should be primarily through economic and financial aid which is essential to economic stability and orderly political processes.

The world is not static, and the status quo is not sacred. But we cannot allow changes in the status quo in violation of the Charter of the United Nations by such methods as coercion, or by such subterfuges as political infiltration. In helping free and independent nations to maintain their freedom, the United States will be giving effect to the principles of the Charter of the United Nations.

It is necessary only to glance at a map to realize that the survival and integrity of the Greek nation are of grave importance in a much wider situation. If Greece should fall under the control of an armed minority, the effect upon its neighbor Turkey, would be immediate and serious. Confusion and disorder might well spread throughout the entire Middle East.

Moreover, the disappearance of Greece as an independent state would have a profound effect upon those countries in Europe whose peoples are struggling against great difficulties to maintain their freedoms and their independence while they repair the damages of war.

It would be an unspeakable tragedy if these countries, which have struggled so long against overwhelming odds, should lose that victory for which they sacrificed so much. Collapse of free institutions and loss of independence would be disastrous not only for them but for the world. Discouragement and possibly failure would quickly be the lot of neighboring peoples striving to maintain their freedom and independence.

Should we fail to aid Greece and Turkey in this fateful hour, the effect will be far reaching to the West as well as to the East.

We must take immediate and resolute action.

I, therefore, ask the Congress to provide authority for assistance to Greece and Turkey in the amount of $400,000,000 for the period ending June 30, 1948. In requesting these funds, I have taken into

RECOMMENDATION FOR ASSISTANCE TO GREECE AND TURKEY   5

consideration the maximum amount of relief assistance which would be furnished to Greece out of the $350,000,000 which I recently requested that the Congress authorize for the prevention of starvation and suffering in countries devastated by the war.

In addition to funds, I ask the Congress to authorize the detail of American civilian and military personnel to Greece and Turkey, at the request of those countries, to assist in the tasks of reconstruction, and for the purpose of supervising the use of such financial and material assistance as may be furnished. I recommend that authority also be provided for the instruction and training of selected Greek and Turkish personnel.

Finally, I ask that the Congress provide authority which will permit the speediest and most effective use, in terms of needed commodities, supplies, and equipment, of such funds as may be authorized.

If further funds, or further authority, should be needed for purposes indicated in this message, I shall not hesitate to bring the situation before the Congress. On this subject the executive and legislative branches of the Government must work together.

This is a serious course upon which we embark.

I would not recommend it except that the alternative is much more serious.

The United States contributed $341,000,000,000 toward winning World War II. This is an investment in world freedom and world peace.

The assistance that I am recommending for Greece and Turkey amounts to little more than one-tenth of 1 percent of this investment. It is only common sense that we should safeguard this investment and make sure that it was not in vain.

The seeds of totalitarian regimes are nutured by misery and want. They spread and grow in the evil soil of poverty and strife. They reach their full growth when the hope of a people for a better life has died.

We must keep that hope alive.

The free peoples of the world look to us for support in maintaining their freedoms.

If we falter in our leadership, we may endanger the peace of the world—and we shall surely endanger the welfare of our own Nation.

Great responsibilities have been placed upon us by the swift movement of events.

I am confident that the Congress will face these responsibilities squarely.

HARRY S. TRUMAN.

THE WHITE HOUSE, *March 12, 1947*.

CONTRIBUTOR'S LIST

LARRY I. BLAND, PH.D. Editor, *The Papers of George Catlett Marshall*, a multivolume documentary edition of General Marshall's papers published by The Johns Hopkins University Press. He holds a B.S. in physics from Purdue University and an M.A. and Ph.D. in U.S. diplomatic history from the University of Wisconsin. He taught at the University of Wisconsin-Milwaukee, Gaston College, Bellmont Abbey College, the Virginia Military Institute, and James Madison University. He is associate editor of *The Journal of Military History*.

PAUL F. BRAIM, PH.D. Professor of American military history at Embry-Riddle Aeronautical University. He received his Ph.D. in American history from the University of Delaware, graduated with honors from the Canadian National Defense College and the U.S. Army Command and Staff College. During his military service he fought in Korea and Vietnam and served in WWII. He has been awarded numerous military decorations including three Silver Stars, the Distinguished Flying Cross, five Bronze Medals, four Purple Hearts and the U.S. President's Volunteer Service Award (1984). After thirty years of service in the U.S. Army he retired with the rank of Colonel. He has authored four books and numerous articles on military affairs, including his recent publication *Global Assessment, 1996-97*, and is currently working on a biography of General James A. Van Fleet. Dr. Braim lectures extensively at U.S. war colleges and universities and civic groups.

DEMETRIOS CARALEY, PH.D. President of the Academy of Political Science, Editor of the journal *Political Science Quarterly*, Janet Robb Professor of the Social Sciences at Barnard College, and Professor of Political Science at the Graduate School of International and Public Affairs at Columbia University. Dr. Caraley has published extensively in the field of national security policy, including the books *The Politics of Military Unification, The President's War Powers,* and *National Security and Nuclear Strategy*. He also specializes in city government, urban problems, the Congress, and democratic political theory, on which he has published numerous books and articles. His latest articles and books include: "Washington Abandons the Cities" and *Critical Issues on Clinton's Domestic Agenda*. His classic article "Elections and the Dilemmas of Democratic Governance" has been reprinted and widely cited. In the academic year 1995-96, he was a Visiting Scholar at the Russell Sage Foundation in New York City.

VAN COUFOUDAKIS, PH.D. Dean of the School of Arts and Sciences, Indiana University - Purdue University, Fort Wayne and Professor of Political Science. He received his Ph.D. in political science, MPA from the University of Michigan and a B.A. from the American University of Beirut. He has written extensively on post-WWII U.S. foreign policy, and the politics, foreign and defense policies of Greece, Turkey and Cyprus. His work has appeared in books and professional journals in the U.S., England, Belgium, Italy, Greece and Cyprus. He edited *Essays on the Cyprus Conflict* (1976) Pella Publishing, NY and is the editor of the *Cyprus Yearbook* (1993-95) Cyprus Research Center,

KYKEM. His latest books include, *Superpower Strategy in the Persian Gulf* (1989) and *The Eastern Mediterranean: Adaptation Strategies in the Foreign Policies of Greece, Turkey and Saudi Arabia,* published by the Foundation for Mediterranean Studies in Athens.

DAVID COLLEY, is a free-lance writer based in Easton, Pennsylvania, has contributed ten articles to *Veterans of Foreign Wars* magazine's Cold War history series. His byline has appeared in a variety of national magazines. Colley was an editor and reporter with several newspapers from 1968-1980, including the Baltimore Evening Sun, before he turned to full-time free-lance writing.

THEODORE A. COULOUMBIS, PH.D. Professor of International Relations, Department of Political Science and Public Administration, University of Athens, Faculty of Law, Economics and Politics and President of the Hellenic Society of International Law and International Relations. He received his B.S. in political science, and M.A. in international relations from the University of Connecticut, and Ph.D. in international relations from American University. He began his career as professor of international relations at the American University (1965-83) and then taught at the Faculty of Law, University of Thessalonike (1983-89). He was a visiting professor at the Pantios School of Political Sciences, Athens; the Diplomatic Academy of the Greek Ministry of Foreign Affairs; and the University of Athens. He is co-editor of the *Yearbook* of the Hellenic Foundation for Defense and Foreign Policy. Dr. Couloumbis has served on several boards of directors including the Hellenic Foundation for European and Foreign Policy and has authored and edited over eighty-five books and articles.

GEORGE ELSEY Speechwriter for President Harry S. Truman. Mr. Elsey served as administrative assistant to President Harry Truman. Subsequently he served as president of the American Red Cross Association. He is currently retired and lives in Washington, D.C.

GENERAL ANDREW J. GOODPASTER, USA (RET.) Chairman of the George C. Marshall Foundation and former Chairman of the American Battle Monuments Commission, the Atlantic Council of the United States and the Eisenhower World Affairs Institute. He graduated from the U.S. Military Academy (1939), received a M.S. in engineering and M.A. and Ph.D. in international relations from Princeton University (1947-50). In 1939 he was commissioned a second lieutenant in the Corps of Engineers and during WWII commanded the 48th Engineer Combat Battalion in North Africa and Italy, receiving the U.S. Distinguished Service Cross for his service. From mid-1944 to mid-1947 he was assigned to the Operations Division, General Staff, War Department, serving a one-year tour with the Joint War Plans Committee of the Joint Chiefs of Staff. During his military service, General Goodpaster was special assistant to the chief of staff, Supreme Headquarters Allied Powers Europe; defense liaison officer and staff secretary to the president; commander of the 8th U.S. Infantry division in Germany; assistant to the chairman, Joint Chiefs of Staff; Director, Joint Staff, Organization of the Joint Chiefs of Staff; director of special studies in the Office of the Chief of Staff; U.S. Army: commandant of the National War College; deputy commander of U.S. Forces in Vietnam; Commander-in-Chief, U.S. European Command and supreme allied commander, Europe. He assisted President Nixon in organizing his administration for the conduct of foreign policy and international security affairs. After retiring in 1974, General Goodpaster was a senior fellow at the Woodrow Wilson International Center for Scholars, Smithsonian Institution, and assistant to Vice President Rockefeller on the Commission of the Organization of the Government for the Conduct of Foreign Policy.

He was recalled to active duty in 1977 and three years later was special representative of President Carter for discussion with the governments of Argentina and Brazil following the Soviet invasion of Afghanistan. He was awarded the U.S. Medal of Freedom as well as military decorations, including the Defense Service Medal with Oak Leaf Cluster; the Army Distinguished Service Medal with three Oak Leaf Clusters; the Navy and Air Force Distinguished Service Medals; the Silver Star; the Purple Heart with Oak Leaf Cluster, the Presidential Unit Citation and the Department of Defense's Medal for Distinguished Public Service. Gen. Goodpaster is the author of *For the Common Defense* and has received honorary degrees from Princeton University, the University of Maryland, McKendree College and The Citadel.

LARRY J. HACKMAN Director, Harry S. Truman Presidential Library, Independence, Missouri. Prior to this appointment he served as New York State's assistant commissioner of education for the Archives and Records Administration. In 1981 he was the first director of the Records Program of the National Historical Publications and Records Commission, previously serving as the director of oral history and senior archivist at the John F. Kennedy Library. Mr. Hackman is a Fellow of the Society of American Archivists and served on SAA's Council and as its annual meeting program chair, the Mellon Fellow in Modern Archives at the University of Michigan, a Littauer Fellow at the School of Government at Harvard. He received the Distinguished Public Service Award of the Rockefeller College of Public Affairs of the State University of New York at Albany. He has written and lectured widely on archival affairs. Currently he serves on the Committee on Professional Associations of the International Council on Archives and on the Governing Board of the Rockefeller Archives.

ALONZO L. HAMBY, PH.D. Professor of History, Ohio University, Athens, Ohio. He received a B.A. from Southeast Missouri State College, M.A. from Columbia University and Ph.D. from the University of Missouri. He has taught at Ohio University since 1965. A specialist in twentieth-century American history, he is the author of four books, editor or co-editor of three others, and the author of numerous articles and reviews. He is perhaps best known for two award-winning works on Harry S. Truman: *Beyond the New Deal: Harry S. Truman and American Liberalism* (1973) [winner of the David D. Lloyd Prize, the Phi Alpha Theta First Book Award, and the Ohio Academy of History Publication Award] and *Man of the People: A Life of Harry S. Truman* (1995) [winner of the Herbert Hoover Book Award and the Harry S. Truman Book Award]. He has held fellowships from the National Endowment for the Humanities, the Harry S. Truman Library Institute, and the Woodrow Wilson International Center for Scholars. Dr. Hamby served as president of the Ohio Academy of History from 1989 to 1990.

JOHN O. IATRIDES, PH.D. Professor of International Politics at Southern Connecticut State University. He received his education in Greece, the Netherlands and the United States. He served with the Hellenic National Defense General Staff (1955-56) and the Office of the Prime Minister of Greece (1956-58). He has taught courses on contemporary Greece at Harvard, Yale, Princeton and New York universities. His publications include: *Balkan Triangle: Birth and Decline of an Alliance Across Ideological Boundaries* (1968), *Revolt in Athens* (1972), *Ambassador MacVeagh Reports: Greece 1933-47* (1980), *Greece in the 1940s: A Nation in Crisis* (1980) and *Greece at the Crossroads: The Civil War and Its Legacy* (1995).

HOWARD JONES, University Research Professor and Chair, Department of History, University of Alabama. A recipient of the John F. Burnum Distinguished Faculty

Award for teaching and research, he teaches courses in American foreign relations and the U.S.-Vietnam War. Dr. Jones received his Ph.D. from Indiana University and taught at the University of Nebraska before coming to the University of Alabama in 1974. He is the author of several books, including *Union in Peril: The Crisis over British Intervention in the Civil War* (1992)—a History Book Club Selection and winner of the Phi Alpha Theta book Award; *Mutiny on the Amistad: The Saga of a Slave Revolt and Its Impact on American Abolition, Law, and Diplomacy* (1987, revised, 1997)—used in writing the screenplay for Steven Spielberg's movie "Amistad," and selection of Book-of-the-Month Club, History Book Club, and Quality Paperbacks Book Club; Prologue to *Manifest Destiny: Anglo-American Relations in the 1840s* (1997)—recognized by Choice magazine as one of the "Outstanding Academic Books for 1997; *Quest for Security: A History of U.S. Foreign Relation*, 2 vols. (1996); *To the Webster-Ashburton Treaty: A Study in Anglo-American Relations, 1783-1843* (1997)—recipient of Phi Alpha Theta Book Award and nominated for Pulitzer and Stuart L. Bernath Book Award; and *"A New Kind of War" America's Global Strategy and the Truman Doctrine in Greece* (1989).

BASIL KONDIS, PH. D. Professor of Modern History at the Aristotle University of Thessalonike and Director, Institute for Balkan Studies, Thessalonike, Greece. He received his Ph. D. in history from New York University in 1975. He has written extensively on Greek-Albanian relations, Greece and the United States in the 1940's and generally on issues of the Eastern Question. He has authored numerous books—including *Greece and Albania: 1908-1914* (1976), *Anglo-American Policy and the Greek Problem: 1945-1949* (1984), *Hellenism in Albania: 1897-1918: Documents from the Historical Archives of the Greek Foreign Ministry* (1995), and *Greek Minority in Albania* (1995).

LAWRENCE J. KORB, PH.D. Director of the Center for Public Policy Education and Senior Fellow in the Foreign Policy Studies Program at the Brookings Institution. Prior to joining the Brookings Institution, he served as dean of the Graduate School of Public and International Affairs at the University of Pittsburgh, and as vice president, Corporate Operations at the Raytheon Company. Dr. Korb served as assistant secretary of Defense (manpower, reserve affairs, installations and logistics) from 1981-85 and for his service he was awarded the Department of Defense's Medal for Distinguished Public Service. He is chairman of the board of the Committee for National Security, and a board member of the Washington Center, the Procurement Round Table, and the National Military Family Association. He is also a member of the Council on Foreign Relations, the International Institute of Strategic Studies, and the National Academy of Public Administration; and is an adjunct professor in national security studies at Georgetown University. In the past he has served as a Consultant to the Office of the Secretary of Defense and to the Office of Education. He was a member of the Defense Advisory Committee for President-Elect Reagan (1980), and a member of the Defense Issues Group for President-Elect Bush (1988). Dr. Korb received his M.A. from St. John's University and Ph.D. from the State University of New York at Albany. He has held several academic positions, among them: assistant professor of political science, the University of Dayton (1969-71), associate professor of government, U.S. Coast Guard Academy (1971-75), and professor of management, U.S. Naval War College (1975-80). He served on active duty for four years as a naval flight officer and retired from the Navy Reserve with the rank of captain. Dr. Korb's fifteen books and over one-hundred articles on national security issues include *The Joint Chiefs of Staff: The First Twenty-Five Years; The Fall and Rise of the Pentagon,* and *American National Security: Policy and Process.*

GEORGE CREWS MCGHEE Petroleum producer and former U.S. government official. He received his B.S. from the University of Oklahoma (1933); Doctorate of Philosophy (Oxon) and (Rhodes Scholar) at Oxford University (1937); Doctorate in Civil Law at Southern Methodist University; LL.D. at Tulane University in 1957 and University of Maryland (1965); and Doctorate of Science at University of Tampa (1969). He began his service in the U.S. Foreign Service as coordinator for aid to Greece and Turkey, Department of State (1947-49). Other posts included: special assistant to the secretary of state (1949); assistant secretary for the Department of State on Near Eastern, South Asian, African Affairs (1949-51); U.S. ambassador, chief, American Mission for Aid to Turkey (1951-53); senior adviser to the North Atlantic Treaty Council, Ottawa Canada (1951); member of the President's Committee to Study U.S. Military Assistance Program (1958-59); and ambassador to the Federal Republic of Germany (1964-68). He authored numerous books including *The U.S.-Turkish-NATO Middle East Connection* (1990), *Life in Alanya: Turkish Delight* (1992), and was editor of *Diplomacy for the Future* (1987). He served on numerous boards including trustee of the American Farm School (1949-61); board of directors and advisory board of the Turkish Friendship Council. He served with the U.S. Naval Reserves (1943-45); lt. col. U.S. Air Force Reserves (1945-72). He has received numerous awards including the Decorated Legion of Merit with three Battle Stars; Order of Cherifien Empire Morocco; recipient of the Distinguished Service award U.S. Junior C. of C. and he was named honorary citizen of Ankara, Turkey (1954). He is an independent explorer and producer of oil and the sole owner of McGhee Production Company

LT. GEN. PHOTIOS METALLINOS (RET.) Special Analyst in International Relations, Hellenic Institute of Strategic Studies. He graduated from the Military Academy of Greece (1957) and the Armor School of Greece (1958) and obtained additional training at the U.S. Armor Maintenance School, West Germany (1960); Special Forces Training and Parachute Fighters School (1963-64), War College (1974-75) and the U.S. Command and General Staff (1983). After thirty-three years of service in the Greek army, serving in Greece and Cyprus, he retired with the rank of lieutenant general. Currently he a member of numerous organizations and institutions, including the Coordination Center of Hellenism, the Hellenic Institute of Strategic Studies, the National Defense School Graduates; Association and the Hellenic Association for Atlantic and European Collaboration. His recent paper on the current history of Greece received the First Prize of the Panhellenic Union of Literature, and his articles on Greek defense issues have been published in several magazines, including the *Parliamentary Inspection, Modern Army* and *Research.*

ADMIRAL HENRY C. MUSTIN, USN (RET.) Defense Consultant. From 1978-80 he served as U.S. Navy, Chief operating officer for all surface navy weapons systems; 1982-84, naval inspector-general; serving as the Secretary of the navy's principle agent for Navy Department corporate structure and management matters and associated relations with OSD, the White House, and Congress. From 1984 to 1986 he served as commander of the U.S. Second Fleet and commander of the NATO Striking Fleet Atlantic, operating as CEO and chief operating officer of the two largest fleets in the U.S. navy and in NATO. From 1986 to 1989 he was in charge of developing rationale for the overall navy structure, conducting business in and with over thirty countries, and served as senior U.S. military representative to the U.N. He was twice awarded the Distinguished Service Medal. He retired from the U.S. Navy in January 1989 as vice admiral. He joined Kaman Corporation, a Fortune 500 company, in 1989 as vice president for international marketing and three years later he joined the Center for Naval Analyses as distinguished fellow. He serves as a trustee of the U.S. Naval Academy Foundation and vice chairman of the Amphibious Warfare Committee of the National Security Industrial Association.

PAUL R. PORTER. He graduated from the University of Kansas in 1928 and worked as a journalist. During most of WWII, he was chairman of a shipbuilding committee of the War Production Board. After serving briefly as an officer of the American military government in Germany, he was appointed deputy chief and then chief of the State Department's Mission for Economic Affairs attached to the American Embassy in London. In 1947, he served as the head of the American resident delegation to the newly created U.N. Economic Commission for Europe in Geneva, Switzerland. He held three positions in the Marshall Plan: chief of its mission to Greece (1949); its assistant administrator (1950); and was appointed to its No. 2 post, the Acting United States Special Representative in Europe, based in Paris (1951). Upon conclusion of the Marshall Plan, he became deputy chief of the American team that negotiated the organization and financing of NATO. In 1953, he founded and was president of Porter International Company which licensed U.S. manufacturing technologies to European manufactures. Upon retiring in 1968, he undertook a study of urban affairs and wrote a book, *The Recovery of American Cities,* which led to his appointment as a professor at Cleveland State University and visiting scholar at the University of Aston in England. He retired a second time in 1986 and since then lives in Florida.

EUGENE T. ROSSIDES, ESQ. Senior Counsel, in the international law firm of Rogers and Wells. He served as assistant secretary of the U.S. Treasury Department (1969-1973) where he supervised the U.S. Customs Service, Secret Service, Bureaus of Alcohol, Tobacco and Firearms, the Mint, and Engraving and Printing, and the Federal Law Enforcement Training Center. He is the founder of the American Hellenic Institute, the AHI Foundation and a member of the board of directors of the Eisenhower World Affairs Institute. He is the editor of the *Handbook on United States Relations with Greece and Cyprus,* the *American Hellenic Who's Who 1994-1995* (5th ed.), co-editor of *Doing Business in Greece* (1996) and author of "Cyprus and the Rule of Law," *17 Syracuse Journal of International Law and Commerce* (1991), 21-90. He is the co-author of the *United States Import Trade Law* (1992), chief import editor since 1979 of BNA's *International Trade Reporter* and author of its *Reference File.* He received his B.A. degree from Columbia College and J.D. degree from Columbia University Law School. Mr. Rossides served as U.S. representative to Interpol (1969-73). In 1982-84, he served as a member of the Executive Committee of the President's Private Sector Survey on Cost Control in the Federal Government—The Grace Commission.

MONTEAGLE STEARNS Ambassador to Greece (1981-1985) and the Republic of the Ivory Coast (1976-1979). He served in the U.S. Foreign Service for over three decades, and was promoted to career minister in 1983. He also served in Athens as minister-counselor (1974-76) and second secretary/political officer (1958-62). He has written extensively on U.S. foreign policy and U.S. relations with Greece. His latest books include, *Talking to Strangers: Improving American Diplomacy at Home and Abroad* (1996) and *Entangled Allies: U.S. Policy Toward Greece, Turkey, and Cyprus* (1992). He served as a United States marine on the U.S.S. West Virginia (1943-45). He received the Presidential Meritorious Service Award (1986) and first prize at the Venice Film Festival for the animated film *Man Learns to Farm* (1953). Ambassador Stearns is currently a Stanley J. Seeger Visiting Research Fellow at Princeton University and fellow at the Center for International Affairs at Harvard University. He is a member of the board of the American Farm School in Thessalonike, Greece and the American Memorial Hospital in Reims, France.

VIRGINIA TSOUDEROS, former deputy minister of foreign affairs of Greece (1991-1993), received M.A. degrees from Oxford University (Sommerville College) and Minnesota State University and Radcliff College-Harvard. She served on the staff of the International Monetary Fund (1949-1958), worked as a columnist for Greek dailies (1958-1967) and served as a member of Parliament for nineteen years (1974-93) and spokeswomen of the New Democracy governing party and a member of the Parliamentary Committee of Foreign Policy and Defense. Ms. Tsouderos was a founding member of the Greek branch of European Movement (1960) and its president in 1977, and a founding member and secretary general of the Committee for the Study of Greek Problems, a European oriented anti-junta private association, the activities of which were considered dangerous to the military dictators who imprisoned her together with other leading members. In 1974 she was a founding member and first vice-president of Amnesty International, Greek branch (1974-1976); in 1975 a founding member and first president (1975-1985) of the Family Planning Association. She is the author of *Foreign Policy* (Athens 1994), *Europe As Our Compass: A Political Discussion* (Athens 1988) *Citizens Power is Democracy's Power* (Athens 1981), *Discussion With A Citizen* (Athens 1978), other books and numerous articles in Greek and foreign dailies and monthlies.

JAMES C. WARREN, JR. Advisor to U.S. firms doing business in Greece. He received his B.A. *magna cum laude* from the Woodrow Wilson School at Princeton University in 1949 and served in the U.S. Army Air Corps. He served as chief, Import Program Office, the Marshall Plan Mission to Greece for over four years. He later made a career in the international petroleum business in Southeast Asia, Japan and New York City, bringing him back to Athens, where he became general manager of Exxon's marketing interests in Greece for eight years. Mr. Warren has served as a trustee of Anatolia College, Thessalonike, Greece, president of the board of American Community Schools, Athens, assistant to the president, Bates College, Maine; vice president of the American Farm School of Greece and member of the Modern Greek Studies Association. He also served as chairman of the Greece and Cyprus Advanced Area Studies for the Foreign Service Institute (1991-94). Currently he is working on a book on the Marshall Plan adventure in Greece and is conducting research at the Truman Library in Independence, Missouri, the National Archives and the Library of Congress. ☐

INDEX